Make That Grade
Irish Criminal Law

Make That Grade
Irish Criminal Law

Kathleen Moore Walsh
and Conor Hanly

Gill & Macmillan

Gill & Macmillan
Hume Avenue
Park West
Dublin 12
with associated companies throughout the world
www.gillmacmillan.ie

© 2005 Kathleen Moore Walsh and Conor Hanly
07171 3744 9

Print origination in Ireland by Carole Lynch

*The paper used in this book comes from the wood pulp
of managed forests. For every tree felled, at least one tree
is planted, thereby renewing natural resources.*

A catalogue record is available for this book
from the British Library.

153, 114
E19

CONTENTS

SECTION 1:
CRIMINAL LIABILITY

1

CRIMINAL LIABILITY

Chapter synopsis

I.   Brief Outline of the Historical Development of Criminal Law
II. The Function of Criminal Law
III. The Criminalisation Decision – Justifications for Punishing
IV. Legal Limits on Criminal Law
V.   Classification of Offences
VI. Punishment

I. Brief Outline of the Historical Development of Criminal Law [1]

A. Before the Common Law

  1. **Primitive societies** were characterised as tribal, rural, hierarchical and familiar, i.e. based on family or clan.
     a. Ancient law in Ireland was Brehon law.
        (1) Society revolved around kin or clan. Law was the customs of the clan and varied from clan to clan.
        (2) No legislature or judiciary.
        (3) Redress for wrongs was primarily left to the victim or kin of the victim.
     b. Two principal concepts were found in most primitive societies.
        (1) Outlawry.
        (2) Blood feuds.
  2. **Outlawry** – dispute between clan members. [2]
     a. If a member committed a wrong against another member of the same clan he or she was deemed an outlaw.
     b. The clan was entitled to attack the outlaw.
     c. Pollock and Maitland: 'It was the right and the duty of every man to pursue the offender, to ravage his land, to burn his house, and hunt him down like a wild beast and slay him.'

3. **Blood feud** – dispute between members of different clans.   [3]
   a. The killing of a member of one clan by a member of another clan was sufficient to initiate a blood feud between the clans.
   b. Blood feuds could be stopped by the payment of compensation, i.e. blood money.
      (1) In Anglo-Saxon Britain, compensation was determined by an independent arbitrator. The greater the amount of vengeance, the greater the amount of compensation.
      (2) Under Brehon law the amount of compensation was based upon the victim's honour price. Every person under Brehon law had an honour price.

B. Norman Invasion – Introduction of the Feudal System   [4]

1. In general.
   a. The Norman invasion of England in 1066 and Strongbow's landing in Ireland in 1172 began the establishment of a feudal structure in both countries.
   b. Society no longer revolved exclusively around the clan.
   c. The feudal system was characterised as a central system of power.
      (1) All power emanated from the king.
      (2) Power moved from the king down through the nobles, then down to the lowest serf.
2. The Crown began to exert control over criminal justice.
   a. The ancient concepts of outlawry and blood feud were not conducive to order and the king's peace. Warring clans would not fight together on the battlefield for the king, etc.
   b. The Crown removed the long tradition of the crime victim to claim compensation and instead took the money for the Royal treasury. (This was the origin of fines.)
   c. By the Assizes of Clarendon 1166 and Northampton in 1179, murder, theft, arson and counterfeiting could only be dealt with in Royal Courts.
   d. Eventually all crimes came under the jurisdiction of the king.

C. Early Common Law   [5]

1. Criminal offences were generally divided into felonies and misdemeanours.
   a. **Felonies** were serious breaches of the king's peace.
      (1) 'Felony' comes from an old word meaning 'wicked' or 'treacherous'.

    (2) Felonies could not be bought off.

    (3) Punishment – offender lost his land, his life and his chattels.

      (a) Chattels are personal property, i.e. livestock, clothing and furniture.

  b. **Misdemeanours** were less serious offences.

    (1) Originally called trespasses.

    (2) Punishment – primarily by fines or corporal punishment.

2. **Importance of early Royal Courts.**   **[6]**

  a. No attempt was made by the early common lawyers to develop a comprehensive theory of criminal liability.

  b. Attention in Royal Courts was directed to procedure. Procedural developments involved:

    (1) Pardons (see [11]).

    (2) Benefit of clergy (see [12]).

  c. Attention to procedure resulted in substantive development, especially in the area of homicide.

    (1) Anglo-Saxon law made no distinction between deliberate and accidental killing. Either could start a blood feud.

    (2) Along with the ecclesiastical courts' insistence of intent, a tripartite distinction in the law of homicide developed in the Royal Courts. See [12].

  d. **Tripartite distinction in homicides.**   **[7]**

    (1) **Deliberate killings** were punished by death and forfeiture.

      (a) Benefit of clergy was not available.

      (b) Similar to modern murder, see [325].

    (2) **Chance medley,** or killings done in spontaneous quarrels.

      (a) Did attract the benefit of clergy and punishment consisted of forfeiture of chattels.

      (b) See modern manslaughter [346] and provocation [336].

    (3) **Accidental killings**, or those done in self-defence.

      (a) A pardon could be granted and forfeiture of chattels was not enforced.

      (b) See modern manslaughter [346].

  e. **Other offences** – developed in a highly fragmented fashion.

    (1) E.g. arson – originally confined to the burning of dwelling houses and barns. Fire damage to other structures was not arson.

    (2) E.g. burglary – consisted of breaking and entering into a house at night. Breaking and entering into a house at any

other time was not a felony. A number of statutes were needed to rectify these anomalies.

D. Early Common Law Trials [8]

1. **Felonies** – based upon information drawn up by a grand jury.
    a. Grand jury was to represent the hundred in which the crime was committed.
        (1) The hundred was similar to the modern electoral district. All English counties were divided into hundreds or groups of villages and hamlets, etc. where 100 men lived.
        (2) Purpose of grand jury was to determine if there was enough evidence to warrant a trial.
            (a) If not, the accused was released.
            (b) If so, according to the Assizes of Clarendon and Northampton the trial would take place on the basis of ordeal.
2. **Trial by ordeal** – [9]
    a. It was believed that God would protect the innocent.
    b. Abandoned – all trials by ordeal were abandoned in 1215 when the Church refused to allow clerics to participate in trials. This led to the creation of the petty jury.
    c. Three trials by ordeal most commonly employed were trial by combat, hot iron or water.
        (1) **Trial by combat** – introduced by the Normans, where the king's champion would fight the accused to the death. Fell into disuse by medieval times, was seldom used by about 1485, but only formally abolished in the nineteenth century when duelling was outlawed.
        (2) **Trial by hot iron** – a red-hot iron was placed into the hand of the accused and the hand bound. After a few days the hand was examined. If the hand had blistered, the accused was guilty.
        (3) **Trial by water** – the accused was bound and thrown into a river or lake. If the accused floated he or she was guilty. This was a favourite trial for women accused of witchcraft.
3. **Trials by jury** – [10]
    a. Petty jury had the burden of deciding the guilt or innocence of the accused.
    b. Originally trial by jury was optional.

(1) The accused could decide to be tried by God and Country (jury trial) or be put in prison *forte et dure* (indefinite imprisonment).

(2) Statute of Westminster I (1275) implemented *prison forte et dure*, but it was misread as *peine forte et dure*, which literally means 'the strong and hard pain'. The trial involved the accused being crushed to death with heavy weights.

c. Early jury trials were very different from the trials of today.

(1) Trials were remarkably brief.

(a) Baker noted that as late as the nineteenth century, the average Old Bailey trial only took a few minutes.

(b) Until the Trials for Felony Act 1836, the accused had no right to counsel. It was feared that allowing counsel would lengthen trials.

(2) The accused could not force witnesses to attend until the Criminal Law Amendment Act 1867.

(3) The accused could not give sworn evidence on his own behalf until the Criminal Evidence Act 1898.

(4) Juries – for a guilty verdict, unanimity was required.

(a) Juries deliberated very little.

(b) The same jury could hear several capital cases in the same day.

E. Punishments under the Early Common Law [11]

1. **Felonies** were punished severely.

a. Originally penalty was mutilation appropriate to the crime, e.g. a thief lost his or her hand.

b. Soon replaced by hanging and forfeiture.

c. Treason penalty was being drawn and quartered as well as forfeiture.

d. Pardons – the accused could avoid the usual penalties by seeking a pardon from the king.

(1) Pardons were often sold and Parliament felt it necessary to enact the Statute of Northampton in 1328, limiting pardons to killings done accidentally or in self-defence.

e. Transportation – from James I (1603–25), a convicted felon could be transported to a colony where he or she could provide slave labour.

2. **Misdemeanours** were usually punished with a whipping and/or fines.

F. *Influence of the Church on the Development of Criminal Law* [12]

1. Outlawry and blood feuds.
   a. While the Crown wanted to get rid of these ancient concepts to consolidate power, etc., the Church wanted to get rid of them to save souls.
2. The birth of *mens rea.*
   a. The Church argued for moral culpability (responsibility) in criminal matters, which led to the beginning of a theory of criminal responsibility.
   b. Equated crime with sin.
      (1) To sin a sinner had to purposely defy the will of God.
      (2) Therefore, to commit a crime an offender had to purposely defy the law.
3. Defences of infancy and insanity were recognised and expanded over time.
   a. McAuley and McCutcheon note that:
      (1) By 1330 lunatics convicted of homicide began to receive a king's pardon.
      (2) Near this time the doctrine of *doli incapax* emerged and the parameters of the defence of infancy began to develop.
         (a) *Doli incapax* – children under the age of seven (first holy communion) were deemed incapable of committing crimes.
         (b) Doctrine of *doli incapax* survived almost in its original fourteenth-century form in Ireland until the Children Act 2001. See [175].
   b. See [179] *et seq* regarding the defence of insanity and [174] *et seq* regarding the defence of infancy.
4. **Escaping punishment.**
   a. **Sanctuary** – places of worship were beyond the remit of the civil authorities. Offenders would seek to escape the harsh justice of the early common law by seeking sanctuary in churches. Civil authorities were reluctant to despoil places of worship with force.
      (1) Parish churches – in small parochial churches a person seeking sanctuary could only be granted forty days of refuge. After forty days the offender could surrender for trial or agree to leave the country. If the offender chose to leave the country he or she would be given safe passage to the nearest port and allowed to leave. If the offender returned he or she could be executed.

(2) Great religious houses, such as the large abbeys, where there was no limit on refuge. Some large religious houses attracted large communities of sanctuarians, much to the annoyance of the Royal authorities. Sanctuary was severely limited and finally abolished in 1623.

b. **Benefit of clergy** – developed in the reign of Henry II after his conflict with Thomas a Beckett. Clerics accused of a crime were handed over to the Church authorities to be tried in ecclesiastical courts under the Cannon law, where punishments were less severe than in the Royal Courts.

(1) Neck verse – the test for determining whether an offender was a cleric was based upon literacy. If the offender could read a particular Psalm, known as the neck verse, he was found to be a cleric and given to the Church to try.

(2) Expansion – the neck verse test was abolished in 1706 and the benefit expanded substantially. The benefit was finally abolished in 1827.

II. *The Function of Criminal Law*   [13]

A. *In General*

1. Aim of criminal law is social control.
   a. However, all law is designed to achieve social control.
   b. Criminal law is distinguished from other areas of law because of punishment.
2. Protection – criminal law protects:
   a. Individuals.
   b. Society.
3. Historically.
   a. Early criminalisation, i.e. the justifications for what conduct should be criminal offences, lacked any theoretical foundation.
      (1) Crimes were created by judges (sometimes Parliament) to stop conduct that threatened the social order.
      (2) Social order was the Crown and Church.
         (a) Treason – reflected the Crown's interest.
         (b) Adultery, murder, sodomy – reflected religious prohibitions.
4. Today, preservation of society is not the only aim – quality of society is of importance.   [14]
   a. By protecting values deemed important enough to need criminal law protection.

b. Reduction of crime.
  (1) This requires actual enforcement of the criminal law.
c. Ashworth has identified the enactment of numerous regulatory offences, e.g. health and safety regulations with strict liability and criminal sanctions.
d. Wilson has identified the protection of both public and private interests.
  (1) Support of public interests in:
    (a) Preventing physical harm, e.g. murder, manslaughter, etc.
    (b) Proscribing personal immorality that are injuries to society's well-being, e.g. bigamy, incest, bestiality, etc.
    (c) Preventing moral corruption of the young, e.g. gross indecency, statutory rape, etc.
    (d) Maintaining the integrity of the State and administration of justice, e.g. treason, perjury, tax evasion, etc.
    (e) Maintaining public order and security through offences, e.g. riot, affray, public intoxication, etc.
  (2) Support of private interests in remaining free from:
    (a) Undesired physical interference, e.g. assault, false imprisonment, etc.
    (b) Being offended through crimes such as indecent exposure.
    (c) Undesired interference with property, e.g. theft, etc.

B. Function of Criminal Law [15]

1. Is to set boundaries for:
  a. Individual behaviour.
  b. The State regarding its power to coerce and punish individuals.
  c. However, Clarkson believes that the function of criminal law is one of maintaining and securing maximum compliance with the values important to society as needing the protection of criminal law.
    (1) When values are maintained, most people do not commit crimes.
    (2) For those who do commit crimes, the law uses stigmatic punishment as a mechanism for preventing or minimising criminal activity.
    (3) The net aim is securing a reduction in crime.

2. **Setting boundaries for individual behaviour.**   **[16]**
   a. By determining the conduct that should be deemed criminal,
      i.e. criminalisation decision.
      (1) Educative deterrence – criminal law is used to reaffirm
          selected important social values.
      (2) Declaring an activity criminal has an influence on con-
          duct and beliefs.
   b. By reserving criminal law to control conduct that cannot be
      regulated by:
      (1) Other means of social controls, e.g. education, religion,
          social convention.
      (2) Other areas of law, e.g. tort, contract, etc.
   c. By defining the circumstances where criminal liability arises.
      (1) Setting forth what conduct is criminal. See criminal lia-
          bility [121].
   d. By structuring the criminal offences – see classification of
      offences [38].
   e. By punishing offenders – individual and general deterrence.
      (1) Individual deterrence – offender will find punishment so
          disagreeable he or she will not reoffend.
      (2) General deterrence – punishment of offender will deter
          others from crime.

3. **Setting boundaries for the State to coerce and punish individuals.**   **[17]**
   a. By determining the conduct that should be deemed criminal
      and therefore limiting power to punish conduct not identified.
      (1) Legality principle – *nullum crimen lege, nulla poena sine
          lege.*
          (a) Translated: 'No crime without law, no punishment
              without law.'
          (b) Meaning: An individual cannot be convicted of a
              criminal offence unless his or her conduct was
              defined as criminal before he or she acted.
      (2) Criminal laws should be clear and precise to allow the
          defendant to adjust his or her conduct.
      (3) Interpretation of imprecise or ambiguous criminal laws
          should be strictly construed, i.e. should be biased in
          favour of the defendant.
   b. By reserving criminal law to control conduct that cannot be
      regulated by other means of social controls or other areas of
      law.

c. By defining the circumstances where criminal liability arises keeps the State from punishing for activities that do not fall within the parameters of the statute, etc.

d. By structuring the criminal offences and thereby setting forth available punishment that can be inflicted for the particular offence.

e. By requiring proportionality between offence and punishment.

C. *Theories of How Criminal Conduct Should Be Identified. Two primary theories have been advocated:* [18]

Liberal theory – respect should be shown to the autonomy of individuals.

Moral theory – criminal law should enforce and reflect morality and only punish behaviour that is morally wrong.

1. **Liberal theory** – associated with the 'harm principle'. [19]
   a. Liberalism – John Stuart Mills (1859).
      (1) The only purpose to which power can be exercised over the will of a member of a civilised community is to prevent harm to others.
         (a) Liberty requires that the only legitimate reason for criminalising behaviour is that it causes harm to others.
         (b) Criminal law should not be used to control conduct that is not harmful or to prevent a person from harming himself.
   b. Reformed liberalism – Jeremy Bentham (1748–1832). [20]
      (1) The primary aim of criminal law is deterrence.
      (2) Argued that for criminal law to be effective in preventing harm to others, it had to act as a deterrent.
      (3) For criminal law to act as a deterrent it requires clarity and predictability.
         (a) Clarity requires that criminal law must be clearly stated.
         (b) Predictability – criminal law must be known in advance.
            i. Critical of common law offences where a judge could declare conduct a crime where before it was not known as a crime.
            ii. Referred to common law as 'dog law' because individuals were summarily punished after acting.

(4) For effective deterrent, proportionality required between crime and punishment.
   (a) Level of punishment has to be equal to the level of harm.
   (b) A rational criminal would conclude that the cost of punishment outweighs the benefits of crime and the criminal would make a rational decision not to commit the crime.

c. Other harm theories.   **[21]**
   (1) Paternalism – conduct should be criminal when it causes harm to others or to the actor himself.
   (2) Offence principle – in attempting to deal with one of the primary criticisms of liberalism (reasonable people can differ on what is harm), Joel Feinberg advocated limiting harm to 'serious offences to a person's interest'.

d. Criticisms of harm principle.   **[22]**
   (1) Difficult to apply and controversial.
      (a) Reasonable people can disagree over what is offensive or insulting.
   (2) Anthropocentic, i.e. human focused.
      (a) Focuses on individual harm rather than harm to the community.
      (b) If there is no harm to humans, State intervention is not justified.

e. Successful use of harm principle as it:
   (1) Influenced debates concerning issues such as consent in rape cases.
   (2) Influenced debates concerning decriminalising homosexuality.
   (3) Influences debates concerning decriminalising prostitution and marijuana.

2. **Moral theory** – associated with Lord Devlin in the 1960s. **[23]**
   a. Criminal law should enforce and reflect morality and only punish behaviour that is morally wrong. Social order requires social solidarity or a widespread consensus that offending is wrong; subjecting offenders to punishment maintains that consensus and discourages future offences.
   b. Criminal law is seen as an expression of moral condemnation and should punish conduct that threatens or undermines the common morality.
   c. Criticism – common morality is derived from Christian teachings and does not reflect a pluralist society. Even among

Christian groups, views differ greatly on such things as abortion, divorce and euthanasia.

3. **Alternative theories of justification for criminal law** [24]
   a. **Welfare theory** – Ashworth has identified feminist theorist Nicola Lacey as having developed an alternative justification for criminal law premised upon the values, needs and interests which a society has decided through its democratic processes are fundamental to its functioning and therefore require protection by criminal law.
   b. **Republican theory** – developed by John Braithwaite and Phillip Pettit – promotes a republican conception of freedom with 'dominion', with freedom being held to be non-domination. Intervention by the law should be a measure of last resort, thus non-legal forms of regulation, such as informal social norms and practices, should be employed because they maximise dominion.
   c. **Radical criminology** – criminal law represents the vested interests of the powerful. Aim of criminal law is the maintenance of social, economic and class structure. Only conduct falling foul of the interests of the elite are criminalised.
   d. **Economic theory** – associated with Possner. Object of criminal law is to discourage 'market bypassing' and thus it discourages 'economically efficient' acts, e.g. stealing a neighbour's television. The thief has bypassed the market where the owner would have received value for his television. Criticism – it does not help to distinguish between crimes and torts and it does not explain victimless crimes. Clarkson opines that it fails to recognise the moral context of criminal law.

III. The Criminalisation Decision – Justifications for Punishing [25]

A. Concerns a Discussion of the Policy Considerations of Making Certain Conduct Criminal

1. What social interest might be furthered by criminalising the conduct?
2. How might the social interest be furthered if the conduct is criminalised?
3. What are the costs of criminalising the conduct, i.e. weigh the costs against the benefits?
4. What is the probable result of balancing the costs and benefits of criminalising the conduct?

B. Applied – John and Mary are unmarried adults and were engaged in consensual sexual intercourse on a bench in the town centre at four o'clock in the morning. They were spotted by a taxi driver, who called the police because he believed that a rape was being committed. Should such conduct be a crime?
[26]

1. What social interest might be furthered by criminalising the conduct?
   a. Liberal view – the role of the criminal law is to prevent and deter harm to others, thus eliminating harm to others is the social interest to be furthered.
      (1) What harm is done to any person when two consenting adults engage in consensual sexual activity in a public place in the middle of the night?
         (a) Is the potential to offend others enough? Some might argue that adult consensual sexual conduct can be viewed on TV at night, so why not in a public area?
         (b) What about the taxi driver who suspected a rape was being committed? Was he harmed by the conduct rather than merely being offended?
   b. Moral view – criminal law should reflect and enforce the core moral values in society.
      (1) What core moral values might be furthered by criminalising two consenting adults engaging in sexual intercourse in a public area at night?
         (a) The basic premise that sexual activity is a private matter and should not be performed in a public place.
2. How could the interests identified be furthered?
   a. Liberal view – criminalising sexual conduct in public will stop most of the activity, therefore it is less likely that others will be offended.
   b. Moral view – criminalising the conduct will reinforce society's belief that sexual activity is a private matter that should not be a public activity.
3. What are the costs of criminalising the conduct?
   a. Liberal view:
      (1) Cost = individuals not allowed to engage in consensual sexual conduct in a public place.
      (2) Benefits = individuals will not be harmed, i.e. offended or upset.

b. Moral view:
  (1) Cost = individuals not allowed to engage in consensual sexual conduct in a public place.
  (2) Benefits = upholding social value that sexual activity is a private matter.
4. What is the probable result of balancing the costs and benefits?
  a. Liberal view – if upsetting or offending another is sufficient 'harm', then conduct should be criminalised.
  b. Moral view – conduct should be a crime.

IV. Legal Limits on Criminal Law – many limits developed in the common law and were incorporated into the Constitution and others come from international sources. [27]

A. Constitution [28]

1. Principle of legality, see [33].
  a. Article 15 – no retroactive criminal laws:
    (1) An individual cannot be convicted of a crime when the activity engaged in was not a crime on the date performed.
    (2) E.g. on 1 June Sean shot a fox that was killing his geese. On 1 July the Oireachtas enacted a statute making it an offence to kill foxes. Sean cannot be convicted under the statute for killing the fox on 1 June.
2. Personal rights. [29]
  a. Article 40.1 provides that every person shall be held equal before the law.
  b. Article 40.4.1 provides that no person shall be deprived of personal liberty except in accordance with law.
    (1) Subsections provide specific procedures for taking a *habeas corpus* case to the High Court.
    (2) *Habeas corpus* – roughly translated, means 'to bring forth the body'. This procedure allows a person who is being denied his or her liberty to be brought before a court to determine the legality of the detention.
    (3) Note: Article 40.4.7 allows for the refusal of bail on the grounds of reasonable suspicion that the accused might commit a serious offence if set free on bail.
  c. Article 40.5 provides that a person's home is inviolable and is not to be forcibly entered except in accordance with law.

3. Criminal trials –   **[30]**
    a. Right to trial by jury – Article 38.5 provides that anyone charged with a criminal offence, other than a minor offence or one to be tried before a special or military court, is entitled to a jury trial.
    b. Right to public trial – Article 34.1 requires that justice must be administered in public except in special and limited circumstances.
    c. Right to due process – Article 38.1 requires that all criminal trials must be conducted in due course of law.
        (1) All criminal trials must be conducted fairly with due regard for the personal rights of the accused.
    d. Independent judiciary – Article 35.2 provides that judges are independent and subject only to the law and the Constitution.
4. Criminal legislation –   **[31]**
    a. Article 40.4 – criminal legislation must respect the right of personal liberty protected by 40.4.
    b. Article 15.2.1 vests exclusive law-making power in the Oireachtas.
        (1) It is no longer possible (as it was under the common law) for the courts to prohibit actions where there is a clear need for prohibition.
        (2) However, the courts still retain the power to declare and expand upon existing common law rules.
    c. 21st amendment (2001) prohibits the reintroduction of the death penalty.
5. Sentencing forms an integral part of the administration of justice. *Deaton* v. *AG* [1963] IR 170.   **[32]**
    a. As a result sentencing must conform to the constitutional requirements of justice, fairness and independence that apply to all aspects of a criminal trial.
    b. Proportionality – Irish courts are constitutionally prohibited from imposing sentences that are excessive in relation to the crime and the degree of blameworthiness of the offender.
    c. *People (AG)* v. *O'Callaghan* [1966] IR 510, Walsh J. held that the concept of personal liberty protected by the Constitution prevents the punishment of any person in respect of any matter of which he or she has not been convicted.
        (1) No preventative justice – an offender cannot receive a sentence that is excessive in relation to the crime committed and the degree of guilt.

(2) Incapacitation theory of punishment (see [42]) is not allowed.

d. Power to pardon – Article 13.6 provides the President with the power to commute or remit punishments imposed by the courts.

B. *Common Law*   [33]

1. Principle of legality requires that an individual cannot be convicted of a crime when the activity engaged in was not a crime on the date performed. This principle was endorsed in the Constitution. Additionally, there are two supporting postulates:
   a. Criminal laws should be clear and precise to allow the defendant to adjust his or her conduct.
   b. Interpretation of imprecise or ambiguous criminal laws should be strictly construed, i.e. should be biased in favour of the defendant.

2. Principle of proportionality is an important and recurring concept in criminal law.   [34]
   a. All justification defences contain a proportionality requirement.
      (1) An individual is not justified in using unreasonable or non-proportional force in defending himself/herself or another.
   b. Punishment is required to be proportionate.
      (1) E.g. Flood J. in *People (DPP)* v. *WC* [1994] ILRM 321 – 'The selection of the particular punishment is subject to the constitutional principle of proportionality…'.

3. Presumption of innocence – the defendant is innocent until proven guilty.   [35]
   a. The burden of proof – the defendant must be proved guilty beyond a reasonable doubt.
      (1) Note: The burden of proof is not the same thing as the standard of proof.
         (a) Burden of proof is concerned with who bears the duty of proof, i.e. the prosecution.
         (b) Standard of proof relates to the level of proof required to convict the defendant, i.e. the defendant must be proved guilty beyond a reasonable doubt.
   b. *Woolmington* v. *DPP* [1935] AC 462 – Viscount Lord Sansky wrote the often quoted statement: '…throughout the web of the English criminal law one golden thread is always seen, that it is the duty of the prosecution to prove the prisoner's guilt.'   [36]

(1) Woolmington Principle – even where the prosecution can establish both elements of the offence (*actus reus* and *mens rea*, see [52 *et seq*]) its duty is not complete. The presumption of innocence also requires that the prosecution negate every explanation or defence consistent with the innocence of the defendant.

(2) Exceptions:

(a) A statute may place on the defendant the burden of disproving certain elements of the offence.

(b) The defence of insanity must be proved by the defence.

(3) Falsity of 'golden thread' quote – per McAuley and McCutcheon: '[a]s we have seen, even if we go back no father than the nineteenth century, this claim is transparently false.' See generally [10].

C. *International Sources* [37]

1. Section 2 of the European Communities Act 1972 – that all treaties and other Acts of the Communities are binding on the State and part of the domestic law of the State.

2. International agreements – the Supreme Court has repeated that with regard to international agreements, Article 29.6 means that in the absence of incorporation the Convention is not part of domestic law. *In Re O'Laighleis* [1960] IR 93.

a. Hogan and Whyte state that the European Convention on Human Rights and other international agreements have had a significant indirect effect in domestic law.

(1) The European Convention for the Protection of Human Rights and Fundamental Freedoms was adopted by Ireland in 1950.

(2) The Convention protects a number of rights, all of which can impact on Irish criminal law and/or justice. For example, the right to marry and found a family has implications for the prison service. The rights protected include:

(a) The right to life.

(b) The right to freedom from torture or degrading treatment or punishment.

(c) The right to freedom from slavery, servitude and forced or compulsory labour.

(d) The right to liberty and security of the person.

(e) The right to a fair and public trial within a reasonable period of time.
(f) The right to freedom from retrospective criminal law and no punishment without law.
(g) The right to respect for private and family life, home and correspondence.
(h) The right to freedom of thought, conscience and religion.
(i) The right to freedom of expression.
(j) The right to freedom of assembly and association.
(k) The right to marry and found a family.
(l) The right to an effective remedy.
(m) The prohibition of discrimination in the enjoyment of the rights as set out under the Convention.

(3) The European Convention on Human Rights Act 2003.
   (a) Generally, it is designed to facilitate bringing cases involving alleged breaches of rights under the Convention in the Irish courts.
   (b) It is hoped that this will allow the cases to be processed faster.

(4) European Convention for the Prevention of Torture and Other Inhuman or Degrading Treatment or Punishment (1987) was ratified by Ireland in 1988.
   (a) A committee of independent experts, one from each State, is mandated to examine the treatment of persons deprived of their liberty.
   (b) Committee makes regular visits to places of detention in Member States and publishes reports. It has highlighted the need for States to make regular inspections of places of detention, etc.

V. *Classification of Offences* [38]

A. *Under the Common Law* (see generally, brief history [5])

1. Felonies are more serious crimes, e.g. murder, rape and kidnapping.
   a. Sentence for felonies was usually the death penalty and forfeiture.
2. Misdemeanours are less serious crimes.
   a. Sentence for misdemeanours was usually fines or imprisonment.
3. Criminal Law Act 1997, section 3 abolished the distinction between felonies and misdemeanours.

B. Criminal Law Act 1997, Section 3 [39]

1. Arrestable offences are any offences that carry a penalty of at least five years' imprisonment.
   a. An arrestable offence also covers attempts to commit an offence that carries a penalty of at least five years' imprisonment.
   b. Section 4(1) and 4(2) provide that a person committing or having committed an arrestable offence may be arrested without a warrant by the police or a private citizen.
   c. A citizen's arrest may only take place to prevent the offender from avoiding arrest by the police.
   d. Section 7(2) provides that it is an offence to impede the arrest of anyone who has committed an arrestable offence.
2. Summary offences are of a minor nature and are tried in the District Court without a jury. They are usually prosecuted by the police or some other State agency, such as the Environmental Protection Agency.

VI. Punishment is what Marks a Criminal Offence from Actions Prohibited by Other Agents of Social Control [40]

A. Theories

1. **Retribution** – punishment is right or wrong. [41]
   a. Historically retribution meant vengeance, i.e. an eye for an eye.
      (1) Punishment is justified on the basis that a crime has been committed.
      (2) *Lex talionis* – the infliction upon the wrongdoer is the same injury inflicted upon the victim.
   b. Modern retribution – is known as 'just desserts'.
      (1) Rejects *lex talionis* – offenders receive punishment simply because they deserve it.
      (2) Central theme is the belief that human beings are free, autonomous beings who act as they choose to act.
      (3) Focus of approach is totally on the past criminal conduct of the offender.
         (a) Future conduct is not relevant.
         (b) Rehabilitation is not relevant.
         (c) Deterrence is not relevant.
   c. Objective of punishment = retribution, i.e. a punishment that is proportionate to the harm caused to the victim.

d. Criticism – it places a limit on the punishment that can be imposed and morally innocent offenders receive the same punishment as offenders who intentionally engaged in the criminal activity.

2. **Utilitarianism** – flows from Bentham's work, see [20]. **[42]**
   a. Simple classical form – holds that human action, either individual or collective, is justified on maximising human happiness or welfare. \153,114
      (1) **Punishment is justified** to the extent that it has the potential result of better consequences than the failure to punish.
      (2) **Basic premise** – punishment is a harm, thus it can only be used if some benefit accrues that would outweigh the harm inflicted, i.e. generally the reduction of crime.
      (3) Deterrence is stressed – utilitarianism looks forward to the future.
         (a) General deterrence – the defendant is punished to send a message to the public to forego criminal activity in the future. The defendant is used as a means to a desired end, i.e. the reduction in crime.
         (b) Specific or individual deterrence – the defendant's punishment is meant to deter the defendant from future criminal conduct. Specific deterrence can occur in two ways:
            i. Incapacitation – the defendant's imprisonment prevents him or her from committing crimes.
            ii. Deterrence by intimidation – after the defendant's release the punishment underwent will remind the defendant that if he or she chooses to commit another offence more pair (punishment) will be inflicted.
   b. **Non-classical utilitarianism** has the same goal to reduce crime. **[43]**
      (1) Rehabilitation advocates the use of punishment to reform the offender rather than attempting to stop criminal conduct by fear of punishment.
      (2) Sentence imposed should be the one most likely to rehabilitate the offender, not the one that the crime required or deserved.
   c. **Objectives of utilitarianism.** **[44]**
      (1) Classical utilitarianism = deterrence and incapacitation.
      (2) Non-classical utilitarianism = rehabilitation.

    d. Basic criticism of deterrence, incapacitation and rehabilitation – there is no necessary connection with the crime committed.

  3. **Hart's mixed theory** – separates the purpose of punishment from the question of who should be punished and how much.   **[45]**

    a. Purpose of punishment – only justified on utilitarian/reductionist grounds.

    b. Who shall be punished and how much – retributionist view that only offenders who have done wrong will be punished and not excessively.

    c. Criticism of mixed theory – offences without moral fault, such as statutory rape and public welfare offences, would not be criminal activities.

B. Sentencing – *judge has almost absolute discretion in imposing sentences.*   **[46]**

  1. Constitutional requirements, see [27].

  2. Statutory requirements –

    a. Criminal Justice Act 1951, section 8 allows courts to take into account offences admitted to by a defendant who has been convicted of another offence.

      (1) Advantages to the defendant is under section 8(2), which prohibits any subsequent prosecution for the offences taken into account.

    b. Criminal Justice Act 1993 contains two provisions that can affect sentencing.

      (1) Section 2 allows the DPP to appeal to the Court of Criminal Appeal any sentence thought to be unduly lenient.

        (a) CCA has the power to substitute a new sentence or to refuse the appeal.

      (2) Section 5 provides that when sentencing a defendant for sexual or violent offences it must take into account the effect of the offence upon the victim.

  3. **Objectives of sentencing** – Irish courts follow an amalgamation of three punishment theories: retribution, deterrence and rehabilitation.   **[47]**

    a. When sentencing, the judge must take into account factors in mitigation, i.e. those factors that would tend to reduce the sentence and result in leniency. See [49].

    b. When sentencing, the judge must take into account facts in aggravation, i.e. those factors that would tend to increase the sentence, e.g. gratuitous violence, offender has previous convictions, an elderly or young victim.

4. Guilty pleas – **[48]**

    a. Discount for early guilty plea – an early guilt plea is a relevant factor to be taken into account when sentencing an offender. *People (DPP)* v. *Tiernan* [1988] IR 250.

        (1) Three justifications have been put forward for allowing the discount.

            (a) Guilty plea may be an expression of genuine remorse.

            (b) By admitting the charge, the defendant spares the victim the ordeal of testifying and being cross-examined.

            (c) An early guilty plea allows the criminal justice system to be more efficient.

        (2) Discount or reduction in sentence is not automatic for an early guilty plea.

    b. Where a defendant does not plead guilty, he or she may not be punished with the imposition of a heavier sentence. **[49]**

    c. Leniency has been granted due to:

        (1) The age of the offender.

            (a) Young offenders are given a chance to mend their ways.

            (b) Elderly offenders or those who find prison life exceptionally difficult through some other personal characteristic, such as illness or race. *DPP* v. *Clark* (1997) unreported CCA – the defendant was a Jamaican who was serving a seven-year sentence. His nationality made prison life difficult. His sentence was reduced to five years.

        (2) Hardship to the defendant's family.

        (3) Co-operation with police.

C. *Types of Criminal Sanctions* **[50]**

1. Prohibited sanctions –

    a. Death penalty – Criminal Justice Act 1990 formally abolished the death penalty and the 21st amendment prohibits its reintroduction.

    b. Corporal punishment – Criminal Law Act 1997, section 12 expressly prohibits corporal punishment.

    c. Teacher immunity – corporal punishment imposed upon a student has been abolished by section 24 of the Non Fatal Offences Against the Person Act 1997.

2. **Sanctions available –** [51]

a. **Fines** may be imposed as a penalty in themselves or in addition to some other penalty.

b. **Imprisonment** – the most severe punishment available under Irish law. In its Report on Sentencing (1996), the Law Reform Commission recommended that imprisonment be viewed as the sanction of last resort.

c. **Forfeiture** – under various Acts property used in furtherance of an offence, e.g. car used in smuggling, or property that directly or indirectly represents the proceeds of crime, e.g. Proceeds of Crime Act 1996, may be forfeited.

d. **Community service orders** – introduced into Irish law by the Criminal Justice (Community Service) Act 1983. Any court may impose a community service order against any offender over the age of sixteen. The order can require between forty to 240 hours of unpaid work performed under the supervision of a probation officer. The offender must consent to the order.

e. **Probation** may be applied to any offender who has been convicted of an offence punishable by imprisonment. There are two forms:

   (1) District Court – absolute discharge. After concluding that the offence has been proved, the defendant is released without formally proceeding to a conviction.

   (2) Conditional discharge – allows any court to release the offender following conviction, subject to the defendant entering into an agreement to keep the peace, i.e. to behave, for a period up to three years. If the offender breaches the agreement he or she must appear and be sentenced for the original offence.

f. **Compensation orders** may be imposed either as an alternative to some other sanction or in addition to another sanction. Under the Criminal Justice Act 1993 the courts have the power to order an offender to pay compensation to the victim, and this should be exercised unless the court has good reason not to impose it.

Review Questions

1. Should it be a criminal offence to cheat on (a) the Leaving Cert exam or (b) university exams?

2. In 2002 the United Nations Human Rights Committee said that it was satisfied that the ban on dwarf tossing was not abusive, but necessary in order to protect public order, including considerations of human dignity. Many dwarfs who previously earned a living by allowing themselves to be thrown as a pub game have fought the ban, saying that it discriminates against them. Should dwarf tossing be a criminal offence?

3. 'Six months for series of nuisance offences', *Irish Times*, 12 July – 'A man who committed a series of public nuisance offences, including having sex on the street, vomiting in a video shop and damaging the door of an amusement arcade, was jailed for six months yesterday…'. Should it be a crime for:

   a. Two consenting adults to engage in sexual activities in a public place?

   b. A person to vomit in a shop?

   c. A person to urinate in a shop, public place or in a private garden?

   d. A person to kick and injure the door of an amusement arcade when he was denied access for being intoxicated?

2

ELEMENTS OF CRIME

Chapter synopsis

I.   *Actus Reus*
II. *Mens Rea*
III. Mistake
IV. Concurrence
V.   Causation

I. Actus Reus   [52]

A. General Principles

1. Definition: The physical or external elements of a criminal offence.
   a. If there is no *actus reus,* there is no crime.
   b. Even if the defendant believes that he or she committed a crime and intended to commit a crime. *R. v. Deller* (1952) 36 Cr App Rep 184 – the defendant believed that a car was mortgaged to a finance company, sold the car with assurances that the car was free of charges. Unknown to the defendant the mortgage document on the car was invalid. The Appeal Court held that while he had the necessary *mens rea* for the offence of obtaining by false pretences, he had been telling the truth. There was no *actus reus* and therefore no crime.
2. *Actus reus* contains three parts.   [53]
   a. Esser has described it as:
      (1) Voluntary act – or failure to act when legally required to act
      (2) That causes
      (3) Social harm.
   b. Lord Hope of Craighead in *AG's Reference (No. 3 of 1994)* (1996):
      (1) The initial deliberate and unlawful act done by the perpetrator.

(2) All the consequences of that act, which may not emerge until many hours, days or even months afterwards.

3. Why require a physical act? [54]
   a. Mere thoughts cannot be criminally punished.
   b. Pragmatically, no ability to read the thoughts of others.
   c. **Theories** – supporting requirement of *actus reus*.
     (1) Utilitarian approach (see [42]) rejects punishing thoughts because:
      (a) No deterrent function – while conduct may be deterred, thoughts cannot be deterred.
      (b) Criminal law should be limited to situations where harm is seriously threatened; it should not be used to excise or clean thoughts.
     (2) Retributive approach (see [41]) – it is morally wrong to punish people for intentions because:
      (a) Punishment is justified for those who freely choose to harm others.
      (b) There is no harm until there is an act.
      (c) Without harm there is no justification for punishment.

4. *Actus reus* must be carried out by a person. [55]
   a. Common law – person referred only to a natural or corporate person; an unincorporated body could not commit a criminal offence.
   b. *DPP (Barron)* v. *Wexford Farmers' Club* [1994] 2 ILRM 295 – High Court held that under the terms of the statute, the unincorporated club could be prosecuted as a person.

B. *Voluntary Acts* [56]

1. For criminal liability to apply, the defendant's acts or conduct must be voluntary.
   a. Rationale for requirement of voluntary acts:
     (1) The defendant does not deserve to be punished.
     (2) No deterrent function – involuntary acts cannot be deterred.
   b. Definition: Voluntary is difficult to define.
     (1) Holmes – willed muscular contraction.
     (2) Austin – movement of the body that follows our volition.
     (3) Hart – were the movements subordinated to the actor's conscious plans of action?

 c. Clarkson has noted that criminal law has tended to adopt the approach that there is a continuum of involuntariness, ranging from complete absence of consciousness through persons acting in a confused or semi-conscious manner, to those who actually know what they are doing but claim their actions were 'morally involuntary' because their will was overborne. (Duress, see [215].) **[57]**

  (1) The courts have been strongly influenced by the context, nature and dangerousness of the conduct in determining involuntary acts.

  (2) Particularly dangerous activities such as driving a car – the law has imposed a strict rule that only absence of consciousness will exempt liability. *AG's Reference (No. 2 of 1992)* (1993) – automatism inappropriate for driver lulled into a trance-like state by the monotonous nature of journey. A defendant must have no awareness at all for the defence to succeed. See automatism [58] and facts of case [61].

  (3) Defendant's conduct overtly abnormal – the law has not imposed a strict rule, i.e. complete lack of consciousness, for conduct to be deemed involuntary.

2. **Automatism** **[58]**

 a. Definition: *Bratty* v. *AG for Northern Ireland* [1961] 3 All ER 523 – an act done by the muscles without any control by the mind, such as a spasm, a reflect action or a convulsion, or an act done while suffering from concussion or while sleep-walking.

  (1) Lord Denning in *Bratty:* automatism is more than just being unable to remember or being unable to control an impulse to commit an act.

  (2) Courts are somewhat suspicious of automatism and limit its exercise.

  (3) Particularly where dangerous activities are involved. See [57] above.

 b. Automatism can arise in two ways: **[59]**

  (1) From internal factors.

  (2) From external factors.

 c. Internal factors are physical or mental conditions that cause the defendant to lose control of his or her actions. **[60]**

  (1) Internal factors constitute a disease of the mind.

  (2) Accordingly treated as a form of insanity, i.e. guilty but insane. See [179] *et seq.*

(3) Where the defendant retains any degree of awareness' automatism will not apply to relieve the defendant of liability. **[61]**

    (a) *O'Brien* v. *Parker* [1997] 2 ILRM 170 – the defendant was involved in a road traffic accident caused by his actions. However, the defendant argued that at the time of the crash he had suffered an epileptic seizure, which had come with no warning. He argued that he should not be accountable on the grounds of automatism. The High Court noted that although it was a civil case there was no reason why automatism should not apply in civil cases subject to the same limits. Because the defendant admitted some awareness he was found liable for the action. A total lack of awareness is necessary for the defence of automatism.

    (b) *AG's Reference (No. 2 of 1992)* (1993) – the defendant was a lorry driver who crashed into a vehicle that was broken down and parked on the hard shoulder. Two people were killed. The defendant was acquitted on the grounds of automatism. The AG sought the opinion of the Court of Appeal on the limits of automatism. (Note: The court's decision would not affect the acquittal.) The evidence suggested that the defendant had been lulled into a trance-like state by the monotonous nature of his journey and was therefore suffering from reduced awareness. The Court of Appeal held that automatism was inappropriate; a defendant must have no awareness at all for such a defence to succeed.

d. **External factors** are conditions that arise from outside the body. **[62]**

    (1) Where an external factor causes an internal factor, the jury is still entitled to conclude that the defendant's automatism was caused by an external factor.

        (a) *R.* v. *T.* [1990] Crim LR 607 – the defendant was raped, which resulted in post-traumatic stress disorder. While in this condition, she was involved in a robbery. It was held that her actions were directly attributable to the rape, which was an external factor, rather than the stress disorder, which was an internal factor. Accordingly, insanity was inappropriate and the issue of non-insane automatism was left to the jury, which convicted her.

(2) **Self-induced automatism** is where the defendant brought about his or her own automatic state, such as through taking drugs.   **[63]**

   (a) Self-induced automatism brought about due to drink or dangerous drugs is not a defence to offences of basic intent, because defendants who use such materials should know of their effect. *R. v. Bailey* (1983) below.

      i. *R. v. Quick* [1973] 3 All ER 347 – the defendant was a diabetic nurse who was charged with assaulting a patient. His defence was that he had taken insulin, did not eat much, then drank too much alcohol and this caused a hypoglycaemic state, i.e. low blood sugar, which affected his consciousness. He wanted to use the defence of automatism, but the trial court ruled that the evidence disclosed a potential defence of insanity. The defendant did not wish to put insanity forward, so he pleaded guilty and appealed. On appeal it was held that his condition was not caused by his diabetes but by his taking of insulin, and this was an external factor. Accordingly the defence of automatism should have been left to the jury.

   (b) Automatism, even where self-induced, may be a defence to specific intent offences (similar to rules of intoxication). See intoxication [200] *et seq.*   **[64]**
R. v. Bailey [1983] 2 All ER 503 – the defendant was a diabetic who did not eat properly after taking insulin, causing a hypoglycaemic condition during which he committed an assault and was convicted of wounding with intent to cause grievous bodily harm, a specific intent offence. On appeal he argued that due to automatism he could not form the intent required for the offence and following the rules of intoxication even if self-induced. It was held that automatism, even where it is self-induced, may be a defence to an offence of specific intent, and in this respect is similar to the rules of intoxication.

C. *Exceptions to Voluntary Acts Requirement* [65]

1. **Status offences** – where an offence is defined in such a way that there is no express requirement of conduct, but rather a state of affairs or a specific situation constitutes the *actus reus.*

    a. *R.* v. *Larsonneur* (1933) 29 Cox CC 673 – the defendant was required to leave the UK. She went to Ireland, from where she was deported back to the UK and handed over to the police. She was charged with and convicted of being an alien found in the UK without permission under the Aliens Order 1920.

    b. *Winzar* v. *Chief Constable of Kent* (1983) – under the Licensing Act 1872 it is an offence to be found drunk on a highway or in a public place. The police were called to remove the drunken defendant from a hospital where he caused a commotion. The police took him out of the hospital, formed the opinion that he was drunk and placed him in their squad car, which was parked on the highway. The defendant was subsequently convicted of being found drunk on the highway. The fact that the offence was effectively committed by the police was not relevant.

    c. It is not certain how Irish courts will decide similar cases.

2. **Vicarious liability** – in limited circumstances the law holds a person criminally responsible even though that person did nothing, but is liable due to the acts of another. [66]

    a. Vicarious liability is not the same as accessorial liability. See [121].

    b. Vicarious liability is discussed in the next chapter. See [141].

3. **Omissions** [67]

    a. **Definition**: The failure to act when legally required to do so.

    b. Historically, the common law has been hostile to punishing a failure to act.

    (1) Reasoning: Criminal law exists to suppress or deter harm.

    c. **A duty to act has been imposed under three categories**.

    (1) **Under contract –** [68]

    (a) Where a person is specifically employed to protect the public. *R.* v. *Pittwood* (1902) 19 TLR 37 – the defendant was a gatekeeper at a railway crossing. Part of his duties consisted of ensuring that the gate was closed when a train was approaching. One day he forgot to close the gate and a person was killed. He was convicted of manslaughter on the basis of his contractual obligations. He was employed specifically to protect the public.

(2) **Under statute** – there are numerous statutes imposed upon people to act. **[69]**

    (a) Failure to act will result in the imposition of criminal liability

    (b) Most common example – Road Traffic Act 1961 (as amended) imposes various duties on drivers, including section 56, a duty to obtain third party liability insurance.

(3) **Under the common law – where four categories have been identified.** **[70]**

- **Public officials owe a duty to members of the public.**

    (a) **Misconduct in a public office.** *R.* v. *Dytham* [1979] 3 All ER 641 – the defendant was a police officer. While on duty he witnessed the deceased being ejected from a nightclub. A fight developed in which the deceased was kicked and beaten to death. At no time did the defendant make any attempt to assist the deceased; he merely stood by and watched. He was charged with misconduct of an officer of justice. He argued that this was an offence unknown to the law. It was held, however, that where the holder of a public office willfully fails to perform any duty that common law or statute requires him or her to perform, he or she is guilty of a common law offence called misconduct in a public office.

    (b) **Endorsement of Dytham.** *DPP* v. *Bartley* (1997) unrep. HC – a woman was sexually abused by her stepbrother for a long time. Early on, the victim made a complaint to the police, one of whom apparently asked her if she enjoyed it. Because of this rejection and the reaction of her parents, the woman was incestuously abused for another twenty-five years. She bore a child by her stepbrother and developed suicidal tendencies and was seriously intimidated and beaten. Carney J. specifically endorsed the holding in *Dytham*. If a member of the police receives a credible complaint of felony, that member is under a common law duty to investigate it. Failure to do so is illegal and will render the officer to criminal prosecution.

- **Family members:** [71]
  (a) Parents –
    (i) Dependent child – *R.* v. *Senior* (1899) 19 Cox
        CC 219 – on religious grounds the defendant
        refused to allow his infant child to be medically
        treated. The child died and the defendant was
        convicted of manslaughter. His conviction was
        upheld on appeal because he was under a duty to
        act because of the close personal relationship
        between him and the child.
    (ii) Independent child – *R.* v. *Shepherd* (1862) 9 Cox
        CC 123 – on religious grounds the defendant
        refused to allow his eighteen-year-old daughter
        to receive medical treatment. It was held that the
        defendant owed no duty to act to his indepen-
        dent eighteen-year-old daughter.
  (b) Other close relatives – see manslaughter [346]. [72]
- **Voluntary assumption – duties are often imposed on
  those who voluntarily assume duties towards another.**
  (a) *R.* v. *Gibbons & Proctor* (1918) 13 Cr App Rep 134 –
      a man's wife left him. He began living with another
      woman, who allowed the man's seven-year-old
      daughter to starve to death. The man and woman
      were convicted of murder. The man had given money
      to the woman for food, etc., but did not intervene in
      the child's lack of care. The man was found to have
      owed a duty to act to his daughter and it was sug-
      gested the woman had voluntarily assumed a duty of
      care toward the child. Both convictions were upheld.
  (b) *R.* v. *Nicholls* (1875) 13 Cox CC 75 – it was held that
      a 'grown up person who chooses to undertake the
      charge of a human creature helpless either from
      infancy, simplicity, lunacy, or other infirmity, he is
      bound to execute that charge without (at all events)
      wicked negligence.' Note: Not limited to relatives.
- **Creation of danger – if a person creates a dangerous
  situation, the law may impose a duty to at least
  minimise the dangers.** [73]
  (a) *R.* v. *Miller* [1983] 1 All ER 978 – the defendant, a
      squatter, fell asleep while smoking. He awoke to find
      the mattress on fire, but failed to take any steps to

put out the fire. He went to another room where he fell asleep again. He was charged and convicted of arson and appealed on the grounds that a failure to put out an accidental fire cannot establish the *actus reus* of arson. The House of Lords found that when he awoke he could have put out the fire with little difficulty or danger to himself. From that moment he had sufficient *mens rea*. It was held that where the defendant created a dangerous situation, he is under a duty to mitigate its effect.

D. Causation [74]

1. Is the causal link between the acts or conduct of the defendant and the required harm specified in the criminal offence?
2. The prosecution must prove that the acts or conduct of the defendant brought about the particular result or harm.
   a. Conduct offences – no result is required. The conduct is the harm. See [76]. [75]
   b. Result offences – causation is required.
3. Classic example – *R. v. White* (1908–10) All ER Rep 340 – the defendant put poison into his mother's drink, intending to kill her. She was later found dead, but the evidence disclosed that she had died from heart failure rather than the poison. The defendant was only convicted of attempted murder because he did not cause the death of his mother.

E. Resulting Harm [76]

1. The law recognises two types of offences – result and conduct offences.
2. Result offences are those where a particular result must occur before criminal liability can attach.
   a. Example: Murder. The defendant cannot be found criminally liable for murder if the victim does not die.
   b. Distinguished from causation: Causation is the required link between the defendant's act and the resulting harm. Thus the defendant cannot be found criminally liable for the murder of the victim if the defendant did not cause the death of the victim.
3. Conduct offences are offences where mere proof of the accused's actions will suffice.
   a. Example: Perjury. The offence is committed as soon as a person makes a false statement under oath, regardless of whether the false statement aids anyone.

b. This is because the social harm resulting from the act is the act itself, i.e. the perjury.

II. Mens Rea [77]

A. General Principles

1. Definition: Guilty mind, the mental element or the internal element of a criminal offence.
2. Historically, in the early common law criminal responsibility was based solely on the commission of the *actus reus*.
   a. As early as the thirteenth century, early common law courts began to require proof that the defendant had a culpable state of mind.
   b. *Actus non facit reum nisi mens sit rea* – an act does not make a person guilty, unless the mind is guilty.
3. Hall has described a six-stage process found in intentional crimes. Sometimes the six steps transpire in seconds and sometimes the perpetrator plans for years.
   a. Perpetrator conceives the idea to commit the crime.
   b. Perpetrator evaluates the idea or plan.
   c. Perpetrator forms the intention to go forward with the crime.
   d. Perpetrator prepares to commit the crime.
   e. Perpetrator commences commission of the crime.
   f. Perpetrator commits the crime.
4. Theories – supporting requirement of *mens rea*. [78]
   a. Utilitarian approach – see [42].
      (1) A person cannot be deterred from committing a crime unless that person realises that he or she may be punished.
      (2) Therefore, punishing one who does not realise he or she may be punished if he or she commits a criminal offence is not productive (as far as individual deterrence is concerned).
   b. Retribution approach – see [41]. [79]
      (1) *Mens rea* requirement flows from society's commitment to individual choice.
         (a) It is morally unjust to punish someone who accidentally caused social harm.
      (2) By convicting a defendant, society denounces the defendant and condemns and punishes the defendant as a wrongdoer. Liberty should not be denied to one who has acted without a culpable state of mind.

5. There must be an element of *mens rea* for each element of the *actus reus*.   **[80]**
6. Note: Motive is not the same thing as *mens rea*.
   a. Motive is why the defendant acted, e.g. why the defendant killed his wife.
   b. Motive is useful for the prosecution in showing that the defendant had a reason for his or her conduct.
7. There are four forms of *mens rea* or states of mind: intention, recklessness, negligence and inadvertence.

B. *Intention*

1. Definition: Where the defendant actually intended to do what he or she did.   **[81]**
   a. *People (DPP)* v. *Douglas & Hayes* [1985] ILRM 25 – 'an intention connotes a state of affairs which the party intending…decides…to bring about, and which in point of probability he has a reasonable prospect of being able to bring about by his own fruition.'
2. Difficulty in determining intention:
   a. Whether the defendant intended to commit the offence is a question of fact for the jury.
      (1) The questions can usually only be answered by drawing inferences from the defendant's conduct.
      (2) *R.* v. *Moloney* [1985] 1 All ER 1025 – 'You cannot take the top of a man's head off and see what his intent was at any given moment. You have to decide it by reference to what he did, what he said and all the circumstances of the case.'
   b. General rule of law – people are presumed to have intended the natural and probable consequences of their actions.   **[82]**
      (1) Presumption of intention applies to all offences.
      (2) Presumption of intention has been given statutory effect in the case of murder under section 4(2) of the Criminal Justice Act 1964.
      (3) Burden of proof is not altered. In other words, it is not the responsibility of the defence to show that the presumption has been rebutted; rather, it is the responsibility of the prosecution to show that the presumption has not been rebutted (beyond a reasonable doubt). *People (DPP)* v. *McBride* [1997] ILRM 233
      (4) *People (DPP)* v. *Hull* (1996) unrep. CCC – the defendant was jealous of the relationship the deceased had with a

young woman. The defendant went to the home of the deceased with a shotgun. Following a row at the front door, the deceased went inside and closed the door. The defendant fired through the door and killed the deceased. The trial judge instructed the jury to break down 4(2) of the CJA 1964 into two parts.

(a) Decide the natural and probable consequences of the defendant's conduct. If it was death or serious injury of the deceased, it could be presumed that the defendant intended them.

(b) Decide whether the presumption had been rebutted. The defendant had said that the discharge of the shotgun was accidental, an argument the prosecution resisted. The defendant was convicted of murder and on appeal his conviction was upheld.

3. There are two types of intention: [83]
   a. **Direct intention** – where the defendant desires to bring about a particular result and deliberately brought about the result.
      (1) Example: Daisy decides to kill her cheating boyfriend Donald. She shoots him and he dies. Daisy had direct intention.
      (2) Direct intention is always sufficient for a conviction.
   b. **Oblique intention** – where the defendant's actions were deliberate, but the defendant brought about a result that he or she did not specifically desire.
      (1) Example: Mickey was upset by the bullying he endured at work from his co-workers. One day Mickey placed several sleeping tablets in the office teapot in an effort to gain some peace. One woman with a weak heart died from drinking the laced tea. Mickey did not intend to kill anyone.

4. **Oblique intention** [84]
   a. English approach – where the defendant acted deliberately but brought about a consequence that he or she did not specifically desire, it may be inferred that he or she intended that consequence only where he or she foresaw it as a virtual certainty.
      (1) *R.* v. *Nedrick* [1986] 3 All ER 1 – the defendant bore a grudge against a woman and threatened to burn her out. One night he poured a flammable substance through her

letterbox and set it alight. The hose was burned down and one of the woman's children was killed. The defendant claimed that he did not want to kill anyone, he merely wanted to frighten the woman.

b. ***Nedrick* rules** – to be applied where the defendant's primary motivation for his or her actions was not to kill but to achieve some other purpose. Jury must answer two questions.　　**[85]**

　(1) How probable was the consequence, i.e. death, that resulted from the defendant's actions?

　(2) Did the defendant foresee the consequence?

　　(a) Where the jury decides that the defendant did not foresee the consequence as a result of his or her actions, he or she cannot be said to have intended it.

　　(b) Where the defendant thought the probability of the consequence was only slight, he or she cannot be said to have intended it.

　　(c) However, where he or she foresaw the consequence as being a virtually certain result of his or her actions, the jury may infer that he or she intended to bring about the consequences even though he or she may not have actually desired it. (The court held that this was the minimum degree of foresight required to raise an inference of intention.)

c. Irish approach regarding oblique intention is uncertain. **[86]**

　(1) *People (DPP)* v. *Douglas & Hayes* [1985] ILRM 25 – defendants were convicted of shooting at another with the intent to kill, contrary to section 14 of the Offences Against the Person Act 1861. It provides that recklessness as to consequences can support an inference of intention.

　(2) *Douglas & Hayes* was heavily influenced by the House of Lords' decision in the pre-*Nedrick* case of *Hyam* v. *DPP* [1974] 2 All ER 41.

　(3) Test of foresight as a virtual certainly should be adopted by Irish courts.

C. Recklessness　　　　　　　　　　　　　　　　　　　**[87]**

1. Definition: The taking of an unjustifiable risk that results in certain harm being caused.
   a. Recklessness is the second most complete form of *mens rea*.
2. Unjustifiable risk is considered:
   a. In light of the defendant's state of mind, or

b. What a reasonable person would have done in similar circumstances.

c. The social utility of the defendant's conduct, and

d. How easily precautions could have been taken to prevent harm.

3. English approach recognises two types of recklessness.   **[88]**

   a. *Cunningham* recklessness – from *R. v. Cunningham* [1957] 2 All ER 412.

      (1) Where the defendant takes a risk that is objectively unjustifiable and the defendant knew of the risk but took it anyway.

      (2) Has been applied to non-fatal offences against the person and accessorial liability.

      (3) *Cunningham* facts – the defendant broke into a gas meter to steal the money inside. He had not turned off the gas and as a result the gas seeped into a neighbour's house, injuring the neighbour. For recklessness to exist the defendant must have known of the risk and decided to take it anyway.

   b. *Caldwell* recklessness – from *Metropolitan Police Commissioner v. Caldwell* [1982] A.C. 341   **[89]**

      (1) Where the defendant takes a risk that is objectively unjustifiable, but the defendant did not consider whether or not there was a risk.

      (2) This test constituted an important extension in the law of recklessness. Facts: The defendant believed that he had a grievance against the owner of a hotel. He got drunk and decided to take his revenge by causing a fire in the hotel. The fire was discovered and extinguished before any serious damage was done.

      (3) Clarkson has noted that this test has been applied to criminal damage, e.g. *Chief Constable of Avon & Somerset v. Shimmen* (1987) 84 Cr App R 7 – the defendant, a martial arts expert, was showing off to some friends and kicked out a plate glass window.

      (4) Legal commentators view *Caldwell* as a move toward objective liability and have attacked it, e.g. Williams, Smith, Law Commission.

         (a) Objections to objective liability – responsibility is based upon choice where the defendant must choose to do harm and this includes consciously running the risk of causing the harm. A defendant who does not see or fails to consider the risk has not exercised a choice. Therefore, he or she is not blameworthy and should not be punished.

  c. The *Caldwell* **lacuna** – gap in the law of recklessness.

    (1) Where the defendant considers the possibility of a risk but mistakenly concludes that there is no risk, the defendant fits neither definition of recklessness. **[90]**

      (a) Under *Caldwell* the defendant must either have appreciated the risk or have failed to consider the possibility of a serious and obvious risk.

      (b) Under *Cunningham* the defendant takes a risk that is objectively unjustifiable and the defendant knew of the risk but took it anyway.

    (2) The existence of the lacuna was acknowledged by the House of Lords in *R.* v. *Reid* [1992] 3 All ER 673.

4. Irish approach to recklessness – **[91]**

  a. Irish courts have traditionally tended towards a more subjective view of the law, thus there should be a leaning towards *Cunningham*.

  b. Leading case on recklessness is *People (DPP)* v. *Noel & Marie Murray* [1977] IR 360.

    (1) *Murray* was decided prior to *Caldwell*.

    (2) *Murray* can be interpreted in a number of ways.

      (a) Walsh J. recognised that recklessness may be found either by applying a subjective test (where there was a conscious taking of an unjustified risk which the defendant knew) or by applying an objective test (where the defendant did not actually know but he or she should have been aware).

      (b) Henchy J. held that for capital murder, *mens rea* is subjective.

      (c) Griffin J. made a distinction between recklessness as to circumstances and as to consequences, and endorsed a purely subjective test.

      (d) Parke and Kenny JJ. appear to have adopted a purely subjective test.

  c. McAleese suggests that the best interpretation of *Murray* is as hesitant support for a *Caldwell* approach to recklessness.

  d. Case law since *Murray* is inconclusive, but there seems to be a drift towards a more objective test. In *Re Heffernon Kearns*

Ltd. [1993] 3 IR 191 Lynch J. reviewed the most recent case law on recklessness in both criminal law and tort and clearly favoured an objective test.

D. Negligence [92]

1. Definition: Falling below the standard of behaviour to be expected of reasonably prudent people.
   a. Lowest form of *mens rea.*
   b. Only results in convictions for certain offences, e.g. manslaughter.
2. Since *Caldwell* there is an overlap between recklessness and negligence.
   a. Prior to Caldwell:
      (1) Recklessness was completely subjective.
      (2) Negligence was completely objective.
   b. Subsequent to *Caldwell*:
      (1) Not easy to know where recklessness ends and negligence begins.
      (2) Case law has indicated that some offences could be established with a *mens rea* less than recklessness.
3. Two types of negligence recognised:
   a. Negligence that results in a manslaughter conviction.
   b. Lower form of negligence for certain statutory offences.
      (1) Both types are objective, i.e. based upon the reasonable person.

E. Inadvertence [93]

1. Definition: Where the defendant reasonably failed to foresee the consequences of his or her actions, i.e. a reasonable accident.
   a. Generally does not result in a conviction.
   b. Example: *R. v. Lamb* [1967] 2 All ER 1282 – the defendant pointed a loaded pistol at his best friend. The defendant was not familiar with firearms and he did not understand the firing mechanism of the gun. Believing that it was safe to pull the trigger he shot and killed his best friend. He argued that the killing had been accidental. On the facts of the case he was not reckless because he did not believe that there was a risk. Three witnesses testified that this mistake had been entirely understandable given the defendant's lack of experience with firearms. The Court of Appeal, while believing there was

evidence of negligence, quashed the defendant's conviction of manslaughter on the grounds that the defendant's defence of inadvertence should have been put to the jury.

III. Mistake   [94]

A. General Principles

1. The law recognises two types of mistake.
    a. Mistakes of law.
    b. Mistakes of fact.
2. Latin maxim – *Ignorantia facti escusat: ignorantia juris non escusat.*   [95]
    a. Translated: 'A mistake of fact will be excused, while a mistake of law will not be excused.'
3. Where the defendant makes a mistake as to fact, the jury must still be satisfied that the defendant did not have the required *mens rea* as a result of the mistake.
    a. Sometimes referred to as the defence of mistake.
    b. It is not a defence, but rather a failure of the prosecution to prove a required element of the offence, i.e. *mens rea.*
    (1) Therefore, similar to intoxication. See [200].

B. Mistake as to Law   [96]

1. General Principles –
    a. Definition: Where a person either does not know that something is illegal or makes a mistake as to the effect of a legal provision.
    b. Generally, a mistake as to the law provides no excuse to a defendant.   [97]
2. Based on policy grounds –
    a. Otherwise every defendant would have a simple and effective defence that would amount to an incentive to turn a blind eye to the law.
    b. Lord Denning in *Kiriri Cotton Co.* v. *Dewain* [1960] 1 All ER 177 – it is not correct to say that everyone is presumed to know the law. The true position is that no one can excuse themselves from doing their duty by saying that he or she did not know the law on the matter.
    (1) Adopted by the Supreme Court in *People (DPP)* v. *Healy* [1990] 1 ILRM 313.
    (2) '...otherwise there would be a premium on ignorance.'

3. Exception – where a mistake as to the law may operate to excuse liability.
   a. Under the Larceny Act 1916, section 1(1) if the defendant took and carried away another person's property under a claim of right made in good faith, the defendant will not be guilty of larceny.
   b. *People (DPP)* v. *O'Loughlin* [1979] IR 85 – it was held that even where the defendant's belief in his claim of right turned out to be wrong in law, he still had a defence as his belief negatived the required *mens rea*.
   c. Note: Although the Criminal Justice (Theft & Fraud Offences) Act 2001 has replaced the Larceny Act 1916, a 'claim of right made in good faith' is retained in the new Act. See [435].

C. Mistake of Fact [98]

1. General principles
   a. Definition: Where a person has a misconception of reality and causes harm because of that misconception.
   b. If because of the mistake the defendant did not possess the particular mental state element required in the definition of the crime, the defendant should be acquitted. [99]
      (1) Because the prosecution failed to prove an element of the offence.
      (2) The prosecution must prove beyond a reasonable doubt that:
         (a) The defendant was not mistaken, or
         (b) That the defendant's mistake did not negate the *mens rea*.
   c. The jury is entitled to have regard as to whether there are reasonable grounds for the defendant's mistaken belief.
   d. An honest mistake will not excuse liability where it is in relation to an element of an offence that does not require proof of *mens rea*, such as an offence of strict liability. [100]
      (1) A genuine mistake as to the girl's age is no defence to statutory rape.
      (2) *People (AG)* v. *Kearns* [1949] IR 358 – the offence of statutory rape was committed even where the defendant genuinely and reasonably believed that the girl was over seventeen. [101]

2. Must be relevant to the elements of *mens rea.*
   a. Clarkson and Keating – to use the popular Boomtown Rats' song, when killing members of one's family because one doesn't like Mondays, it is not relevant that the defendant has made a mistake and it is in fact Tuesday.
3. A mistake of fact can be: **[102]**
   a. Subjectively reckless,
   b. Objectively reckless,
   c. Negligence, or
   d. Honest.
4. A genuine mistake of a relevant fact will excuse liability for most offences.   **[103]**
   a. Note: The mistake must be genuine.
   b. The type of mistake must be less than the *mens rea* of the offence for an acquittal.
      (1) Example: If an offence requires intention, then a negligent mistake of fact will result in an acquittal.
   c. *DPP* v. *Morgan* [1975] 2 All ER 347 – a man invited three of his friends to have sex with his wife. He told them that she liked that kind of thing and that she would pretend to struggle in order to increase her enjoyment. The three men had sexual intercourse with the wife and she resisted them. The men were convicted of rape and appealed on the grounds that they had made a genuine mistake regarding the woman's consent.
      (1) Law Lords held that a man who has sexual intercourse on the basis of an honest but unreasonable mistaken belief in the woman's consent is not guilty of rape, because the mistake prevents the man from having the required *mens rea.*
         (a) The fact that the mistake of fact is not reasonable is not relevant so long as the mistake of fact is genuine.
      (2) The defendants' appeal was dismissed and their convictions were not overturned. The Law Lords believed that the trial judge's instructions to the jury did not cause prejudice. In essence, they concluded that the defendants knew that the woman was not consenting and the jury would have reached the same decision had they received the proper instruction.
   d. The legal effect of a genuine mistake of fact is not limited to rape cases. *R.* v. *Kimber* [1983] 3 All ER 316.

IV. Concurrence [104]

A. General Principles

1. The *actus reus* and *mens rea* must coincide in terms of time.
   a. Example: At the time Monica kills Joey she must have the required *mens rea*.
   b. For a conviction it is not sufficient that the defendant had the required *mens rea* before or after the *actus reus*.

B. Continuing Act [105]

1. In some cases there is a continuing *actus reus* and all that is necessary is that the *mens rea* exist at any stage during this extended *actus reus*.
2. Under this approach a number of nominally separate acts can be seen as one continuing act.
   a. *Fagan* v. *Metropolitan Police Commissioner* [1968] 3 All ER 442 – the defendant accidentally parked on a police officer's foot. The defendant refused to move. He argued that he was not guilty of assault because his first action was accidental and therefore he did not have the required *mens rea*. Divisional Court held that the assault was one continuing action that began with the accidental parking on the foot and ended with the removal of the car.
   b. *Kaitamaki* v. *R.* [1984] 2 All ER 435 – the defendant was having sexual intercourse with a woman under the mistaken impression that she was consenting. He realised that this was not the case, but he did not withdraw. It was held that the *actus reus* of rape was a continuing action that began at penetration and ended at withdrawal. When the defendant realised that the woman was not consenting he formed the *mens rea* necessary for rape, and because the *actus reus* continued until withdrawal the *actus reus* and *mens rea* coincided.
3. Duty approach – can be used in similar circumstances. [106]
   a. *R.* v. *Miller* [1983] 1 All ER 978 involved a squatter who fell asleep while smoking and started a fire. See [73] for facts. The Court of Appeal upheld his conviction for arson, employing the continuing action approach. The House of Lords upheld the conviction and discussed the continuing act and duty approach. It was held that the duty approach was preferable, as it would cause less confusion to a jury.

4. **The supposed corpse rule –**   **[107]**
   a. Developed by the English courts to deal with situations where
      the defendant commits two or more acts and there is no co-
      incidence of the *actus reus* and *mens rea*.
   b. *Thabo Meli* v. *R.* [1954] 1 All ER 373 – the defendant and
      others seriously assaulted the deceased and thought that they had
      killed him. They threw the deceased over a cliff, but it was the
      fall and the resulting exposure that actually killed the deceased.
      (1) It was argued that the *actus reus* that caused the death was
          throwing the body off of the cliff. At that time the defen-
          dant did not have the *mens rea* of murder. The defendant
          thought that he was disposing of a corpse.
      (2) Argument rejected – what had occurred was one series of
          acts and the defendant had the required *mens rea* when
          the deceased was assaulted.
   c. Two actions were part of a series of acts designed to achieve a
      harmful result and thus are a single transaction.   **[108]**
      (1) *R.* v. *Church* [1965] 2 All ER 72 – the defendant assault-
          ed a woman who had been taunting him. He knocked her
          unconscious and when he was unable to revive her, in a
          panic, thinking that he had killed her, the defendant
          threw her into a river. The deceased died of drowning
          rather than the assault. Court of Criminal Appeal held
          that a murder conviction was possible if the jury con-
          cluded that the two actions were part of a series of acts
          designed to cause death or grievous bodily harm.
   d. A single action can be established where the second action is
      designed to cover or conceal the first act.   **[109]**
      (1) *R.* v. *Le Brun* (1991) 4 All ER 673 – the defendant and
          his wife were on their way home when a heated argument
          developed. The defendant punched his wife, knocking
          her down. The defendant then tried to move her to pre-
          vent detection. In attempting to lift her he accidentally
          dropped her and this killed her. There was no precon-
          ceived plan and the defendant did not think that the
          initial assault had killed his wife. On appeal his convic-
          tion for manslaughter was upheld on the basis of the two
          acts being one transaction.
          (a) The court held that where the second event is
              designed to cover or conceal the first event, a single
              transaction can be established.

(b) Issue of what would have happened if the second action had been designed to assist the victim rather than to avoid detection.

(c) Suggested that the chain of causation would have been broken, i.e. no liability.

V. *Causation* [110]

A. *General Principles*

1. Definition: Causation is the required causal link between the acts or conduct of the defendant and the required harm specified in the criminal offence.
2. The prosecution must prove that the acts or conduct of the defendant brought about the particular result or harm. See resulting harm above [76].
   a. Conduct offences – it is not necessary to establish causation in a conduct offence.
      (1) This is because no result is required to establish the offence.
      (2) The act or conduct is the social harm, i.e. perjury.
   b. Result offences – causation is essential.
      (1) The prosecution must prove that the defendant brought about the particular result (harm) specified by the offence.
      (2) No causation, no criminal liability.
3. Classic example – *R. v. White* [1908–10] All ER Rep 340 – the defendant put poison into his mother's drink, intending to kill her. She was later found dead, but the evidence disclosed that she had died from heart failure rather than the poison. The defendant was only convicted of attempted murder because he did not cause the death of his mother.
4. Note: Issue of causation does not arise often and when it does it is usually in a homicide case.
5. Causation – there are two types of causation:
   (a) Actual causation, or cause-in-fact.
   (b) Proximate causation, or legal cause.

B. *Actual Causation* [111]

1. Sometimes referred to as cause-in-fact.
2. **No liability** – there can be no criminal liability unless it can be shown that the defendant's conduct was a cause-in-fact of the prohibited result.

3. **But for test** – or *sine qua non* test.   **[112]**
   a. Function of test is to eliminate certain forces from responsibility for the resulting harm.
   b. But for the defendant's acts the victim would not have died.
      (1) Applied to *R. v. White* (above) – but for the defendant placing the poison in his mother's tea his mother would not have died.
      (2) This is not a true statement. The mother did not die of the poison.
      (3) Therefore, there is no causation and therefore no criminal liability.
      (4) Note: The defendant was not held criminally liable for his mother's death, but he was held criminally liable for his attempt to kill her.

C. Proximate Cause   **[113]**

1. The defendant's act or conduct must be the legal cause (as well as the factual cause) of the prohibited harm.
   a. Sole cause of the prohibited result is not required.
   b. Operating and substantial or significant cause is sufficient.
2. Example: *R. v. Hennigan* [1971] 3 All ER 133 – the defendant was driving a car at about 80 m.p.h. at night in a restricted area. As he drove through an intersection he crashed into another car, killing two occupants. The issue before the Court of Appeal was whether the defendant was responsible for the collision and therefore the two deaths. The trial judge had directed the jury that the defendant's actions did not have to be the sole cause of the collision, providing that it was a substantial cause. Substantial meant that his conduct must have been more than a remote cause of the deaths – it must have been an appreciable cause.
   a. *R. v. Cato* [1976] 1 All ER 260 – Court of Appeal held that it is not necessary to use the word 'substantial' so long as the jury is aware from the direction that something more than a minor contribution is required.

D. Novus Actus Interveniens – New Intervening Acts   **[114]**

1. Definition: Where an independent force causes prohibited harm to another after the defendant's voluntary act has been committed.
   a. An independent force may be:
      (1) The conduct of a third party,
      (2) The victim, or
      (3) A natural force, such as the weather.

2. Legal issue – under what circumstances will the intervening conduct of a *novus actus interveniens* relieve the defendant of criminal liability? [115]
3. There are four requirements that must be met to break the chain of causation to relieve the defendant of criminal liability. [116]
   a. Where it is alleged that the conduct of a third party is a *novus actus*, the third party's conduct must be voluntary.
      (1) *R. v. Pagett* [1983] Crim LR 394 – the defendant used his sixteen-year-old pregnant girlfriend as a shield during a standoff with police. The girl was killed in the crossfire. The defendant was convicted of murder and appealed. Issue: Whether the police, who were the immediate cause of the death, could constitute a *novus actus interveniens*. His murder conviction was upheld on a number of reasons, including the fact that police intervention was involuntary. The police were acting in reasonable self-defence. Goff L.J. found that there is no distinction between a reasonable attempt to escape violence and a reasonable attempt to resist violence by defending oneself.
   b. The defendant must not have brought about the *novus actus*. [117]
      (1) Where a third party performs a reasonable act to preserve his or her life against the violence of the defendant, there is no *novus actus*. *R. v. Pagett.*
      (2) Where a reasonable action is undertaken as a result of a legal duty no *novus actus* arises. *R. v. Paget.*
   c. Where the actions of the third party were foreseeable by the defendant, a *novus actus* will not arise.
      (1) *R. v. Williams & Davis* [1992] 2 All ER 183 – the defendants gave the victim a lift. They attempted to rob the victim and he jumped from the car and was killed.
         (a) The Court of Appeal held that a victim's response will not excuse a defendant's liability if it could reasonably have been foreseen by a reasonable person.
         (b) Only where the action was so daft as to make it the victim's own voluntary act will the chain of causation be broken.
   d. The intervening act must be independent of the defendant's conduct and must effectively be the cause of the prohibited result. [118]

(1) The prohibited result, following a normal medical treatment required because of the defendant's unlawful conduct, is not a *novus actus interveniens*. *R.* v. *Jordon* (1956) Cr App R 152.

(2) The prohibited result, following an abnormal medical treatment required because of the defendant's unlawful conduct, may be a *novus actus interveniens*.

   (a) *R.* v. *Jordan* (1956) 40 Cr App Rep 152 – the defendant stabbed the victim. The victim was hospitalised, where he received antibiotics for his wound. He was allergic to the antibiotic, yet he was again treated with the antibiotic and a large amount of liquids were given to him intravenously. His lungs became waterlogged and he died of pneumonia. The death was not due to the stab wound, but the medical treatment.

   (b) *Jordan* has been limited to its facts. *R.* v. *Smith* [1959] 2 All ER 193 – the victim was a soldier stabbed with a bayonet during a fight with other soldiers. Unknown to anyone his lung was punctured. He was taken to a first aid station, where the busy doctor failed to appreciate the seriousness of his injuries and he died. While the medical treatment was not appropriate the chain of causation was not broken, i.e. the victim was stabbed in the back, his lung was punctured, he died within a few hours due to the lung injury.

(3) Limited to extraordinary and unusual treatment – that it is so significant that it completely overshadows the original injury. **[119]**

   (a) *R.* v. *Cheshire* [1991] 3 All ER 670 – the victim was shot in the abdomen and thigh. After developing breathing difficulties a tracheotomy was performed. He died two months later from complications arising from the tracheotomy, while his gunshot wounds had healed. The court held that the complications that caused the victim's death were a direct result of the gunshot wounds and the attempts by the doctors to deal with the wounds. Only extraordinary and unusual treatment could constitute a *novus actus*, and even then only if the jury is satisfied that this treatment was so significant a cause of death that it completely overshadowed the original injury.

E. Eggshell Skull Rule [120]

1. The rule – the defendant must accept the victim as the victim is.
2. It is no defence that the victim suffers from some abnormality that accentuates the injury.
3. *R. v. Blaue* [1975] 3 All ER 446 – the defendant attacked an eighteen-year-old Jehovah's Witness who refused his sexual advances with a knife. She refused medical treatment involving a blood transfusion and died. The defendant argued that her refusal was unreasonable and should constitute a *novus actus* that broke the chain of causation.
    a. The Court of Appeal noted that the policy of the law has always been that those who inflict violence upon others must take their victim as they find them.
    b. This includes the religious and spiritual values held by those victims.

Review Questions

1. Bart has always been jealous of his sister Lisa. While his parents were away on an extended holiday Bart was house sitting for them. Every day he looked at Lisa's prized saxophone and became more jealous and angry. One day Bart took the saxophone to a car boot sale and sold it for €1. Within a week of selling the saxophone Bart was consumed with guilt and went to the local police station and confessed what he had done. Under the local statutes Bart is charged with theft. The police begin to investigate and discover that before their parents left on their extended holiday Lisa had joined a religious cult and gave away all of her possessions. She gave her saxophone to Bart, but the parents forgot to tell Bart.
    (a) Did Bart have the *mens rea* for theft?
    (b) Did Bart perform a voluntary act?
    (c) Can Bart be successfully prosecuted for theft? Why or why not?

2. As James was walking along the quays late at night he was attacked by Les, who wielded an iron pipe. Surprised and dazed, James fought back and ultimately overpowered Les. James wrestled the pipe from Les and James hit Les in the head with it. Les fell into the street, bleeding profusely. Thinking that he had killed Les, James fled the scene. Later, Tony hit a pothole and, looking in his rearview mirror, he saw Les lying in the road. Believing that he had killed Les with the taxi, Tony picked Les up and threw him into

the river. In fact, Tony's taxi did not strike Les. The following morning both James and Tony went to the police and confessed to killing Les. A post mortem revealed that Les died as a result of drowning. Will the supposed corpse rule apply to

(a)   James and/or

(b)   Tony?

3.   Ken was angry with his girlfriend, Barbie, as she had been unfaithful. Ken asked Richard to rape Barbie to teach her a lesson. Richard agreed. Richard lay in wait for Barbie near her home. Richard saw a woman approach and, believing her to be Barbie, attacked and raped the woman. In fact, the woman attacked was not Barbie, but her friend, Madge. Will Richard be convicted or raping Madge in view of the holding in *DPP* v. *Morgan*?

4.   Joe pushed his way into Gráinne's apartment and pointed a gun at her. He put her in the bedroom and told her to stay quiet. Fearful, Gráinne attempted to escape by climbing onto a nearby roof. Unfortunately, a roof tile gave way and Gráinne fell to her death. When apprehended, Joe stated that he had no intention of injuring Gráinne and was shocked that she climbed out the bedroom window and fell to her death. Will Joe be convicted of a criminal offence since he did not kill Gráinne?

5.   Carmel believed that her aunt was wealthy. When her aunt became elderly Carmel took her aunt into her home to care for her. However, when Carmel learned that her aunt was not wealthy, Carmel stopped feeding her aunt. Her aunt died shortly thereafter from malnutrition. Can Carmel be held criminally liable for the death of her aunt if she did not strangle, stab, poison or by some other violent means kill her aunt?

6.   Joan discovered that her sister Julie had been having an affair with Joan's husband, Roger. Without thinking, Joan grabbed her car keys and the sharpest knife in the house. She drove toward Julie's house intending to kill her sister. On the way to Julie's house, Joan's car was hit by a lorry and pushed onto the footpath. To Joan's horror her car ran over a person who was standing on the footpath. Unknown to Joan the woman killed was her sister Julie. When told the news, Joan danced around in glee. Will Joan be held criminally liable for Julie's death?

7.   Mary belongs to a new religious group called The Wave. It is the teaching of The Wave and Mary's firm belief that no male can see her body or touch her except her husband. One day Mary is attacked by a young man, who stabs her in the arm with a sharpened

screwdriver to get her to release her handbag. Mary is taken to the hospital by the police, but refuses to allow the male doctors to see or treat her wound. By the time a female doctor is located and rushed to the hospital, Mary has bled to death. Will Mary's actions be a *novus actus interveniens,* relieving her attacker of criminal liability for her death?

8. Rip Van Salem was in a coma for over seven years. He awoke one day and went home to his surprised but delighted family. Itching for a cigarette, he went to his desk and found some old tobacco and began making cigarettes. Later, he went to the local pub and was arrested for smoking in the pub. When Rip went into the coma, smoking in a pub was not illegal. What Latin phrase should you recite to Rip regarding his situation?

9. Amanda hates her rival, Yvonne, so Amanda makes an elaborate plan to murder Yvonne and jots her plan down in her diary. Has Amanda performed an *actus reus* for murder?

10. Rhonda and Ralph have been married for thirty years. Yesterday, Rhonda made a funny face at lunch and would not respond to Ralph. Suddenly, Rhonda picked up a steak knife and plunged it into Ralph's hand, causing a severe injury. Medical tests have revealed that Rhonda suffered a mild stroke and she has no memory of injuring Ralph. Did Rhonda perform the *actus reus* of aggravated assault?

3

SCOPE OF CRIMINAL LIABILITY

Chapter synopsis

I.   Complicity
II. Vicarious Liability
III. Strict Liability
IV. Transferred Intent

I. *Complicity*   [121]

A. *In General*

   1. Liability for a crime is not restricted to the person who actually committed the crime.

      a. Anyone who provided assistance to that person may also be prosecuted for assisting either:

         (1) Before,

         (2) During the commission of the crime, or

         (3) After the commission of the crime.

   2. This is referred to as *secondary participation* in a crime.

B. *Historically*   [122]

   1. Under common law there were four categories of participation.

      a. **Principle in the first degree** – applied to felonies and misdemeanours.

         (1) The actual perpetrator of the offence.

         (2) Known in modern terms as the principal offender.

      b. **Principle in the second degree** – applied to felonies and misdemeanours.

         (1) A person who aids and abets the commission of a crime at the time of the commission of the crime.

         (2) Example: A lookout.

         (3) Treated the same as a principal offender.

  c. **Accessory before the fact** – applied to felonies and misdemeanours.

    (1) A person who assisted the commission of a crime before
it was actually committed.

    (2) Example: A person who gave the burglars her employer's
security codes to disable the alarm system.

    (3) Treated the same as a principal offender.

  d. **Accessory after the fact** – applied to felonies.

    (1) A person who knows that a felony has been committed
and provides shelter to the felon.

    (2) Did not apply to misdemeanours.

    (3) Under common law a wife could not be an accessory after
the fact to a crime committed by her husband.

      (a) She was considered to be under his control and pre-
sumed to have acted under his coercion.

2. Common law participation has been overtaken by statute – for
all offences there is little distinction between the principal
offender and a secondary participant.   **[123]**

  a. Section 8 of the Accessories and Abettors Act 1861.

    (1) Provided that where a person aided, abetted, counseled or
procured the commission of a misdemeanour, that person
was liable to be treated the same as a principal offender.

    (2) This Act was repealed by the Criminal Law Act 1997.

  b. Criminal Law Act 1997.

    (1) Re-enacted section 8 with respect to indictable offences.

    (2) Any person who aids, abets, counsels or procures the
commission of an indictable offence is liable to be indicted, tried and punished in the same way as the principal
offender.

  c. Section 22 of the Petty Sessions (Ireland) Act 1851.

    (1) Makes a similar provision in respect of summary offences.

C. Modern Complicity   [124]

1. General principles –

  a. Complicity concerns the imposition of criminal liability on a
person who did not personally commit a harm, but is held
accountable for the acts of another.

  b. Generally arises in two ways:

    (1) **Accomplice or accessory liability** – where a person may
be held liable for the acts of another if he or she assists the
other in committing an offence.

(2) **Doctrine of common design** – a person may be held accountable for the conduct of a co-conspirator who commits a crime in furtherance of their criminal agreement or joint enterprise.

D. Modern Accomplice or Accessory Liability   [125]

1. General principles –
   a. Criminal Law Act 1997 – section 7(1).
      (1) Definition: Any person who aids, abets, counsels or procures the commission of an indictable offence is liable to be indicted, tried and punished in the same way as the principal offender.
      (2) Accessories after the fact – section 7(2) provides that if a person believes another to have committed an arrestable offence, any action done with the intent of preventing the arrest of that person is an offence (updates common law definition of accessory after the fact).
         (a) Section 7(3) provides that if a person is charged with an arrestable offence which is shown to have been committed, but there is not enough evidence to convict as a principal offender, he or she may, if the evidence warrants it, be convicted under section 7(2).
   b. English approach – the terms 'aid', 'abet', 'counsel' and 'procure' were thought to have distinct meanings. *AG's Reference (No. 1 of 1975)* (1975) Eng.
      (1) Clarkson has noted that it is now widely accepted that, with the possible exception of procuring, the terms are simply synonyms embracing all forms of helping or encouraging the principal offender.
         (a) Prosecutions allow for an accessory in language which uses all four terms without having to specify which precise category is alleged.
         (b) Contrary to the House of Lords' opinion that the true nature of the case against the defendant should be made clear in the indictment. *Maxwell* v. *DPP for N.I.* (1979) 68 Cr.App.R 128.
      (2) Irish courts have not specifically addressed the issue of whether the terms have distinct meanings or are interchangeable.

c. Aiding and abetting – **[126]**
    (1) Requires the secondary participant to be present at the time the crime is committed.
    (2) English approach:
        (a) *Gillick* v. *West Norfolk & Wisbech Area Health Authority* [1985] 3 All ER 402 – the House of Lords considered whether a doctor who prescribed contraceptives for an under-age girl without the consent of her parents, which was allowed in exceptional circumstances by UK guidelines, had committed a crime. The Lords decided that a crime could be committed depending upon the doctor's intention. Aiding and abetting could occur even though the doctor would not be present when the offence of unlawful sexual intercourse was committed.

d. Counselling – **[127]**
    (1) Generally requires help or advice given prior to the commission of the crime.
        (a) Precise form of help required is not clear.
    (2) No requirement that there is a causal connection between the assistance given and the commission of a crime.
        (a) *R.* v. *Calhaem* [1985] 2 All ER 266 – the defendant was infatuated with her solicitor and instructed a man to kill a woman who was alleged to be having an affair with the solicitor. The prosecution case was that the defendant counselled or procured the murder. She appealed, alleging that there was no causal connection, on the facts, between anything she might have said to the killer and what actually happened, therefore she concluded that she could not be said to have counselled the murder. The court held that all that was required was the prosecution show a contact of some sort between the defendant and the killer, and that the killer acted within the scope of the contact.

e. Procuring – **[128]**
    (1) Generally regarded as bringing about a desired result through one's efforts.
        (a) Example – Mr Wilson is aware that Dennis is allergic to peanuts. Mr Wilson is tired of Dennis, as he is such a menace to Mr Wilson's sanity. Mr Wilson would like to be rid of Dennis permanently. If Mr Wilson

persuades Mrs Wilson to make a peanut butter cake for Dennis's birthday, if Dennis has an allergic reaction and dies, Mr Wilson has procured Dennis's death. Not only does Mr Wilson desire Dennis's death, but he took steps to bring about the result.

(2) Does not require a formal agreement between the procurer and the principal offender.

   (a) Principal offender may be unaware of the efforts of the procurer.

   (b) *AG's Reference (No. 1 of 1975)* (1975) – the defendant spiked a friend's drinks with spirits. The friend was arrested for being over the limit while driving home. The defendant was charged with aiding and abetting, counselling or procuring the offence of driving while intoxicated. The Court of Appeal held that procuring does not require a conspiracy or agreement between the procurer and the principal offender.

2. *Actus reus* – [129]

   a. Requires proof of actual assistance given to the principal offender.

      (1) *R. v. Brown* [1968] SASR 467 (Australian) – the defendant's action was a simple cough that acted as a warning to a killer that the victim was leaving his room and therefore vulnerable to attack. The cough was intended to assist in the commission of the crime.

   b. Encouragement to the principal offender may be a sufficient act. [130]

      (1) *R. v. Gianetto* [1996] Crim LR 722 – the Court of Appeal held that any involvement in a crime 'from encouragement upwards would suffice' for a conviction. In that case, the trial judge in his summation to the jury stated as an example that if someone told the defendant that he was going to kill the defendant's wife and the defendant patted him on the back, nodded and said, 'Oh goody,' that would be sufficient for a conviction.

   c. **Omissions** – generally a failure to act, such as merely being at the scene of a crime or not preventing the commission of a crime, does not give rise to secondary liability. [131]

      (1) Example: Mr Wimpie is an expert in martial arts. Recently, while eating a hamburger in his favorite fast food restaurant he watched a young man threaten the

staff and make off with all the cash in the till. Although Mr Wimpie could have easily stopped the young man, Mr Wimpie was more interested in finishing his hamburger. Mr Wimpie has incurred no criminal liability for his failure to act.

(2) Exception – a failure to act may constitute secondary participation where the defendant is under a duty to act or is in a position of authority. **[132]**

  (a) *R. v. Dytham*, see [70] – the defendant was a police officer who watched as a man was kicked to death and did nothing to intervene. He was convicted of misconduct in a public office, but it is submitted that on the facts, he could have been charged with complicity in the murder.

  (b) *Tuck* v. *Robson* [1970] 1 All ER 1171 – the owner of a pub allowed a customer to continue drinking after closing time, thereby breaching the licensing laws. The publican's failure to act was held to constitute aiding and abetting as he was in control of the premises, knew of the situation and was under a legal duty to act.

(3) Exception – sometimes mere presence during the commission of a crime may be sufficient if the defendant derived encouragement from the presence and the presence was not accidental and intended to encourage. **[133]**

  (a) *R. v. Clarkson* [1971] 3 All ER 344 – a woman recently out of hospital went to a party given by members of the British army on duty in Germany. While there, she was raped violently by a number of soldiers. At some point during the rapes, a number of other soldiers, including the appellants, entered the room eagerly, having heard the woman's screams, and remained there for some time. Some even assisted by holding the woman down. The appellants, however, did not commit any such positive act to assist the rapists. The Courts Martial Appeal Court acknowledged that their presence was not accidental; they entered the room because they heard the woman screaming. However, this was not enough. Nor was the fact that the rapists derived encouragement from their presence. Held: Additionally, it would have to be shown that appellants intended their presence to encourage the commission of the crime.

3. *Mens rea* –   **[134]**
   a. Intention – encouragement or assistance is given intentionally.
      (1) All authorities agree that secondary participation requires intention.
      (2) Neither recklessness nor negligence is sufficient.
      (3) Example: *The People (AG)* v. *Ryan* (1966) 1 Frewen 304 – the defendant was convicted of aiding and abetting a murder. The defendant and two others had been involved in an altercation with another group who were attending a dance. Later, after the dance ended the two groups met again. The defendant's group was armed with various car tools. The ringleader of the defendant's group killed one member of the other group and seriously injured another. The evidence indicated that the defendant had been one of the men who had been armed. Simply standing around with a weapon in hand could constitute an act sufficient to impose liability.
   b. Knowledge of the offence planned –   **[135]**
      (1) All authorities agree that secondary participation requires knowledge of the offence planned.
      (2) Authorities are in conflict over how much knowledge is required.
      (3) English approach:
         (a) General knowledge of violent activities sufficient. *DPP for NI* v. *Maxwell* (1978) – the defendant was a member of the UVF and led others to a public house. The men he led threw a bomb at the building, but the owner's son foiled the attack by throwing it away. The defendant was convicted of doing an act with intent to cause an explosion likely to endanger life and appealed. He argued that he was only involved in the UVF in respect of welfare matters and had no idea what the purpose of the operations would be. House of Lords held that this defendant was a member of an organisation that continually performs acts of violence. He must have known that he was on a military operation and would have involved the use of guns, bombs or incendiary devises. Because of this knowledge he aided and abetted in whatever form

the attack took. His conviction was upheld.

(b) An intention to go through with the offence is not necessary under English law. *R. v. Rook* [1993] 2 All ER 955 – a husband recruited the defendant and another man to kill his wife for money. The defendant then recruited a fourth man and all four planned the killing. On the day of the killing, however, the defendant did not turn up, but the killing went ahead anyway. Held: He had intended to assist or encourage the comission of the crime, he could be convicted where he believed that the offence would probably be committed. In order to withdraw from participation, the defendant must give timely communication to the other parties of his withdrawal.

(4) Irish approach – appears more restrictive than English approach.

  (a) The defendant is required to know the nature of the intended crime. **[136]**

    i. *People (DPP) v. Madden* [1977] IR 336 – Court of Criminal Appeal held that it was necessary to establish that the defendants had intentionally given assistance to the commission of a crime of which they had known, or the commission of a crime of a similar nature.

    ii. *People (DPP) v. Egan* [1989] IR 681 – the defendant was told that a 'small stroke' was planned. He was asked to have his garage available. He agreed. While he knew that a theft was planned, he did not know that it was an armed robbery, something which he alleged that he would never have agreed to. Held: On the basis of *Maxwell & Madden* that it was not necessary to show that he had known the precise means of the theft, he just had to know the nature of the intended crime. Because he knew that some form of theft was planned his conviction was upheld.

      • Distinguished from *Maxwell* – knowledge of violent activities alone would not be sufficient under *Egan*. Required to know the nature of the intended crime under *Egan*.

Common Law Criminal Law Act 1997   [137]

Common Law			Criminal Law Act 1997	
		Criminally liable?		Criminally liable?
Principal in first degree	Actual perpetrator	Yes	Principal offender	Yes
Principal in second degree	Aids and abets the commission of the crime at the time of the crime.	Yes	S. 7(1) accomplice – aids and abets, counsels or procures the commission of an indictable offence.	Yes
Accessory before the fact	Assists before the crime is committed.	Yes		
Accessory after the fact	Knowing felony was committed and provides help and shelter for felons to avoid arrest.	Yes intent to or	S. 7(2) acting with the impeding the arrest of a principal offender.	No, under s. 7(1). Yes, under s. 7(2).

E. Doctrine of Common Design

1. General principles –   [138]
   a. Definition: 'Where two people embark on a joint enterprise, each is liable for the acts done in pursuance of that joint enterprise…that includes unusual consequences if they arise from the execution of the agreed joint enterprise but…if one of the people goes beyond what was tacitly agreed as part of the common enterprise, the other person is not liable for the consequences of the unauthorized act.' *R.* v. *Anderson & Morris* [1966] 2 All ER 644.
   b. Also known as joint enterprise.
   c. Not the same as secondary participation. *R.* v. *Stewart & Schofield* [1995] 3 All ER 159. Note: Irish authorities have not addressed this issue.

(1) Secondary participation –
   (a) A person who aids and abets, etc. is a secondary party to the commission of whatever crime it is that the principal has committed, although he or she may be charged as a principal.
   (b) The parties are treated as principals.
(2) Common design/joint enterprise –
   (a) Where the allegation is common design or joint enterprise, the allegation is that one defendant participated in the criminal act of another.
   (b) The parties are principals.

2. Joint responsibility – **[139]**
   a. People are jointly responsible for any act done in furtherance of a crime.
   b. However, no joint responsibility if one person acts beyond the crime as originally planned.
   c. Example: *People (DPP)* v. *Noel & Marie Murray* (1977), see [91]. The Supreme Court recognised that there was no evidence that the need to shoot a Garda had been discussed and agreed by the defendants in planning their raid. For this reason, the Supreme Court held that, on the fact of this case, there could be a common design in relation to murder, but it could not extend to capital murder.

3. Withdrawal from common design – **[140]**
   a. *R.* v. *Mitchell* (1998) unrep CA – held that to withdraw from secondary participation a person must clearly communicate his or her intention.
   b. *Mitchell* – if violence is spontaneous, communication may not be possible; withdrawal may be communicated by simply walking away.

II. Vicarious Liability

A. General Principles **[141]**

1. Definition: Where one person is held criminally liable for the crimes committed by another person imposed because of the relationship between the defendant and the perpetrator.
   a. Unknown in common law.
      (1) '...[A] master cannot be criminally liable for an offence committed by his servant.' Collins J. in *Hardcastle* v. *Bielty* [1892] 1Q.B. 709.

    (2) Vicarious liability is part of Irish criminal law per the Supreme Court in Re Employment Equality Bill 1996 [1997] 2 I.R. 321, where the Court struck down the vicarious liability provisions of the Bill.

  2. Distinguished from: **[142]**
    a. Accomplice liability.
      (1) Accomplice liability is not vicarious.
      (2) An accomplice's liability is based upon his or her participation in the crime.
    b. Strict liability –
      (1) Strict liability reduces the *mens rea* requirement.
      (2) Vicarious liability eliminates the requirement of an *actus reus*.

B. Legislative Intent   **[143]**

  1. Whether a statute imposes vicarious liability depends on legislative intent.
  2. Courts generally assume that vicarious liability was not intended.
  3. In practical terms vicarious liability usually arises in employer-employee circumstances.

C. Employee/Employer

  1. Generally limited to employers being held liable for the criminal acts of their employee committed within the scope of the employee's employment. May arise in three ways.
  2. Statute may expressly impose vicarious liability.
  3. The Delegation Principle.   **[144]**
    a. Applies to rare statutory offences where liability may only be applied against persons of special status, such as the owner, occupier or licensee of premises.
    b. Wilson has noted that due to the narrow drafting of statutes the delegation principle developed.
      (1) For example: Section 4(1) of the Intoxicating Liquor Act of 2003 provides that it is an offence for a licensee, on licensed premises, to supply or permit any person to supply intoxicating liquor to a drunken person or to any person for consumption by a drunken person.
    c. Rule: A licensee who delegates the performance of his or her duties to another also delegates their potential liability for the other's default.   **[145]**

(1) Knowledge of employee may be imputed to employer.
   (a) *Allen* v. *Whitehead* [1930] 1KB 211 – the licensee of a café hired a manager and then only visited the café infrequently. The licensee was warned by the police that prostitutes were likely to congregate in the café. He instructed the manager to refuse entry to prostitutes and placed a notice to this effect in the café. The manger ignored his instruction and continued to allow known prostitutes to congregate in the café. The licensee was convicted of knowingly allowing prostitutes to congregate on his premises, notwithstanding his lack of knowledge and efforts to exclude the prostitutes.
   (b) *Howker* v. *Robinson* [1973] QB 178 – it was held that a licensee of a pub who was serving in one room was liable when his employee sold alcohol to a minor in another room.

4. Judicial interpretation – courts interpret words in a statute so that the act of an employee is deemed to be the act of his or her employer. **[146]**
   a. Clarkson has noted that this has been important in pollution offences where the only effective way of enforcing the law is by making the company liable. *National Rivers Authority v. Alfred McAlpine Homes East Ltd.* [1994] Crim LR 760.

D. Criticisms [147]

1. An employer can be held criminally liable where the employer has done everything within his or her power to prevent the wrongdoing.
   a. *Harrow LBC* v. *Shah* [1999] 2 Cr.App.R. 457 – an employer took every possible precaution to ensure that lottery tickets were not sold to persons under sixteen. However, a prohibited sale took place and the employer was held vicariously liable.
2. Justification for imposing vicarious liability is based on the fact that the employer is in the best position to prevent wrongdoing. It is the employer who hired, trained and has control and authority over the employee. **[148]**
   a. Criminal liability ensures that an employer will maintain careful control over an employee.
   b. Clarkson has pointed out that in pollution cases it is generally a failure of the employer's system and operations and it would be unfair to hold an employee liable for the failure.

III. Strict Liability

A. In General

1. Strict liability arises in two ways –   **[149]**
   a. *Strict liability doctrine* – where a rule of criminal responsibility that authorises the conviction of a morally innocent person for violation of an offence that, by definition, requires proof of a *mens rea.*
      (1) Example: Ignorance of the law does not excuse. A person may be convicted of an offence where he or she genuinely had no intention to commit an offence. See [95].
   b. *Strict liability offences* – offences that by definition do not contain a *mens rea* for one or more elements of the *actus reus.* **[150]**
      (1) Example: See statutory rape [100] and [413].
      (2) Note: Strict liability offences are not the same as status or 'state of affair' offences. See status offences [65].
         (a) State of affair or status offences require no *mens rea* and are rare.
         (b) Strict liability offences do not require *mens rea* for one or more elements of the *actus reus.*
2. Historically –   **[151]**
   a. *Malum in se* – refers to conduct that is inherently wrongful.
   b. Until about the middle of the nineteenth century offences generally focused on *malum in se.*
      (1) Examples: Murder, rape and larceny.
      (2) Conviction required proof of *mens rea.*
         (a) Conviction was stigmatising.
         (b) Penalties were severe.
      (3) Exception – there were some early strict liability offences, such as statutory rape (see [413]), where a male could be convicted even where he believed that the female was over the age of consent.
   c. The Industrial Revolution brought about changes that required legislation to ensure public health, safety or welfare.
                                                                    [152]
      (1) Conduct that was not morally wrong could have a huge impact on public health, safety or welfare.
         (a) Examples: Early Factories Acts, traffic regulations, consumer protection, control of adulterated foods, drugs, health and safety at work, environmental protection, etc.

    (b) Traditional principle of *mens rea* was not incorporated into these statutes because:

        i. Norrie has argued it was the only way to get magistrates to convict 'their own kind', i.e. the factory owners.

        ii. Clarkson has reasoned that a *mens rea* requirement would have undermined the effectiveness of the law because due to increased complexity in components it would be difficult to prove that a manufacturer or merchant knew that the good did not conform to standards.

(2) *Malum prohibitum* conduct – conduct that is wrong because it is prohibited. **[153]**

    (a) Became known as public welfare offences.

    (b) In common law only two offences of strict liability were recognised:

        i. Public nuisance.

        ii. Criminal libel.

    (c) All other strict liability offences were recreated by statute and depended upon the wording of the statute.

        i. Ashworth has noted that about half of the 8,000 criminal offences recognised under English law are strict liability offence.

3. Theories **[154]**

  a. Retribution – does not support strict liability, see [41].

    (1) *Mens rea* requirement is consistent with the retribution principle that a person who does not choose to cause social harm and who is not otherwise morally to blame should not be punished.

    (2) Society balances the interest of the blameless person who causes harm above its concern for deterring social harm by requiring proof of the person's *mens rea*.

  b. Utilitarian arguments in support of strict liability, see [42].

    (1) The lack of a *mens rea* requirement may provide a desirable effect of keeping a large class of people from engaging in dangerous activities that may adversely impact on others.

    (2) Those who do choose to engage in dangerous activities will act with greater care due to the strict liability nature of the law.

(3) Criticism –
    (a) Little evidence that strict liability makes people more careful.
    (b) Offenders often treat fines as costs of doing business, thus same deterrence could be achieved through non-criminal means.

c. Barbara Wooten's proposal –   **[155]**
  (1) Wooten has advocated that all requirements of *mens rea* for all crimes be abandoned.
  (2) Conviction would simply require proof that the defendant caused the required social harm.
  (3) Consideration of the defendant's *mens rea* or lack of *mens rea* would occur after a finding of guilt in order to determine what punishment is appropriate.
  (4) Based on utilitarian considerations – the *mens rea* requirement hampers the modern goal of the criminal justice system to prevent harm.
  (5) Criticism –
    (a) Hart has noted that there is a utilitarian justification for retaining the *mens rea* requirement. Without *mens rea* nearly every action might result in criminal inquiry and this would result in a waste of police resources and increase policing of individuals' lives.

B. Modern Strict Liability   [156]

1. Determining if statute imposes strict liability.
  a. Lord Scarman in *Gamman Ltd.* v. *AG for Hong Kong* [1984] 2 All ER 503 suggests five points when trying to determine whether an offence is a strict liability offence.
    (1) There is a general presumption that the legislature intended that *mens rea* be required.
      (a) This presumption of a *mens rea* requirement was endorsed by the High Court in *Maguire* v. *Shannon Regional Fisheries* [1994] 2 ILRM 253.
    (2) This presumption is very strong when dealing with an offence that is 'truly criminal' in character, as opposed to one that is essentially regulatory.
      (a) If the offence is found in a regulatory scheme and enforced by a regulatory agency it will generally be regarded as relating to public welfare.

    (b) Public welfare offences are more likely to be regarded as strict liability offences.

(3) The presumption can be rebutted only where the statute clearly says as much or does so by necessary implication. **[157]**

    (a) In other words, offences require *mens rea* unless the statute clearly states that the offence is one of strict liability, or

    (b) Where a statute creates criminal offences dealing with the same or similar subject, if five of the offences require *mens rea*, the necessary implication if the sixth is silent is that the omission of a *mens rea* requirement is that the legislatures meant for the sixth to be a strict liability offence.

(4) The presumption can only be rebutted where the statute is in respect of a matter of social concern.

    (a) Clarkson has noted that courts are inclined to rebut the presumption in favour of *mens rea* if potential victims are vulnerable.

    (b) Applies where the public has no choice, for example consuming food or breathing the air,

    (c) Or where children are vulnerable to exploitation by adults.

(5) Even where such matters are the concern of the statute, strict liability must be an effective requirement in order to achieve the purpose of the statute. **[158]**

b. Language used in statute –

(1) Certain words suggest that *mens rea* is required.

    (a) For example: Adverbs such as 'intentionally' or 'recklessly' always establish a *mens rea* requirement.

    (b) For example: Other words, such as 'knowingly', 'wilfully' or 'maliciously', also have been found to establish a *mens rea* requirement.

IV. Transferred Intent

A. General Principles   **[159]**

1. **Concurrence,** see [104 *et seq*].

a. The *actus reus* and *mens rea* must coincide in terms of time.

(1) Example: At the time Monica kills Joey she must have the required *mens rea*.

2. Doctrine of Transferred Intent –   **[160]**
    a. Developed to deal with situations where the defendant per-
        formed the *actus reus*, but did not have the required *mens rea*
        to harm the victim.
        (1) Example: Richard Kimball is trying to strike Larry with a
             lamp. Unfortunately, when Richard throws the lamp at
             Larry he hits Lt. Philip Gerard instead. Richard had the
             intention to criminally assault Larry, but instead crimi-
             nally assaulted Philip.
    b. Wilson has described transferred malice: 'If the defendant
        intends a particular consequence, he is guilty of a crime of
        intention even though his act takes effect upon an object
        (whether person or property) that was not intended.'
        (1) Wilson has noted that the principle probably applies to
             transfer recklessness as well as intention.
    c. Hanly – the doctrine applies to all offences in Ireland. **[161]**
        (1) Doctrine given statutory effect in section 4(1) of the
             Criminal Justice Act 1964. See [325].

B. Similar Mens Rea Requirement   **[162]**

1. For transferred intent to apply, the *mens rea* for the intended offence
    can only be transferred to an offence that has a similar *mens rea*.
    a. Example: Glenda is angry that her boyfriend has dumped her.
        She drives slowly by his house, intending to throw a stone
        through his window. Unfortunately, her aim is not good and
        she throws a stone through Father Cavanagh's window.
        Glenda's intent to damage her boyfriend's window is trans-
        ferred to the damage she caused to Father Cavanagh's window.
    b. Classic example: *R. v. Pembliton* (1874) 12 Cox CC 607 – the
        defendant was drinking with a group in a pub. The entire
        party was asked to leave because of disorderly conduct. A fight
        began outside the pub, in which the defendant was involved.
        The defendant picked up a large stone and threw it at the
        people he was fighting. The defendant missed and broke a
        pub window. He was convicted of a statutory offence of caus-
        ing criminal damage despite the fact that the jury concluded
        that he had intended to hit people, not the window. On
        appeal, the conviction was quashed due to the lack of *mens
        rea*. He did not have the *mens rea* to damage property.
    c. *AG's Reference (No. 3 of 1994)* (1996) (English) – the defendant
        stabbed a pregnant women in the abdomen, knowing that she

was pregnant. He pleaded guilty to a charge of wounding with intent to cause grievous bodily harm. He admitted to intending to cause the women serious injury, but denied any similar intent with respect to the foetus. As a result of the stabbing the woman went into premature labour and the child only lived 121 days. The House of Lords wrestled with the issue of whether the defendant could be prosecuted for murder or manslaughter of the child who died as a result of being born prematurely. The House of Lords refused to find that the malice of the defendant toward the mother could be transferred to the foetus, which could in turn be transferred to the child once born. They did accept that the defendant could be guilty of manslaughter as no issue of transferred intent arises under that charge.

C. Criticism [163]

1. Ashworth believes that people should be punished according to what they intend rather than for the accidents of fate arising from the execution of that intention.
2. Glanville Williams believes that the doctrine of transferred intent is contrary to principle and suggests that liability should not be imposed unless the defendant was at least negligent as to the outcome occurring.

Review Questions

1. Ken was angry with his girlfriend, Barbie, because she had been unfaithful. Ken asked Richard to rape Barbie to teach her a lesson. Richard agreed. Richard lay in wait for Barbie near her home. Richard saw a woman approach and, believing her to be Barbie, he attacked and raped the woman. In fact, the woman was not Barbie, but her friend, Madge.
   (a) Under modern complicity principles, is Ken criminally accountable for the rape of Madge?
   (b) Will the doctrine of transferred intent apply to Richard?
2. A young woman was suicidal. She stood on a ledge outside of her office, which was located on the fourth floor of an office building. Soon a crowd gathered and Larry, Mo and Curly began to yell to the young woman, 'Jump', 'Aw come on, just jump', 'One, two, three, jump' and finally Larry yelled, 'Just close your eyes and jump.' Assume that suicide is a criminal offence in Ireland (it currently is not).

(a) If the young woman jumps to her death, can Larry, Mo and Curly be convicted of aiding and abetting the offence of suicide?

(b) If the young woman jumps to her death, can Larry, Mo and Curly be convicted of counselling the young woman to commit the offence of suicide?

(c) Can the other members of the public who were present but were not shouting encouragement for the young woman to jump be held criminally accountable under modern complicity principles if the young woman does commit suicide by jumping?

3. Bonnie and Clyde planned to rob the bank on the quays using toy pistols that look very authentic. Unknown to Clyde, Bonnie obtained a real machine gun that she pulled from under her coat during the robbery. Terrified of Bonnie in possession of a real gun, Clyde grabbed a bag of collected money and fled out the back door of the bank, leaving Bonnie to fend for herself and make her way to the getaway car near the front door.

(a) If Bonnie shoots and kills a man who tries to stop her as she gets into the getaway car, under the doctrine of common design, will Clyde be held criminally liable?

(b) Will Clyde escape criminal liability for the robbery because he withdrew from the scene?

(c) If Clyde withdrew from the plan prior to entering the bank and told Bonnie that he was not going to participate in the robbery, does he escape all criminal liability if she proceeds to rob the bank and kill the man in front of the bank?

4. If a statute is introduced that makes it a criminal offence to toss or bowl consenting dwarfs for amusement in pubs or elsewhere, would this be:

(a) an example of a status offence?

(b) an example of a strict liability offence?

(c) an example of vicarious liability?

SECTION 2: CRIMINAL DEFENCES

4

EXCUSE DEFENCES

Chapter synopsis

I.   Criminal Defences – General Principles
II. Excuse Defences – General Principles
III. Infancy
IV. Insanity
V. Intoxication
VI. Duress

I. Criminal Defences – General Principles   [164]

A. There are two types of defences recognised in criminal law.

1. General defences, which are complete defences to any criminal charge.
   a. Most defences are general defences.
   b. E.g. insanity, infancy and self-defence.
2. Partial defences are defences that only apply to a specific offence and may not be a full or complete defence, e.g. provocation.
   a. Provocation only applies to murder.
   b. Not a complete defence – if provocation defence is successful, the defendant is not acquitted, but rather he or she is convicted of manslaughter. See provocation [336].

B. Two Theories – For All Defences   [165]

1. **Excusatory defences** – excuses the defendant from moral blame and punishment.
   a. Concession to human frailty – the defendant's conduct is criminal, but the defendant's conduct is excused.
   b. The defendant's conduct is excused because of:
      (1) Involuntary behaviour, e.g. duress.
      (2) Lack of capacity, e.g. automatism, insanity, infancy.

    c. Concedes the wrongfulness of the conduct, but asserts that the circumstances under which the conduct was done are such that the conduct should not be punished.

2. Justificatory defences – justifies the conduct of the defendant. See Chapter 5. **[166]**

    a. Definition: A justification defence is where what would normally be criminal conduct is not because the existing circumstances make the conduct socially acceptable and/or desirable and therefore lawful.

    b. Challenges the wrongfulness of an action that technically constitutes a crime.

       (1) Hart has described a justified act as one that 'the law does not condemn, or even welcomes.'

    c. Punishment is viewed as incompatible with the social approval bestowed on the conduct, e.g. commandeering a car and breaking traffic laws to rush an accident victim to the hospital, or a young woman who awakes to find herself being attacked in her own home and seriously injures her male attacker using excessive force in her self-defence.

3. Distinctions between excuse and justification defences arose at common law. **[167]**

    a. Lawful killings were justified, but accidental killings were merely excused (and subject to forfeiture). See [6].

    b. Forfeiture was abolished in 1828 – distinction lost significance.

    c. Revival of interest due to two factors:

       (1) The American Model Penal Code adopted the distinction.

       (2) George Fletcher, *Rethinking Criminal Law* and other legal commentators have clarified the nature of the concepts of justification and excuse.

          (a) Have also demonstrated how the two types of defences differ.

          (b) Explain why we should care about the differences.

          (c) E.g. George Fletcher, 'Should Intolerable Prison Conditions Generate a Justification or an Excuse for Escape?' (1979) 26 *UCLA Law Rev.* 1355, wherein it is argued that justification involves 'right conduct'.

C. Burden of Proof – the prosecution bears the burden of disproving any defences raised by the evidence.   **[168]**

II. Excuse Defences – General Principles

A. Definition: An excuse defence is where the defendant has performed criminal conduct, but it is deemed that the defendant should not be blamed or punished for the conduct, which is viewed as involuntary.   **[169]**

B. Theories Supporting Excuse Defences

1. **Deterrence theory** – there is no reason to punish a defendant if deterrence cannot be achieved. See utilitarianism [42].   **[170]**
    a. Classical utilitarianism – Jeremy Bentham recognised excuse defences because they identify the circumstances in which conduct is not deterrable. To punish an insane person who committed a crime is wrong because it is inefficacious.
    b. Hart has criticised the classical utilitarian approach – he believes that excuse defences are necessary as they limit criminal liability to voluntary wrongdoing, which in turn allows individuals to avoid criminal sanctions by obeying the law.
2. **Causation theory** – the defendant should not be blamed for his or her conduct if the conduct was caused by factors outside the defendant's control.   **[171]**
    a. This is a non-utilitarian theory.
    b. This theory is rejected by most legal commentators as being so broad as to allow no one to be blamed or punished for a wrongful act.
    c. E.g. assume that scientists have found that a high proportion of violent offenders have an abnormal V gene not found in the majority of the non-offending population. Joe is a young man who has admitted to killing several women, but he cannot say why he killed the women. If Joe was born with the V gene, he could avoid punishment because his conduct was caused by the V gene, which is outside his control.
3. **Character theory** – punishment should be proportional to the defendant's moral desert and that desert should be based or measured on the defendant's character.   **[172]**
    a. Reinforces basic premise that individuals who commit crime are bad people, e.g. if John robbed a bank because he has an

addiction to fine living well beyond his means, John would be viewed in general as having a bad character. However, if John robbed the bank under duress because a local gangster threatened to kill his child, his actions are not generally taken to mean he has a bad character.

   b. Criticisms.

     (1) Difficult to measure a defendant's character.

     (2) Individuals with good characters would not be punished for the same conduct as others who would be punished.

  4. **Free choice theory** – an individual can only be punished for his or her conduct if the individual had the capacity and opportunity to freely choose whether to violate the law.   **[173]**

   a. Free choice exists if at the time of the criminal conduct the defendant had the capacity and opportunity to:

     (1) Understand the facts relating to the conduct.

     (2) Appreciate that the conduct violated the law.

     (3) Conform conduct to the law.

   b. In other words, individuals who do not have the ability to reason, e.g. insanity or infancy.

   c. Criticisms – the proponents of the character theory believe that the free choice theory is too narrow.

III. Infancy   **[174]**

A. Historically

  1. From the earliest times, common law recognised that children should be fully accountable for their actions. See *doli incapax* [12].

   a. Recognised that young children were not able to form the required *mens rea*.

   b. While the punishment of child offenders has changed dramatically, the rules relating to the prosecution of child offenders have remained the same for centuries.

  2. The common law recognised three categories of children with regard to criminal liability:

   a. Those under seven.

     (1) Considered *doli incapax* – incapable of crime.

     (2) Child under seven cannot be prosecuted for any crime.

   b. Those aged between seven and fourteen.

     (1) Presumed *doli incapax*.

     (2) Rebuttable presumption – presumption may be rebutted

by showing that the child knew the difference between right and wrong.

    (a) Prosecution required to show that the child knew that what he or she was doing was seriously wrong. *R.* v. *Gorrie* (1919) 83 JP 136.

    (b) Seriously wrong test endorsed by the Irish High Court. *KM* v. *DPP* [1994] 1 IR 514.

  c. Those aged fourteen or over –

    (1) Law conclusively presumes that the child is able to distinguish between right and wrong.

    (2) Child may be prosecuted in the same way as an adult.

B. The Children Act 2001 [175]

  1. Generally –

    a. Philosophy of the Act is that children in conflict with the law must be treated as children first.

    b. Detention should only be used as a last resort.

  2. Children Act 2001, section 52(1) – *doli incapax.* [176]

    a. Age of criminal responsibility raised from age seven to age twelve.

    (1) Children under the age of twelve are *doli incapax*, i.e. unable to commit crime.

    (2) Age twelve is the lowest age of responsibility in Europe.

  3. Children Act 2001, section 52(2)– rebuttable presumption. [177]

    a. A child who is twelve but not yet fourteen is considered incapable of committing any offence, but this presumption may be rebutted by showing that the child knew the difference between right and wrong.

    b. Prosecution is required to show that the child knew that what he or she was doing was seriously wrong. *R.* v. *Gorrie* (1919) 83 JP 136.

    c. Seriously wrong test endorsed by the Irish High Court. *KM* v. *DPP* [1994] I IR 514.

  4. Children aged fourteen or over are still conclusively presumed to be able to distinguish between right and wrong. Child may be prosecuted in the same way as an adult.

  5. Note: Section 54 – Aiding, Abetting, Counselling or Procuring a Child for Crime – [178]

    a. Where a child under fourteen is responsible for what would normally be considered a criminal offence, any person who

aids, abets, counsels or procures the child in relation to it shall be guilty of that offence.
b. Any person aiding, abetting, counselling or procuring a child under fourteen to commit a criminal offence will be held liable to be tried and punished as a principal offender for that offence.

IV. Insanity [179]

A. Historically

1. Early common law –
   a. First recognised in the fourteenth century. See [12].
   b. Chief Justice Coke wrote that insanity was no defence unless the defendant resembled a beast rather than a man.
   c. Hale would have allowed the defence where a man had the understanding of a child under fourteen.
2. Historical development of modern insanity – [180]
   a. *R. v. Hadfield* (1800) 27 St Tr 1281 – the defendant believed he had to die in order to save the world. Because suicide was a sin he could not kill himself, so he fired a shot at the king, which he knew was a capital offence. It was held that he was not accountable for his actions because of insanity. He was acquitted.
   b. *R. v. M'Naghten* [1843–60] All ER Rep 229 – the defendant suffered from an insane delusion that Sir Robert Peel was persecuting him. The defendant believed that Peel had to be killed. However, the defendant killed Peel's secretary instead. At his trial, the defendant was acquitted because of insanity. The decision caused such public outrage that the House of Lords asked the Law Lords a series of questions designed to explain the defence of insanity. The judges complied, although protesting the impropriety of having to do so outside a case. The answers to these questions have become known as the *M'Naghten* Rules and they have continued to form the basis of the defence of insanity ever since.
      (1) The *M'Naghten* Rules. [181]
         (a) Rule 1: A partial delusion will be no defence if the defendant still knew, despite the delusion, that his or her actions were against the law.
         (b) Rule 2: Every person is presumed to be sane and therefore accountable for his or her actions until the

contrary is proven.

    (c) Rule 3: To establish insanity, the defendant must show that at the time the act was committed, he or she was suffering from a defect of reason arising from a disease of the mind such that he or she did not know the nature and quality of his or her actions, or if he or she did know, he or she did not know that they were wrong. Wrong in this respect means contrary to the law.

    (d) Rule 4: A person suffering from a partial delusion only should be treated as if the facts of the delusion were real.

3. Trial of Lunatic Act 1883   **[182]**

    a. Section 2 provides that where a defendant has been found insane, the jury should return a special verdict of guilty but insane.

    b. *People (DPP)* v. *Gallagher* [1991] ILRM 339 held that the special verdict was actually a verdict of acquittal.

4. Henchy Committee Report (1978) made recommendations concerning the insanity, but none were implemented.

    a. Redrafting the provisions relation to insanity verdicts.

    b. Setting up a system of tribunals to monitor and advise on the release of defendants found not guilty by reason of insanity.

    c. Introduction of diminished responsibility.

B. Current Law on Insanity   **[183]**

1. *M'Naghten* Rules still form the basis of the insanity defence, but in Ireland it is not the sole and exclusive test. See [187].

    a. Presumption of sanity – Rule 2 – all persons are considered sane and accountable for his or her actions until the contrary is proven.   **[184]**

        (1) Rebuttable presumption – if the defendant cannot prove that he or she is 'insane', the defendant will be held accountable for his or her actions.

        (2) Onus or burden of proving the defence of insanity rests upon the defendant.

            (a) Unique among defences, as this requirement is an exception to the *Woolmington* principle. See [36].

    b. Standard of proof required of the defendant in proving insanity is on the balance of probabilities.   **[185]**

        (1) Civil rather than criminal standard of proof used.

(2) Rationale: Defendants do not have the power or resources of the State.

  c. No medical or psychiatric experts required.

    (1) However, McAuley has noted that there are no recent reported cases where the defence of insanity was successfully raised in the absence of medical evidence.

  d. Finding of fact for the jury to decide whether or not a defendant was legally insane at the time of the commission of the offence.

2. *M'Naghten* Rule 3 contains threefold test for establishing defence of insanity. **[186]**

  a. The defendant must be suffering from a disease of the mind.

  b. The disease of the mind must cause the defendant's defect of reason.

  c. Because of the disease of the mind and defect of reason, the defendant did not know the nature and quality of his or her acts or did not know the acts were wrong.

    (1) Litmus test of insanity is the defendant's knowledge.

3. *M'Naghten* Rules are not the sole and exclusive test for insanity in Ireland. *People (AG)* v. *O'Brien* [1936] IR 236. **[187]**

  a. Note: Irish courts have expanded the *M'Naghten* Rules further than the English courts.

  b. Example: *Doyle* v. *Wicklow County Council* [1974] IR 55 – a seventeen-year-old burned down an abattoir while suffering from a mental disorder. The plaintiff, who owned the abattoir, claimed compensation from the defendant. The Supreme Court ruled that the *M'Naghten* Rules are not the 'sole and exclusive test' for determining insanity. Reasoning: The questions asked of the Law Lords were limited to insane delusions and the answers should be similarly limited. Situations that do not fit precisely within the Rules may still amount to legal insanity.

C. *Defect of Reason from Disease of the Mind – Rule 3*   **[188]**

1. Legal question, not medical question – whether the defendant was suffering from a disease of the mind.

2. Defence of insanity.

  a. Exists to provide a defence to those who commit acts through no fault of their own, i.e. their conduct is excused.

  b. Therefore, the defence of insanity:

    (1) Excludes external cause of actions, such as drinks or drugs.

(a) See self-induced automatism [63].

(b) See intoxication [200].

(2) Excludes some internal cause of actions, such as anger, forgetfulness or carelessness. *R.* v. *Clark* (1972) (facts below).   **[189]**

c. Requires loss of power to reason.

(1) *R.* v. *Clark* [1972] 1 All ER 219 – defendant charged with larceny for failing to pay for items from a supermarket. Her defence was that she had taken the items without paying for them due to absentmindedness brought on by depression. The trial judge held that this raised the issue of insanity, but this was rejected on appeal. The Appeal Court held that insanity only applies to people who have lost their powers of reasoning due to a disease of the mind. It does not apply to those who retain the power of reasoning but who in moments of confusion or absent-mindedness fail to use their powers to the full.

3. Disease of the mind – not limited to psychiatric conditions. **[190]**

a. Essence of disease of the mind is a malfunctioning of the mind caused by a disease. *R.* v. *Quick* [1973] 3 All ER 347.

(1) *R.* v. *Sullivan* [1983] 2 All ER 673 – the defendant had epilepsy and kicked an eighty-year-old man in the head during a seizure. The defendant wanted to raise the defence of non-insane automatism rather than insanity. The House of Lords expressed sympathy for the defendant's desire to avoid being labeled insane, but endorsed the approach taken in *Kemp* and *Quick*.

b. A physical condition can be a disease of the mind if it impairs the defendant's ability to reason.   **[191]**

(1) *R.* v. *Kemp* [1956] 3 All ER 249 – the defendant suffered from arteriosclerosis, a lack of blood to the defendant's brain such that he lost consciousness. While in this state the defendant attacked his wife with a hammer. He was a man of excellent character and he and his wife had been regarded as a devoted couple. The prosecution argued that arteriosclerosis is not a disease of the mind. It was held that for insanity purposes, mind was concerned with the mental faculties of reason, memory and understanding. A condition that impaired these faculties was a disease of the mind for insanity purposes.

(2) External causes are not diseases of the mind for insanity purposes. **[192]**

    (a) *R. v. Quick* – the defendant was a nurse who assaulted a patient. He argued that he was diabetic and had not followed medical instructions in the taking of his insulin. The defendant took the insulin, did not eat much and then went out drinking. He claimed that he had suffered a hypoglycemic shock and had no knowledge of his actions at the time. He argued that he should be acquitted on the grounds of automatism. See [58]. The trial judge directed that his defence was consistent only with insanity and the defendant pleaded guilty. On appeal it was held that the essence of a disease of the mind is a malfunctioning of the mind caused by a disease. A malfunction of the mind caused through the use of an external factor such as drink or drugs did not arise as a result of a disease. The defendant's condition did not result from his diabetes, but his failure to follow medical advice. The causative factor was external rather than internal.

c. Condition is not required to be permanent, it is only required to be present at the time the offence was committed and operated to deprive the defendant of the defendant's power to reason. *R. v. Sullivan.* **[193]**

D. Nature and Quality of the Act – M'Naghten *Rule 3*   [194]

1. After establishing that he or she was suffering from a disease of the mind at the time of the act, the defendant must also prove that the disease caused an impairment of his or her ability to reason.
2. This can be done in either of two ways:
   a. By showing that the defendant did not know the nature and quality of his or her actions.
   (1) This means that the defendant cannot comprehend the physical nature of his or her actions.
   (2) Examples:
       (a) If Sandra cut Paul's hand thinking that she was cutting up a chicken, Sandra does not know the nature and quality of her act.
       (b) Throwing a baby on a fire thinking that the baby is a log of wood.

> (c) Beheading another, thinking it would be entertaining to watch the victim search for his or her head.

b. The defendant did not know his or her acts were wrong. **[195]**

> (1) Wrong in this sense means illegal.
>
>> (a) *R. v. Windle* [1952] 2 All ER 1 – the defendant killed his wife by giving her an overdose of aspirin. His wife had complained many times about her life and frequently mentioned committing suicide. When he surrendered to the police he said, 'I suppose they will hang me for this.' At trial, the doctors giving evidence were satisfied that the wife was insane. Doctors were equally satisfied that the defendant was suffering from a form of communicated insanity that might constitute a disease of the mind. However, the court held that because the defendant knew that his acts were illegal he knew they were wrong. The defendant could not use the defence of insanity.

3. Additionally, Irish law recognises irresistible impulse – where the defendant is fully aware of his or her actions and knows full well that they are wrong, but due to some mental impairment he or she is unable to prevent himself or herself from committing the criminal offence. **[196]**

a. *People (AG)* v. *McGrath* (1960) 1 Frewen 192 – the defendant committed an assault from which the victim later died. The defence appealed against the conviction on the basis that the killing was due to an uncontrollable impulse. The defence was rejected.

b. *People (AG)* v. *Hayes* (1967) unrep. CCC – the defendant killed his wife and claimed that he had been unable to stop himself. Henchy J. held that although the defendant knew the nature and quality of his acts and knew that they were wrong, because of a disease of the mind he could not stop himself. The defendant would be allowed to use the defence of insanity.

c. *Doyle* v. *Wicklow County Council* (1974) – see [187] for facts. Supreme Court endorsed *Hayes* decision.

d. English approach – more restrictive.

> (1) *R. v. Codere* (1916) 12 Cr App Rep 21 – the defendant, an officer in the Canadian army, killed a fellow soldier. He was convicted of murder, but he argued that nature and quality suggested different aspects of the test for

insanity. Nature, he argued, referred to the physical nature of the act, while quality referred to its moral character. Court of Appeal held that the defendant's ability to discern the moral character of his actions was not relevant, i.e. if he knew he was killing but believed that the killing was justified, he could still be convicted.

(2) *R. v. Dickie* [1984] 3 All ER 173 – the defendant set fire to a wastebasket, knowing what he had done. There was evidence that he was suffering from a manic-depressive episode at the time, but he had known what he was doing. The fact that he was not able to appreciate the consequences and dangers of his actions was not material.

E. Partial Insane Delusions – Rules 1 and 4 [197]

1. A defendant suffering from a partial delusion will be treated as if the delusion was real.
2. Then a determination must be made as to whether the law recognises the delusional situation as a defence to the offence.
3. Example: Breda has a delusion that her neighbour George is a serial rapist and is going to attack her. While George is taking out the trash, Breda is startled and hits George in the face and runs away.
   a. Step 1: Partial delusion treated as if real – George is a serial rapist and is going to attack Breda.
   b. Step 2: The law does recognise that Breda has the right to use reasonable force to defend herself and she is not required to wait for George to land the first blow. See self-defence [236] *et seq.*

F. Consequences of Insanity [198]

1. Trial of Lunatics Act 1883, section 2 provides that upon a finding of insanity the jury should return a special verdict of guilty but insane.
   a. *People (DPP) v. Gallagher* [1991] ILRM 339 – special verdict is in reality an acquittal.
2. Section 2(2) provides that the defendant should be detained in a psychiatric hospital during the government's pleasure.
   a. *Gallagher* – the defendant was found guilty but insane of a double murder. He was detained in Dundrum Central Mental Hospital. The Supreme Court held that the release or other-

wise of the defendant was not part of the administration of justice, but a matter for the executive. Also:

    (1) Any defendant who is guilty but insane has the right to apply to the government for release on the grounds that he or she is no longer a danger.

    (2) Government is obliged to hold a full and fair enquiry into all the circumstances of the case before reaching a decision.

    (3) The decision of the inquiry is not reviewable by the courts.

b. The decision-making process for the release of defendants who were found guilty but insane must conform to the constitutional requirements of natural justice. *Kirwan* v. *Minister for Justice* [1994] 1 ILRM 444.

    (1) Facts: The defendant sought release from Dundrum Hospital and sought legal aid for the preparation of his required statement for release. It was held that sought legal assistance was excessive, but recognition was made that the defendant required a solicitor, which was not excessive.

G. Reform [199]

1. Generally, all legal commentators agree that insanity is in urgent need of reform.

2. The Criminal Justice (Mental Disorder) Bill 1996 was introduced, but has not yet been enacted.

3. The Criminal Law (Insanity) Bill 2002 was introduced.

  a. Sets out to affirm and codify Irish criminal law on insanity.

    (1) Section 4(1) codifies the common law rules regarding when the defence is available (from *M'Naghten* and *Doyle*, see [181] and [187] above).

      (a) The defendant did not know the nature and quality of his or her acts.

      (b) The defendant did not know what he or she was doing was wrong, or

      (c) The defendant was not able to refrain from committing the acts.

  b. Provides for mental disorder as an excusing mental illness.

    (1) Section 1 defined as including mental illness, mental handicap, dementia or any disease of the mind.

    (2) Intoxication is specifically excluded.

c. Introduces diminished responsibility.
   (1) Is a lesser form of insanity – it operates as a partial defence to murder, and if successful reduces murder to manslaughter.
       (a) It was introduced into English law by section 2 of the Homicide Act 1957.
   (2) Applies where the defendant can show that at the time of the murder the defendant was suffering from an abnormality of the mind that substantially impaired his or her mental responsibility for his or her acts.
       (a) Abnormality of the mind means a state of mind so different from that of ordinary people that a reasonable person would deem it abnormal. *R. v. Byrne* (1960).
       (b) Test is objective.
       (c) Irresistible impulse is a form of diminished responsibility.
   (3) *R. v. Byrne* [1960] 3 All ER 1 – the defendant was a violent psychopath who strangled a young woman and mutilated her corpse. The medical evidence disclosed a long history of violent perverted desires that were stronger than normal sexual desires.
   (4) Note: Diminished responsibility is not recognised in Irish law (until the enactment of the Criminal Law (Insanity) Bill 2002).

V. Intoxication   [200]

A. General Principles

1. The law pertaining to intoxication does not distinguish between alcohol and other substances.
2. The relationship between intoxication and crime is well documented.   [201]
   a. Per Lord Elwyn-Jones in *DPP* v. *Majewski* [1976] 2 All ER 142, 'Self-induced alcoholic intoxication has been a factor in violence…throughout the history of crime in this country…voluntary drug taking with the potential and actual dangers to others it may cause has added a new dimension to the old problem…'.
3. Common law rules regarding intoxication as a defence are strict.   [202]

     a. Traditional common law attitude – no regard for a defendant who committed an offence while intoxicated.

     b. Hale stated that the defendant should 'have the same judgment as if he were in his right senses.'

  4. Modern approaches –   **[203]**

     a. English approach – intoxication is not a defence to a criminal charge unless the offence requires proof of specific intent. See specific intent [208].

     b. Modern Irish approach is unclear.

  5. *Mens rea* – intoxication as a defence arises most often where the defendant was so intoxicated that he or she was not able to form the necessary *mens rea*.   **[204]**

     a. Not a true excuse defence, but rather a failure to prove a required mental element of offence.

       (1) Therefore similar to mistake of fact. See [98].

     b. Sometimes through long-term abuse the defendant's brain is damaged such that he or she cannot form the require*d mens rea* for an offence. Insanity defence may apply. See [179] *et seq.*

B. Definition   **[205]**

  1. The American Law Institute in its Model Penal Code provides that intoxication is 'a disturbance of mental or physical capacities resulting form the introduction of substances into the body.'

  2. Definition adopted by the Law Reform Commission in its Consultation Paper and Report on Intoxication (1995).

     a. Definition describes more than drunkenness.

       (1) Drunkenness is never a defence to any charge. *DPP* v. *Beard* (1920) below.

       (2) Drunkenness may be an aggravating factor resulting in a heavier sentence.

  3. Two types of intoxication:

     a. Voluntary, and

     b. Involuntary.

C. Voluntary Intoxication   **[206]**

  1. Definition: Where the defendant deliberately ingested alcohol or drugs.

     a. Also includes where the defendant deliberately took an intoxicant but was not aware of its strength. *R.* v. *Allen* [1988] Crim LR 698.

2. **Basic intent** – intoxication is *not* a defence to offences of basic intent. **[207]**
   a. Reasoning: The effect of alcohol upon the body is well known, and therefore anyone who intoxicates himself or herself must know what may happen.
   b. Becoming intoxicated is deemed to be a reckless thing to do and proof of recklessness is sufficient for offences of basic intent.
3. **Specific intent** – intoxication may be a defence to offences of specific intent. **[208]**
   a. Examples of offences of specific and basic intent.
      (1) Specific intent: Murder, attempts, theft, robbery, burglary.
      (2) Basic intent: Manslaughter, rape, assault.
   b. *DPP* v. *Beard* [1920] All ER Rep 21 – the defendant raped a girl and then suffocated her to death. He argued that intoxication is a defence to any criminal charge and this was accepted by the Court of Appeal. The House of Lords held that this contention was too broad and did not represent the law as it was not based on authority. Decision highlighted differences between drunkenness and intoxication. Intoxication is only a defence if the defendant was incapable of forming the specific intent required to constitute the offence.
   c. *DPP* v. *Majewski* [1976] 2 All ER 142 – the defendant was convicted of three counts of assault occasioning actual bodily harm and three counts of assaulting a police officer, all arising out of a brawl. The defendant's defence was that prior to the incident he had consumed a considerable amount of alcohol and drugs and he therefore had no *mens rea,* nor any memory of the incident. House of Lords held:
      (1) Common law rule that intoxication is never a defence still existed, but was no longer applied absolutely.
      (2) Where an offence required proof of specific intent, intoxication could operate as a defence if it negated that specific intent.
      (3) Where the offence required proof of basic intent, intoxication was not relevant.
      (4) Theories behind opinion –
         (a) Where a person causes himself or herself to be in a position where his or her self-control is removed, he or she should not be permitted to benefit from it.

      (b) One of the purposes of the criminal law is to protect people from unjust attack: if intoxication were to be a general defence, the public's level of protection would necessarily be reduced.

    (5) The Lords acknowledge that the distinction between specific and basic intent was not logical, but it was an attempt to balance policy with principle.

    (6) Decision has been criticised.

  d. Definition of specific intent – at least three definitions have been advanced.   **[209]**

    (1) *Majewski* – Lord Simon equated it with direct intent or a particular purpose implied in the definition of the crime.

      (a) Problems with definition – murder is an offence of specific intent and does not require any purposive element, while rape, which is an offence of basic intent, does.

    (2) *Morgan* – Lord Simon had defined offences of specific intent as those that require proof of an ulterior intent. For offences to specific intent, the elements of the *mens rea* extend beyond those of the *actus reus*, while offences of basic intent were defined as those in which the elements of the *mens rea* extended no further than the elements of the *actus reus*.

      (a) Problem with this definition – many specific intent offences such as murder do not have an extra element of *mens rea*.

    (3) *Majewski* – Lord Elwyn-Jones defined offences of basic intent as those that can be established by proof of recklessness, while offences of specific intent are those that require proof of intention. For basic intent offence, the act of voluntarily becoming intoxicated is a reckless thing to do and this is sufficient for a conviction. Such recklessness is not enough for intention (specific intent), thereby intoxication is a defence.

      (a) This definition was adopted by the majority of the House of Lords in *MPC* v. *Caldwell* [1981] 1 All ER 961.

4. Irish approach – not entirely clear.   **[210]**

  a. Holdings in *Manning* and *McBride* suggest that intoxication is a defence to any criminal charge providing it is sufficient to negate *mens rea*.

(1) *Manning* – intoxication is no defence unless the defendant had consumed so much as to 'render him incapable of knowing what he was doing at all, or if he appreciated that, of knowing the consequences or probable consequences of his actions.' *People (AG)* v. *Manning* (1953) 89 ILTR 155.

(2) *McBride* – drunkenness is not a defence to any charge – *People (DPP)* v. *McBride* (1997), however it is relevant as to whether or not the defendant was capable of forming the required intent.

5. Dutch courage – **[211]**

   a. Definition: Where the defendant deliberately consumes an intoxicant in order to give himself or herself the courage to commit an offence.

   b. *AG for N. Ireland* v. *Gallagher* [1961] 3 All ER 229 – the defendant wanted to kill his wife. He bought a knife and a bottle of whiskey. He drank the whiskey to give himself courage, then he stabbed her to death. The House of Lords held that his conviction for murder should be upheld. Lord Denning held that where the defendant forms the intention to kill, prepares to do so, then drinks alcohol to give himself courage, he cannot then claim to have been incapable of forming *mens rea*.

     (1) Note: Smith and Hogan have correctly pointed out that *mens rea* and *actus reus* must coincide in terms of time. See [104].

     (2) At the time the defendant killed his wife it is possible that the defendant was so intoxicated he could not form the required *mens rea*.

     (3) It could be held to be evidence of a continuing intent. See [105].

     (4) Public policy – the decision is better than allowing a defendant to get away with murder.

D. Involuntary Intoxication   **[212]**

1. Definition: Where the defendant became intoxicated, but the defendant was not aware of ingesting alcohol or drugs, e.g. drink spiked.

2. Under the common law, where involuntary intoxication was shown, the defendant would not be held responsible for his or her conduct.

3. Modern approach – *R.* v. *Kingston* [1994] 3 All ER 353. **[213]**

    a. Where involuntary intoxication results in an inability on the part of the defendant to form *mens rea*, it is a complete defence to any criminal charge. *R.* v. *Kingston* [1994] 3 All ER 353.

    b. Where involuntary intoxication results in the defendant still being able to form a drugged intent, it is still an intent and the necessary *mens rea. R.* v. *Kingston.*

4. *R.* v. *Kingston* – the defendant had paedophiliac tendencies. Another man planned to blackmail him. To do this he lured a fifteen-year-old boy to his flat, spiked the defendant's drink and invited the defendant to abuse the boy. Both the defendant and the blackmailer were charged with indecent assault. The defendant argued that his actions were brought about by the spiked drink. The trial judge directed the jury that the defendant could only be acquitted where the intoxication negatived *mens rea* and the defendant was convicted. The Court of Appeal quashed the conviction because the conduct of the defendant was brought about because of the fraud of another. The House of Lords ruled that the original conviction should be reinstated. Held: Although the defendant surrendered to his tendencies he knew what he was doing. A drugged intent is still an intent. He had the necessary *mens rea*, thus his conviction was valid.

E. *Reform* [214]

1. In its 1995 Consultation Paper on Intoxication, the Law Reform Commission indicated that the issue of voluntary intoxication could be approached in one of two ways.

    a. Intoxication could not be a defence to any charge.

    b. Intoxication could be a defence to any charge, but a new offence of committing an offence while intoxicated could be created.

2. Recommended – statutory provision enacted ruling out intoxication as a defence to any charge.

3. Involuntary intoxication recommendation – defence to any charge where the level of intoxication is such that the defendant could not form the necessary *mens rea*.

    a. Expanded to include:

        (1) Where the defendant took drugs for medicinal purposes on medical advice and according to directions or was unaware that it would or might create aggressive or uncontrollable behaviour.

VI. Duress [215]

A. In General

1. There are two types of duress.
   a. Duress by threats or duress *per minas*.
   b. Duress by circumstances.
      (1) Basically similar to necessity. See the defence of necessity [228]. [216]
2. Definition: Where '[t]hreats of immediate death or serious personal violence so great as to overbear the ordinary power of human resistance should be accepted as a justification for acts which would otherwise be criminal.' Murnaghan J. in *People (AG)* v. *Whelan* [1934] IR 518.
   a. 'Concession to human frailty' (*R.* v. *Howe* [1987] 1 All ER 771 (House of Lords)).
      (1) The defendant committed a criminal offence because he or she was forced to do so, either because of threats to himself/herself or his/her family.
      (2) The defendant intended to commit the criminal offence, i.e. had the *mens rea,* but the law does not hold the defendant fully responsible.
   b. ***Whelan* Rules –** [217]
      (1) The will of the defendant must have been overborne by the threats.
      (2) The defence does not apply to murder (but the court explicitly left open the question of which offences may be met by evidence of duress).
         (a) More recently, the English Court of Appeal, in *R.* v. *Pommell* (1995) 2 Cr App Rep 607, held that duress of circumstances should be available to meet any charge other than murder, attempted murder and some forms of treason.
         (b) Also, in *R.* v. *Howe* (1987) the House of Lords ruled that it is not available to charge of secondary participation in a murder.
      (3) The duress must be operating when the offence is committed.
      (4) If there is an opportunity for the individual will to reassert itself and it is not taken, a plea of duress will fail.

3. **The test** – not clear what test the Irish courts will use.   **[218]**
   a. In *Whelan*, Murnaghan J. referred to the 'ordinary power of human resistance.'
      (1) Suggests some degree of objectivity.
   b. Court in *R. v. Howe* [1987] 1 All ER 771 compared duress with provocation.
      (1) Charleton notes that duress and provocation are different.
         (a) Duress involves a loss of self-control.
         (b) Provocation involves a rational choice between what the defendant sees as the lesser of two evils.
      (2) *People (DPP) v. MacEoin* [1978] IR 27 – provocation held to be decided according to a subjective test.
   c. Objective English test – two-step process –   **[219]**
      (1) Jury must be satisfied that the defendant acted on a reasonable fear of immediate danger.
      (2) The jury must be satisfied that a sober person of reasonable firmness, sharing the relevant characteristics of the defendant, would have acted in a similar fashion under similar duress.
         (a) Relevant characteristics – *R. v. Hegarty* [1994] Crim LR 353, age, gender and state of physical health.
      (3) Criticisms – English Law Commission.
         (a) A weak-willed person will not be able to resist the threats, thereby making the test useless as a means of law enforcement.
         (b) The objective test demands unreasonable standards from a weak person, which undermines the whole purpose of the defence.
4. Will must be overborne –   **[220]**
   a. To avail of defence, the defendant must show that he or she faced some serious and imminent danger.
      (1) Serious means a threat of injury or death.
         (a) Does not include threat to property.
         (b) Does not include a threat to embarrass.
      (2) Imminent does not appear to mean immediate commission.
         (a) *R. v. Hudson and Taylor* [1971] 2 All ER 244 – the defendants were prosecution witnesses in a criminal trial arising from a bar room brawl. They were threatened by an associate of the accused and consequently failed to identify the accused, who was acquitted. The

defendants were convicted of perjury and appealed. The Court of Appeal quashed the convictions, holding that the fact that the threat could not be carried out immediately in the courtroom was not relevant. The threat was a present one that could have been carried out very shortly after the trial.

- b. Motivation of the defendant to commit the crime must have been the threat. **[221]**
  - (1) Presence of other motivations to commit the crime will not defeat the defence if the jury is satisfied that the crime would not have been committed but for the threats of injury.
    - (a) *R. v. Valderrama-Vega* [1985] Crim LR 220 – the defendant was under financial pressure and was then threatened with disclosure of his homosexuality. He then received threats of death or serious harm. Court held that first two threats were not sufficient to constitute duress on their own, but the cumulative effect on the defendant in combination with the other threats could be considered by a jury.
  - (2) Greed – as other motivation. **[222]**
    - (a) *R. v. Ortiz* (1986) 83 Cr App Rep 173 –the defendant was a Columbian involved in the fashion industry. He met a Columbian drug lord who demanded that the defendant act as a courier for drugs and threatened to harm the defendant's family if he refused. The defendant agreed and subsequently received huge sums of money. The defendant pleaded duress, but was convicted. On appeal the defendant argued that it was possible for a man to commit a criminal act partly out of fear and partly out of greed. Appeal rejected and court suggested that it would be difficult in practice for a jury to conclude that the defendant's will had been overborne if he was also acting out of greed.
- c. Note: Per *Whelan*, duress lasts only as long as the threat is present and exerting an influence over the defendant. If there is an opportunity for the defendant's will to reassert itself, the opportunity must be taken.

5. Voluntary duress – **[223]**
  - a. Where the defendant voluntarily exposes himself or herself to duress, he or she cannot then use that duress as an excuse or defence to his or her criminal conduct.

b. Duress is not available to someone who has voluntarily joined a criminal organisation with knowledge of its nature.   **[224]**

   (1) *R. v. Sharp* [1987] 3 All ER 103 – the defendant took part in the robbery of several post offices. A murder was committed during one of the robberies. The defendant argued that he did not want to go on the robberies when he learned that guns would be used, but he lost his nerve when the ringleader threatened to kill him.

   (2) Principle in *Sharp* may not be appropriate in all circumstances. Court of Appeal in *R. v. Shepherd* (1987) 86 Cr App Rep 47 – the defendant had joined a group that stole cartons of cigarettes from shops. After willingly participating in the first episode, the defendant attempted to withdraw from the gang. He did not because of the threats of the ringleader.

   (3) *R. v. Hegarty* [1994] Crim LR 353 – the defendant escaped from police custody and was offered accommodation by a group of men. He lived there for three months. One night the men violently assaulted the defendant and threatened his family. The defendant was then forced to participate in a series of armed robberies. It was held that duress is available where the original association was not voluntary.

Review Questions

1. Tyron loves to collect women's shoes. He prefers the right shoe but sometimes he will take a left shoe. Currently, Tyron has over 10,000 shoes filling one complete room of his home from floor to ceiling. Tyron saw a lovely baby blue pump with a three-inch heel on Anne's foot. While Anne was visiting the gym Tyron crept into the changing room and took her shoe. Does Tyron have a valid defence to a charge of theft?

2. John went into the hospital for an operation. After the surgery, while still under the effects of the anaesthetic, John got out of his bed and staggered into a nearby ward, where he climbed into bed with Karen and sexually assaulted her, believing that Karen was his wife. Will John be successful if he relies upon the defence of intoxication?

3. Brian joined a Bible study group at university. Unknown to Brian, the group was connected to a cult. Soon Brian was completely under

the control of the leader of the cult, Brother Bob. Brother Bob conditions his followers by whipping them if they do not follow his every order. Brother Bob ordered Brian to kill Bob's ex-wife, Louise. When Brian appeared reluctant to kill Louise, Brother Bob threatened to kill Brian and his parents. Brian reluctantly killed Louise. Does Brian have a valid defence to a charge of killing Louise?

4. On Christmas Day 1995 Mary had a baby boy that she named Noel. Noel was a mischievous boy and on St Stephen's Day 2001 Noel took his mother's cigarette from an ashtray and poked his little cousin in the face, burning him. Noel caused the baby to suffer a severe burn and laughed happily when the baby screamed in pain. Does Noel have a defence to a criminal charge of assault?

5. 'Driven to it', *Irish Independent,* 14 September 2002, p. 28 – 'A German got drunk and drove erratically through a town in the east of the country – specifically so he could lose his license. He told police in Georgsmarienhuete that he did it because he was sick and tired of having to take his wife everywhere. They obliged by banning him.' Assume that these events took place in Ireland. Would the defendant have the defence of duress *per minas*?

6. Colin was obsessed with vampires. He read about vampires, he dressed completely in black, collected vampire movies, refused to go outside during daylight hours and went so far as to have his teeth altered to look like fangs. His girlfriend Mortica allowed him to draw blood from her arm and drink it. When Mortica's blood was not enough for him, Colin carefully planned the murder of his mother to drink her blood. When he realised that he would not be able to kill her without drawing attention to himself, he selected a homeless teenager and killed her instead.

   (a) Will Colin be able to avail of the defence of insanity for the death of the teenager?

   (b) What defence, if any, might Colin be able to avail of if he is charged with assaulting Mortica?

   (c) What offence, if any, did Colin commit by planning his mother's murder?

7. Simon was upset at the way he was being treated at work. He went to his local pub and began drinking. When the pub closed he tried to walk home, but kept stumbling out into the street. When a man named Luke attempted to help, Simon picked up a stone and hit Luke in the head. A police officer observed Simon hitting Luke and arrested Simon. Simon cannot remember the incident. Does Simon have a valid defence to a charge of assault?

8. Georgette has three sons. Michael is fourteen, Larry is twelve and Joe is ten. Recently, all three boys were arrested while vandalising cars. What criminal responsibility, if any, will be applied to (a) Michael (b) Larry and (c) Joe?

5

JUSTIFICATION DEFENCES

Chapter synopsis

I.   *General Principles* [225]

A. *Definition:* *A justification defence is where what would normally be criminal conduct is not because the existing circumstances make the conduct socially acceptable and therefore does not attract criminal liability.*

1. For example, if Sandra intentionally hit Paul in the eye it is normally an assault. See assault [359]. However, if Sandra was acting in self-defence to stop Paul from dragging her off of the footpath into a dark alley, the existing circumstances means that Sandra's conduct is not morally wrong nor criminal.

B. *Historically* [226]

1. In early English legal history the distinction between justifications and excuses was a matter of practical significance.
   a. Felonies – a justified defendant was acquitted and excused. Defendant was subject to the same punishment as a convicted offender (the death penalty and forfeiture of his property). See [11]. A defendant could escape the death penalty with a pardon from the king.
   b. Over time the distinction blurred.
2. Today, justified and excused defendants are treated the same by the criminal courts, i.e. acquitted.

C. Theories Supporting Justification Defences   [227]

1. **Public benefit theory** – under the early common law this was the dominant theory. Conduct was only justified if it benefited society.

2. **Moral forfeiture theory** – an individual's conduct is justified so long as it does not result in a socially undesirable result.
   a. Individuals have certain moral rights or interests that society supports through criminal law, e.g. liberty, but which may be forfeited by the individual.
   b. Note: Forfeiture of a right such as liberty is not the same thing as waiving that right.
   c. Applied – if Steve is attacked by Les, whose intent is to kill Steve, if in defending himself Steve kills Les, Steve's conduct is deemed justified. Les's moral choice to kill Steve is wrong, therefore Les has forfeited his right to life. The death of Les is not viewed as a socially undesirable result.
   d. Criticism – many believe that the killing of a human being is always socially undesirable.

3. **Moral rights theory** – an individual's conduct may be justified on the grounds that the individual has a right to protect a particular moral interest.
   a. Contrasted with moral forfeiture:
      (1) Moral forfeiture theory focuses on Les's wrongdoing.
      (2) Moral rights theory focuses on the rights of the defendant, Steve.
   b. Under this theory Steve has an affirmative right to protect himself, thus Les's death is not treated as being socially irrelevant.
   c. Criticism – this theory has the potential to allow disproportional responses to any harm threatened.

4. **Lesser harm theory** – a defendant is authorised to act when the defendant's interests are greater than those of the person harmed. This theory is consistent with the utilitarian goal of promoting individual conduct that reduces harm. See utilitarian theory [42].
   a. Interests are graded, e.g. preserving human life is more important than preserving property.
   b. Criticism – in the heat of the moment it is often difficult to weigh and correctly respond, e.g. Steve and Les both have the right to life. Under this theory, when Les attacked Steve, Steve's conduct (preservation of life) is justified so long as he pursues a lesser harm, i.e. injures but does not kill Les.

II. Necessity [228]

A. Definition: *The defence of necessity arises where the defendant intentionally commits a crime to prevent some greater evil where there is no reasonable alternative.*

1. Similar to the defence of duress, see [215].
   a. Necessity – the defendant chooses to commit a crime because of circumstances.
   b. Duress – will of the defendant is overborne by threats of another person.
2. Example – while walking home late one evening, Finbar tripped over a man lying severely injured in the street. If Finbar breaks into the nearest house to use the telephone to call for an ambulance and takes kitchen towels to stem the injured man's wounds, Finbar may be able to avail of the defence of necessity.
3. Some commentators question whether the defence of necessity still exists. [229]
   a. There are some recent English cases where duress by circumstances, i.e. necessity, has been allowed.
      (1) E.g. *R.* v. *Pommell* (1995) 2 Cr App R 607 – the defendant took a submachine gun from another man to prevent him from committing a murder with it. The defendant took the gun away late at night and gave evidence that he was going to give it to his brother the next morning to take to the police. The defendant was charged with being in unlawful possession of a firearm. It was held that the defence of necessity was available because of his 'commendable' action in preventing the far worse offence, i.e. murder.
      (2) Note: Clarkson notes that duress of circumstances may not be the same as necessity. Pointing to the English Court of Appeal decision *Re A (Conjoined Twins 2000)* [2000] 4 All ER 961 – in this case the doctors owed conflicting duties to conjoined twins. The doctors were justified in choosing the lesser of two evils, i.e. the death of one twin and not both.
   b. There is also statutory recognition of a defence in relation to criminal damage in: [230]
      (1) Section 6(2)(c) of the Criminal Justice Act 1991 as amended by section 21 of the Non-Fatal Offences Against the Person Act 1997.

(2) Section 18(3)(b) of the NFOAPA 1997, which deals with the justifiable use of force against a criminal act and provides that this occurs where the actor would have a defence on the grounds of duress, whether by threats or circumstances.

B. Restrictions on Use of Defence [231]

1. Necessity does not apply to murder.
   a. *R.* v. *Dudley & Stevens* (1884) Cox CC 624 – the defendants were in a lifeboat with a young boy and another man. After about twenty days without food or water, the defendants killed the boy, who was very weak and dying. All three men fed on the boy's body. They were rescued four days later and the defendants were charged with murder. The jury made a finding that the boy would have died anyway and shortly thereafter the defendants would have died. It was held that there was no rational basis for deciding who should live and who should die. The decision would invariably be made by the strongest at the expense of the weakest, and it is the weakest who are most in need of the greatest protection of law. Defendants were convicted of murder and their mandatory death sentence was commuted to six months' imprisonment.
2. There must be no alternative to the defendant's actions. [232]
   a. If Finbar (see [228] above) found the severely injured man at the entrance to the local hospital he would have had a reasonable alternative, i.e. run into the hospital and seek medical help for the injured man rather than break into a nearby home and take tea towels.
   b. *DPP* v. *Rogers* [1998] CRIM LR 202 – the defendant was speeding and was followed by a police car. Eventually the defendant stopped and expressed no surprise that the car following him was the police. At trial he attempted to use the defence of necessity, alleging that he was speeding to avoid his large, aggressive neighbour who he thought was following him to assault him because of a domestic dispute. The court rejected his defence because he had reasonable alternatives to breaking the law.
3. The defendant's actions must not go any further than necessary. [233]
   a. Once Finbar telephoned for an ambulance and took the tea towels to stem the blood from the injured man, he cannot

return to the house and make himself a sandwich while he waits for the ambulance to arrive.

4. **Self-induced necessity** – the defence is not available if the defendant brought about the circumstances. **[234]**
   a. If Finbar had earlier hit the injured man with his car, Finbar cannot avail of the defence of necessity if he decides to break into the house in an effort to save the man.

C. The Test – *the jury must be satisfied that the defendant committed the crime out of a reasonable belief of necessity and that a sober person of reasonable firmness, sharing the characteristics of the defendant, would have acted the same way.* R. v. Pommell *(1995) 2 Cr App Rep 607.* **[235]**

1. Uses objective and subjective elements – both must be met for a successful defence.
   a. Subjective – defendant committed the crime out of a reasonable belief of necessity, i.e. to prevent a great evil when there was no alternative to committing the crime.
   b. Objective – a sober person of reasonable firmness, sharing the characteristics of the defendant, e.g. gender, age, skills and abilities, would have acted in the same way.

III. Self-defence [236]

A. In General

1. Common law –
   a. Under the common law an individual is allowed to use reasonable force to:
      (1) Defend himself or herself.
      (2) Defend another.
      (3) Defend his or her property or the property of another.
      (4) Prevent the commission of a crime.
   b. Force – required to be objectively reasonable.
      (1) Lethal force – allowed so long as objectively reasonable.
      (2) Reasonable force requires:
         (a) That the force be immediately necessary, and
         (b) The force used must be proportionate.

B. Non-Fatal Offences Against the Person Act 1997 [237]

1. Sections 18–20 largely restate the common law.

2. **Section 18 – justifiable use of force** – provides a defence where:
   a. **Section 18(1)(a)** – the defendant used reasonable force to protect himself or herself from injury, assault or detention that is caused by a criminal act.
      (1) **Section 18(3)** – criminal acts are deemed to have occurred even if the person committing the criminal conduct would be acquitted on the grounds of automatism, duress, infancy, intoxication or insanity.
   b. **Section 18(1)(b)** – the defendant used reasonable force to protect himself or herself from a trespass to his or her person.
   c. **Section 18(e)** – the defendant used reasonable force to prevent a crime or a breach of the peace.
3. **Section 19(1) – lawful arrest** – allows the use of reasonable force by an individual to make a lawful arrest.   **[238]**
   a. **Section 19(3)** – whether or not the arrest is lawful will be judged according to the circumstances as the defendant believed them to be.
   b. Therefore, if the defendant acts under a mistaken belief of the facts, the lawfulness of the arrest will be judged according to that mistaken belief.
   c. E.g. Tom, a taxi driver, was driving down the quay one afternoon when he saw two men wearing masks run from a bank with sawed-off shotguns. The men ran toward a group of small schoolchildren waiting at a bus stop. Tom quickly pulled his taxi directly into the path of the running men and both ran into the car and were injured. Tom leapt from his taxi and grabbed the shotguns from the injured men. Unfortunately, the men were actors recreating a bank robbery for a television crime show. Because Tom believed the men were armed robbers running toward schoolchildren, his act of driving into the path of the running men would probably be considered reasonable.
4. **Section 20 – defines use of force** – for purposes of sections 18 and 19 as including: **[239]**
   a. The application of force or the causing of an impact upon another person's body or property,
   b. The threats of such force, or
   c. The detention of another person without the use of force.
   d. Section 20(3) provides that a threat of force may be reasonable although the actual use of force may not be.

5. **Section 22** abolishes the common law defences within the meaning of sections 18 and 19.
   a. Does not adequately address whether the common law has been totally replaced by the NFOAPA 1997.
   b. Given the title of the Act it appears that sections 18–20 deal only with self-defence in cases other than homicide, i.e. death of a human.
   c. In homicide cases the common law defence should be used.

C. Mistake [240]

1. Under the common law –
   a. Where there is a mistaken but genuine belief that a threat to oneself or another exists, the defendant is entitled to be judged according to his or her mistaken view of the circumstances.
   b. E.g. *R.* v. *Williams (Gladstone)* [1987] 3 All ER 411 – the defendant saw a man dragging a youth along the street. The man struck the youth and the youth called for help. The man falsely stated that he was a police officer. However, he had captured the youth after the youth stole a lady's handbag. When the man could not show any identification the defendant struggled with the man, causing him injury. The defendant was charged and convicted of assault causing actual bodily harm and appealed, arguing that he honestly believed that the victim was assaulting the youth so he went to the defence of the youth. The Court of Appeal held that the defendant was entitled to be judged according to his mistaken view of the circumstances.
2. Under the NFOAPA 1997 – [241]
   a. **Section 18(1)** provides that the use of force is not an offence if it is reasonable according to the circumstances as the defendant believes them to be.
   b. **Section 18(5)** provides that whether or not the defendant faced one of the threats which would justify the use of force is to be determined according to the defendant's view of the events.
   c. **Section 19(1)** provides that a person may use force in effecting or assisting in a lawful arrest so long as the force is reasonable under the circumstances.
   d. **Section 19(3)** provides that the question of whether the arrest is lawful is determined according to the circumstances as the person using the force believes them to be.

e. **Section 1(2)** provides that in relation to sections 18 and 19 it is not material that the defendant's belief turns out to be unjustified.

D. *Raising the Defence* [242]

1. **General rule** – there must be evidence before the jury that raises an issue of self-defence.
   a. Raised by either party – the evidence raising self-defence may be raised by either party, e.g. *People (AG)* v. *Quinn* [1965] IR 366 held that it was not material whether the evidence was raised by the prosecution or the defence. Once raised, the judge must instruct the jury on the applicable law and the jury must consider it. The burden rests on the prosecution to disprove the defence once it is raised. [243]
   b. Exception – the Supreme Court in *O'Laoire* v. *Medical Council* (unrep. SC 1997) held that the defendant must introduce some sort of evidence to raise the issue. If this is not done the judge does not have to instruct the jury to consider it.

E. *Issue of Fact* [244]

1. **General rule** – once self-defence is raised it is a matter for the jury to decide whether the defendant acted reasonably.
2. While giving jury instructions the judge has a duty to review the evidence, but the judge must avoid influencing the jury's decision in any way.
   a. *People (DPP)* v. *Clarke* [1994] 3 IR 289 – the deceased attacked the defendant, then threatened to cut his head off with a hatchet and then attack his family. The defendant went home and got a gun. During another confrontation, the defendant shot and killed the deceased. The judge stated that while theoretically an acquittal on the grounds of self-defence was justified, the facts of the case would hardly allow such a result. The Court of Criminal Appeal quashed the defendant's conviction and ordered a retrial on the grounds that the judge's comments amounted to a misdirection.

F. *Motive* [245]

1. Force is only justified if used in the face of immediate dangers.
   a. Revenge – force used out of revenge is never justified.

b. *People (AG)* v. *Coffey* (1966) 1 Frewen 314 – the defendant had allegedly been assaulted by a number of men. He went to his car with a number of friends, where they armed themselves with various tools and then went looking for the other men. Self-defence would not apply.

2. Where the defendant provoked the attack – it is not clear if the defence exists under the common law.   **[246]**

   a. *R.* v. *Browne* [1973] NI 96 – it was held that defensive action must not have been created by the conduct of the accused in the immediate context of the incident which was likely or intended to give rise to that action.

      (1) Example: If the defendant provokes the victim by racially insulting the victim and the victim then reacts violently toward the defendant, the defendant will not be able to avail of self-defence if he or she injures or kills the victim.

   b. *People (DPP)* v. *Doran* (1987)(unrep. CCA) – the defendant broke into the victim's home, but he ran when confronted by the victim. The victim chased the defendant along the street and hit the defendant several times with a golf club. The defendant pulled out a knife and stabbed the victim several times, killing the victim. The Court of Criminal Appeal did not disapprove of the defendant's attempt to rely on self-defence, apparently because the victim's reaction was excessive in relation to the threat faced.

3. **Section 18(7), NFOAPA 1997** provides that under the Act:

   a. General rule – the defence of self-defence will not apply to a defendant who causes conduct or a state of affairs with a view of using force to resist or terminate it.   **[247]**

      (1) Dennis knows that Johnny is a Kilkenny hurling fanatic. Knowing that Johnny will react physically, Dennis places a large Clare flag in Johnny's front garden the morning of the All Ireland between Kilkenny and Clare. If Johnny takes down the flag and throws it in Dennis's face, Dennis will not be able to avail of the defence of self-defence if he uses force against Johnny for throwing the flag in his face.

   b. Exception – the defence may apply where the defendant did something lawful, but knew that it would cause conduct or a state of affairs with a view of using force to resist or terminate it.   **[248]**

      (1) Although Dennis knows that his neighbour Johnny is a Kilkenny hurling fanatic, Dennis put a large Clare flag in

his own front garden the morning of the All Ireland between Kilkenny and Clare. When Johnny saw the flag he became angry and removed the flag and threw it in Dennis's face. If Dennis uses force against Johnny, such as pushing him out of his garden, Dennis will be able to avail of the defence of self-defence.

G. Retreat [249]

1. **Common Law –**
   a. A failure to retreat is not conclusive evidence that the defendant had not acted in self-defence, although he or she would still have to show a reluctance to fight. *R.* v. *McInnes* [1971] 3 All ER 295.
   b. It is not necessary to show a reluctance to fight, but rather unwillingness would be only one factor to be considered by the jury in deciding if the defendant had acted reasonably in the circumstances. *R.* v. *Bird*.
      (1) *R.* v. *Bird* [1985] 2 All ER 513 – the defendant, a woman, was pinned against a wall by the victim, who was holding a glass. In self-defence the defendant hit the man with the glass.
   c. Irish approach –
      (1) *People (AG)* v. *Dwyer* [1972] IR 416 – the principle in *McInnes* was quoted with approval.
      (2) The court would likely have upheld *Bird* had the case been decided at the time.
2. **Section 20(4) NFOAPA 1997** provides that the fact that the defendant had an opportunity to retreat but failed to take it is only one factor to be taken into account in deciding whether or not the force used was reasonable. [250]

H. Preparation

1. **Common Law –**
   a. 'A person has a right to defend himself, and to strike a blow in his defence without waiting until [his attacker] has struck.' (*Russell on Crime*, 10th ed., 1950). [251]
      (1) Quoted with approval in *People (AG)* v. *Keatley* [1954] IR 12.
   b. Reasonable steps to prepare for an attack.
      (1) *R.* v. *Fegan* [1972] NI 80 – the defendant married a woman of a different religion and faced threats from a

number of sources. He illegally bought a gun and ammu-
nition with a view of defending himself and his family. It
was held that his purpose in holding the weapon could be
lawful provided that:

(a) The threat must have been genuinely and reasonably
anticipated – not founded on fancy or an aggressive
motive.

(b) The threat should be of a nature that cannot be met
by other means.

(c) The steps taken by the defendant must be proportionate to the threat anticipated.

(2) *AG's Reference (No. 2 of 1983)* (1984) – the defendant, a
shopowner, made a number of petrol bombs at a time
when severe riots were breaking out around his shop.
[252]

(a) Held: The defendant was justified in arming himself
to meet a threat, and this justification could extend
to the manufacture of petrol bombs if the bombs
were reasonable in the circumstances.

(b) However, once the threat passed, there was no longer
a justification to retain the petrol bombs.

c. Irish approach – appears to endorse the English approach.**[253]**

(1) *Ross* v. *Curtin* (unrep. HC) (1989) – in this civil case it
was found that the defendant shopkeeper held a .22 rifle
to protect himself and his property, and this was held to
be justifiable.

(2) *People (DPP)* v. *Kelso* [1984] ILRM 329 – the defendant
and two of his friends were members of the RUC who
went drinking in the Republic of Ireland while carrying
RUC-issued weapons. They were attacked by a hostile
crowd and they drew their weapons to scare the crowd
away. They were charged with the possession of firearms
for unlawful purposes.

(a) Held: It was held that it was not unlawful for the
defendants to carry weapons if they had an honest
and reasonable belief that their lives might be in
danger, and

(b) The only way to protect their lives was to carry
firearms.

(3) *People (AG)* v. *O'Brien* (1969) 1 Frewen 343 – the defendant knew that the victim wrongly blamed him for an

assault. The defendant gave evidence that he was frightened of the victim, who had a violent reputation. The defendant started carrying a knife to protect himself. When the victim attacked the defendant, the defendant stabbed the victim several times in the chest, killing him. The defendant's conviction for manslaughter was upheld, the court holding that a knife is not a defensive weapon. The court did not dispute the defendant's right to carry a knife in appropriate circumstances.

2. **Section 20(2) NFOAPA 1997** [254]
   a. Sections 18 and 19 apply equally to acts that are immediately preparatory to the use of force.
      (1) Section 18 – justifiable use of force, see [237].
      (2) Section 19 – justifiable use of force in effecting/assisting in a lawful arrest, see [238].
   b. Key word – immediately. [255]
      (1) Appears to allow the defence of self-defence where the defendant took some action to prepare for an attack, but only where this preparation is immediately connected to the use of force.
      (2) Appears that statute is more restrictive than the common law rules.

I. *Excessive Force* [256]

1. Where a defendant knowingly used more force than was necessary in the circumstances, the defendant will have no defence.
2. What force is reasonable?
   a. Objective standard – based upon what a reasonable person would think or believe is reasonable under the circumstances.
   b. Law recognises that a person being attacked cannot be expected to be totally rational.
      (1) 'Detached reflection cannot be demanded in the presence of an uplifted knife.' (Holmes J. in *Brown* v. *US* (1921))
3. Objectively unreasonable force – where the defendant uses more force than is reasonably necessary and the target of the force dies as a result.
   a. But where the defendant used no more force than he or she honestly thought necessary, the defendant should be convicted of manslaughter. See [344].
   b. And where the defendant knowingly used more force than necessary, the defendant should be convicted of murder. See [325].

(1) *People (AG)* v. *Commane* (1975) 1 Frewen – the defendant was attacked by the victim. The defendant successfully knocked out the victim by fracturing his skull. However, the defendant then strangled the victim and killed him. It was held that the defendant had at that point already rendered the attacker incapable of further violence. Any further force used was excessive and the jury was entitled to infer that he must have known that it was excessive. His murder conviction was upheld.

IV. Defence of Others [257]

A. Common Law

1. Under the common law an individual is allowed to use reasonable force to:
   a. Defend another.
   b. Prevent the commission of a crime.
2. Force – required to be objectively reasonable.
   a. Lethal force – allowed so long as objectively reasonable.

B. Non-Fatal Offences Against the Person Act 1997, sections 18–20 [258]

1. Section 18(1)(a) allows the use of reasonable force in the protection of not only himself or herself but also family members or others from criminal acts causing:
   a. Injury,
   b. Assault, or
   c. Detention.
2. Section 18(1)(b) allows the use of reasonable force to protect not only himself or herself but also another from:
   a. Trespasses to the person.
   b. Note: When using reasonable force to protect another from a trespass to the person, the defendant must have acted with the authority of that other person.
3. Section 18(6) – the defence of self or another is not available where the defendant knew that:
   a. The force is used against a member of the Gardaí acting in the course of his or her duties.
   b. The force is used against another who is assisting a police officer acting in the course of his or her duties.
   c. Exception – unless the defendant believed the force to be immediately necessary to prevent harm to himself or herself or another.

4. **Section 19 – justifiable use of force in effecting/assisting in a lawful arrest.** [259]
   a. Section 19(1) – a person may use reasonable force in effecting or assisting in a lawful arrest.
   b. Section 19(3) – whether the arrest is lawful is determined according to the circumstances as the defendant believed them to be. See [238].

C. *Section 20 defines use of force for purposes of sections 18 and 19 as including:* [260]

1. The application of force or the causing of an impact upon another person's body,
2. The threats of such force, or
3. The detention of another person without the use of force.

D. *Raising the Defence* – *see [242] above* [261]

E. *Issue of Fact* – *see [244] above*

F. *Motive* – *see [245] above*

1. Exam hint: The defendant comes to the aid of a woman being beaten by her husband.
   a. General rule – section 18(7) – the defence of another does not apply to a defendant who causes conduct or a state of affairs with a view of using force to resist or terminate it.
   b. There is little doubt that a defendant who intercedes to stop a husband from beating his wife is going to cause the husband to turn on the defendant.
   c. Note that even if the defendant knowingly interceded with the hope and desire that the husband would turn on the defendant so the defendant would be justified in using force on the 'wife beater' husband, the defence of another should still apply. (So long as the force used by the defendant was reasonable.)
   d. This is true even if the wife pleads with the defendant not to intercede. The defendant should still be able to avail of the defence of another so long as the defendant is using reasonable force to defend her from a criminal act, i.e. the assault.
   e. If there was no criminal act (only a trespass to the person) the defendant could not rely upon the defence of another unless

the wife gave the defendant authority to act on her behalf (section 18(b)).

G. Retreat – *see [249] above*

H. Preparation – *see [251] above*

I. Excessive Force – *see [256] above*

V. Defence of Property [262]

A. The Common Law

1. Protection of home –
   a. Under the early common law a 'man's home was his castle'.
   b. A person could use lethal force to defend his or her home.
   c. At some point if the resident resisted the invasion of his or her home, the resident would be engaging in self-defence as well as defence of home.
2. Protection of other property –
   a. Under the common law a person could use reasonable force to protect personal property from theft or damage.
   b. Under the common law a person could use reasonable force to eject trespassers from his or her lands after asking the trespasser to leave.

B. NFOAPA 1997 [263]

1. Section 18(1)(c) – the defendant may use reasonable force to protect his or her property from:
   a. Appropriation,
   b. Destruction, or
   c. Damage caused by a criminal act or from a trespass or infringement.
2. Section 18(1)(d) – the defendant may use reasonable force to protect the property of another from appropriation, destruction or damage:
   a. Caused by a criminal act, or
   b. With the authority of the other person caused by trespass or infringement.
3. Property –
   a. Section 1 defines property as meaning property of a tangible

nature, whether real or personal, including money and animals that are capable of being stolen. See theft [435].
4. Section 18(3) – criminal act.
   a. Criminal acts are deemed to have occurred even if the person committing the criminal conduct would be acquitted on the grounds of automatism, duress, infancy, intoxication or insanity.
5. Section 18(8) – property belongs to (under section 18(1)(c) and 18(1)(d)).
   a. Section 18(8)(a) – any person having the custody or control of it.
   b. Section 18(8)(b) – any person having any proprietary right or interest in it.
      (1) Does not include equitable interest arising only from an agreement to transfer or grant an interest in it.
   c. Section 18(8)(c) – any person having a charge on the property.
      (1) Trust – where the property is subject to a trust, the persons to whom it belongs shall be treated as including any person having a right to enforce the trust.
      (2) Corporate property shall be treated as belonging to the corporation notwithstanding a vacancy in the corporation.

C. Section 20 – Meaning of 'Use of Force'   [264]

1. Section 20(1)(a) – a person uses force in relation to another or property where that person:
   a. Applies force to the person or property of another, or
   b. Causes an impact on the body of that person or property.
      (1) E.g. *R. v. Renouf* [1986] 2 All ER 449 – it was held that forcing a car off the road in order to arrest the occupant could be a reasonable use of force and not constitute reckless driving.
2. Section 20(1)(c) – a person is treated as using force in relation to property if he or she threatens a person with the use of the property.

D. Raising the Defence – *see [242] above*

E. Issue of Fact – *see [244] above*

F. Motive – *see [245] above*

G. Retreat – *see [249] above*

H. Preparation – *see [251] above*

I. Excessive Force – *see [256] above*

Review Questions

1. Natalie owns the Wild Rover Pub and often leaves her premises late at night with a large amount of money. Early one morning Natalie leaves the pub and as soon as she is on the empty street she hears footsteps. When she slows down the other person slows down. Desperately, Natalie searches her handbag for anything to use as a weapon to defend herself. Suddenly Natalie is grabbed from behind by a large man who tries to knock her to the ground. In a blind terror Natalie pulls her extra-strength hairspray from her handbag and sprays it directly into the face of her attacker. Natalie escapes and when she returns with the police they find her attacker dead. An autopsy reveals that the man died from an asthmatic attack brought on by the hair-spray. Does Natalie have a defence to a charge of manslaughter?

2. As James was walking along the quays late at night he was attacked by Les, who wielded an iron pipe. Surprised and dazed, James fought back and ultimately overpowered Les. James wrestled the pipe from Les and hit Les in the head repeatedly, killing him. Will James be convicted of murder?

3. Santa and his senior elf, Herbie, were flying to Las Vegas for a little holiday after the Christmas rush. Unfortunately, the plane began to develop engine problems and there was only one parachute. Knowing that millions of children would be disappointed if some-thing happened to Santa, Santa strangled Herbie, put on the para-chute and landed safely. Can Santa avail of the defence of necessity?

4. Wenceslas, a law student, returned from his class Christmas party in time to see a strange man dressed in red kissing his mother under the mistletoe. Believing that his mother was being attacked, Wenceslas sprang into action and grabbed the pointy star on top of the Christmas tree and stabbed the intruder in the back, killing him. To Wenceslas's horror, his mother turned over the body of the intruder and removed the white whiskers to reveal that the intruder was in fact Wenceslas's father. Will Wenceslas be able to avoid criminal liability for killing his father?

5. Tim and Tom are twins. They love to play practical jokes on people. Recently, their neighbour Rose got married and had a small reception in her parents' home. The twins saw her wedding cake in the kitchen. They quietly opened the kitchen window and stuck a long-handled pitchfork into the cake and brought it out the window. Rose entered the kitchen in time to see the cake go out the window. She ran outside and threw stones at the boys, trying to stop them from running off with her cake. Both boys were injured, as was the cake.

   (a) If Rose is charged with assault, will she be able to avail of any valid defences?

   (b) If the boys are charged with theft, will they have a valid defence?

6. Joan is desperate. Her husband has left her and she has no money to feed her six small children. She has applied for various aid, but no money is forthcoming and the children are hungry now. She asks for credit at the local shop, but the owner cannot afford to extend any more credit to her. In desperation, Joan goes to a large supermarket and is caught trying to leave the supermarket with a carton of milk and a large bag of porridge. Can Joan avail of the defence of necessity to a charge of theft?

7. Alan was waiting for his friends when he was threatened by a group of men outside his local pub. Later, Alan saw the ringleader of the men who had threatened him earlier on his own and gave the ringleader a clout with his fist. If Alan is charged with assault, can he avail of the defence of self-defence?

8. Bertha is a large woman and often physically abuses her timid husband, Richard. One afternoon, Richard's sister, Pearl, observed Bertha verbally abusing and slapping Richard. Pearl ordered Bertha to stop abusing Richard, although Richard told Pearl to mind her own business. When Bertha made a lunge for Pearl, Pearl hit her with the rolling pin she was using to roll out pastry. Will Pearl be able to avail of the defence of another after Richard indicated that he did not want Pearl's help?

SECTION 3:
CRIMINAL OFFENCES

6

INCHOATE OFFENCES

Chapter synopsis

I.   General Principles
II. Attempts
III. Conspiracy
IV. Incitement

I. General Principles   [265]

A. Inchoate Means 'Just Begun'

1. The defendant has formed the *mens rea*, but the defendant has not attained or completed the unlawful goal.
2. See Hall's six-stage criminal process; see [77]. Inchoate offences fall between steps four and six.
3. Sometimes inchoate offences are described as imperfect or incomplete offences.

B. The Most Common Inchoate Offences

1. Attempts.
2. Incitement.
3. Conspiracy.

C. Why Punish Inchoate Offences?   [266]

1. There are two primary competing theories regarding criminal liability. See liberal and moralistic views [18].
2. Subjective analysis – follows directly from liberalism.
   a. Criminal law should focus on the defendant's subjective intentions (*mens rea*), which highlight the defendant's danger to society and bad character. Anyone who attempts or plans a crime is dangerous.
   b. To focus on the defendant's act is only important as it verifies the *actus reus*.

3. Objective analysis – is social protectionism. **[267]**
   a. The focus is on the defendant's act or conduct. Conduct should only be punished when criminality is objectively discernible at the time it occurs. Thus, if a person attempts an act that is objectively criminal, that person should be punished.
   b. Fletcher described this as meaning a third party observer could recognise the activity as criminal even if that person had no special knowledge of the offender's intention.
   c. Note: Subjectivists and objectivists will often reach the same result regarding criminal liability using different reasoning.
4. Utilitarian analysis – flows from Bentham and Mills, see [19 *et seq*]. **[268]**
   a. Threat of punishment can reduce crime. Any deterrent effect of threatened punishment comes from the full offence.
   b. Because threatening punishment for an inchoate offence has no added influence, it is not effective punishment and therefore should not be inflicted.
5. Retributive analysis – moralistic approach. **[269]**
   a. Punishment is justified when it is deserved.
   b. Subjective retributionists focus on culpability of criminal attempts. A person who shoots at his or her victim but misses is as morally culpable as the person who succeeds in shooting his or her victim.
   c. Objective retributionists – a person attempting a crime disturbs the order of things and punishment is necessary to restore public order (Ashworth).
6. Inchoate offences are valuable for preventative law enforcement. Such offences provide a basis for police intervention to prevent the full offence.

II. Attempts [270]

A. Historically

1. As early as the fourteenth century, judicial opinions contained some language favouring the punishment of inchoate conduct.
2. The offence of attempt was first recognised in *R. v. Scofield*, Caldecott 397 (1784), where a candle was lit and placed under the stairs with the intention of burning the building.
3. Hall describes the pre-1784 criminal climate as 'a miss was as good as a mile'.
4. Originally, attempt was a misdemeanour, regardless of the seriousness of the offence the defendant wanted to commit.

5. Modern law has developed from *R.* v. *Eagleton* (1855) Dears CC 515. Facts: The defendant supplied bread to a Poor Law Authority. The bread was below the contract amount, but the defendant submitted an account for the full amount. The fraud was discovered before the defendant was paid for the bread. The defendant was convicted of attempting to obtain money by false pretences.

B. *General Principles of Attempts*   [271]

1. *Actus reus* of attempts –
   a. Requires an *act* that progresses sufficiently toward the commission of the complete offence.
      (1) The only difference between an attempt and the complete offence is the fact that the attempt was not successful.
      (2) Thoughts (*mens rea*) are not sufficient, regardless of how evil the thoughts. See [54].
      (3) E.g. Fred West sat down one Saturday afternoon and planned out in minute detail how he would entice a hitch-hiker into his vehicle, overpower her, rape her and then strangle her. Fred West cannot be held criminally liable for his thoughts and plans to rape and kill.
   b. Purely preparatory conduct is not sufficient.   [272]
      (1) There is great difficulty in determining where purely preparatory conduct ends.
      (2) The requirement of more than mere preparation has been described as requiring the defendant after preparations to make a direct movement toward the commission of the complete offence. *People (AG)* v. *Thornton* [1952] IR 91.
      (3) Example of preparatory conduct – *R.* v. *Ilyas* (1983) – the defendant reported to the police that his car was stolen and he obtained claim forms from his insurance company. The defendant did not fill out the forms. Held: The defendant's acts were merely preparatory.
2. *Mens rea* **for attempts** –   [273]
   a. Requires two elements:
      (1) The defendant must have the intention to commit the complete substantive offence, and
      (2) The defendant must have the required *mens rea* for the substantive offence.
   b. Recklessness is not enough.

(1) This is true even where recklessness is sufficient for the complete offence.

    (a) E.g. Ted Bundy was charged with attempted rape. The prosecution must show that Ted intended to rape the victim. This is true even though the *mens rea* for rape is knowingly engaging in sexual intercourse with a female who the defendant either knew was not consenting or the defendant was reckless as to whether she was consenting. (See recklessness [87] and [91] and specific intent crimes [208].)

C. The Required Act [274]

1. **The Last Act Test** was traditionally used – the *actus reus* of attempts required the defendant to have done everything necessary to achieve his or her intent, e.g. *R.* v. *Eagleton* (1855) Dears CC 515 – facts above.

  a. Last Act Test was rejected in *DPP* v. *Stonehouse* [1977] 2 All ER 909 as being too restrictive in some cases and too broad in others.

    (1) Lord Edmund-Davies found that a person could have done the last act but still not sufficiently progress toward the commission of the offence to justify criminal liability.

    (2) *DPP* v. *Stonehouse* facts: The defendant, a British politician, decided to fake his own death in order to start a new life in Australia. He named his wife as his life insurance beneficiary but did not tell her of his plan. In Australia his plan was discovered before any demand was made on his policy. The defendant was charged with attempting to obtain property by deception.

      (a) Famous quote in case – Lord Diplock described the *actus reus* of an attempt as the defendant having 'crossed the Rubicon and burnt his boats…'. In other words, the defendant must have reached the point of no return, which is slightly less than having done everything necessary to achieve the goal.

2. **Proximity test** – the required act must be proximate or close to the commission of the complete offence. [275]

  a. Formulated by Holmes J. in *State* v. *Peaslee* (1900) 177 Mass. 267 – the defendant put material in a building intending to return to light it. The defendant abandoned his plan on the way back to the building, but was held guilty of an attempt.

   b. Endorsed by the Irish Supreme Court in *People (AG)* v. *Sullivan* [1964] IR 169.
      (1) *People (AG)* v. *Sullivan* facts: The defendant, a midwife, filed a claim for fictitious patients. Her fraud was discovered before she was paid. The SC held that what the defendant did was beyond mere preparations once she handed in the false forms.
3. **Crossed the Rubicon test** – some legal commentators advocate the requirement that the defendant must have reached the point of no return, which requires slightly less than the last clear act test.   **[276]**
   a. Lord Diplock's famous quote regarding proximity that for an attempt there must be evidence that the defendant 'crossed the Rubicon and burnt his boats…' (*DPP* v. *Stonehouse*).
4. **English approach to attempts** – statutory.   **[277]**
   a. Criminal Attempts Act 1981, section 4(3) declares that a step beyond mere preparation will be sufficient. Whether the defendant's actions are more than merely preparatory is a legal question for the judge.
   b. Clarkson describes the English approach after statute as 'objectivist', focusing on the actions of the defendant.
   c. Statute rejects Diplock's 'crossing the Rubicon' because the statute allows for criminal liability to incur before the defendant has reached the point of no return.
5. **Attack on legally protected interest test** –   **[278]**
   a. In 1996 Duff described the proper test for the *actus reus* of an attempt to occur where there is an attack on some legally protected interest.
   b. *R.* v. *Jones* [1990] 3 All ER 886 – the defendant got into the victim's car and pointed a gun at the victim. Held: The defendant's actions were more than mere preparation when he got into the car and confronted or attacked the victim.
   c. Criticism – such a test cannot deal effectively with all attempt offences.
6. **Equivocality test** is used in civil law jurisdictions such as France and Germany and is contained in the US Model Penal Code.
                                                                  [279]
   a. The *actus reus* must be *res ipsa loquitur* with respect to the intention to commit the full offence. In other words, the conduct itself must show the intention of the defendant to commit the full offence.

  b. E.g. *Davey* v. *Lee* [1967] 2 All ER 423 – the defendants cut through four fences to enter a compound containing copper. The defendants were charged with attempting to steal the copper. Held: The conduct could not be reasonably regarded as having any other purpose than to steal the copper.
  c. Criticism – the rule is arbitrary and leads to inconsistent applications.

D. Consequences/Circumstances   [280]

1. The defendant must intend the result or consequences of an offence requiring a specific result. See [76] regarding result offences.
2. However, the defendant is not required to have intention as to all circumstances of the offence.
   a. E.g. *AG's Reference (No. 3 of 1992)* (1994) – the defendant threw a petrol bomb at a car, but instead it hit a wall. Held: Recklessness with regard to circumstances is sufficient for attempting 1) arson with the intent to danger life, and 2) recklessness as to whether life was endangered.
   b. E.g. *R.* v. *Khan* [1990] 2 All ER 783 – the defendant was convicted of attempted rape. The trial judge directed the jury that recklessness as to the victim's consent was sufficient for conviction. The defendant argued that intention was needed for both the consequences, i.e. completing the offence, and circumstances, i.e. engaging in sexual intercourse knowing that the victim did not consent. The appeals court held that attempted rape could be established by recklessness as to circumstances, i.e. whether the victim was consenting.
3. The Law Commission in the UK originally believed that a distinction between consequences and circumstances would not be workable.   [281]
   a. It recommended that intention should be required as to all elements of the offence.
   b. Ultimately, this position was abandoned and the Commission has recommended that recklessness as to circumstances is sufficient if it is sufficient for the substantive offence.
4. **Beware** – attempted murder.   [282]
   a. Requires an intent to kill although the *mens rea* for murder is an intent to kill or to cause serious injury. *People (DPP)* v. *Douglas & Hayes* [1985] ILRM 25.
   b. E.g. if Lola shoots Connie with the intention of causing serious

injury and disfigurement, Lola *cannot* be convicted of attempted murder. However, if Connie dies from the gunshot wound, Lola could be convicted or murder.

E. *Impossibility* [283]

1. Definition: Impossibility is where the defendant intends to commit a crime but cannot commit the crime.
2. **General rule** – impossibility is generally a defence to a criminal charge. There are two types of impossibility: [284]
   a. Legal impossibility.
   b. Physical impossibility.
3. **Legal impossibility** – where the defendant attempts to do something believing it to be illegal, but the activity is not illegal. [285]
   a. E.g. *Haughton* v. *Smith* [1973] 3 All ER 1109 (HL) – the police intercepted stolen meat but allowed it to continue to the defendants. The defendants were charged with receiving stolen property. Held: The meat came under police control before the defendants had possession, therefore it was no longer stolen. The conviction for attempting to handle stolen goods failed.
   b. **Remember** – the intention of the defendant to commit a crime does not criminalise an act that is not criminal. [286]
      (1) E.g. *R.* v. *Taafe* [1984] 1 All ER 747 – the defendant imported cannabis into the UK believing that he was importing cash. Importing money is not a crime, although the defendant thought that it was an offence. Held: The defendant could not be guilty of an attempt.
   c. Australian approach –
      (1) *Britten* v. *Alpogut* (1987) – the defendant thought that he was smuggling cannabis when he was actually smuggling something that was not illegal. Per Murphy J. – at common law if the intent was to commit a recognised crime and the act was not merely preparatory, then at that stage the attempt to commit the full offence was committed. Therefore, the defendant could be convicted of attempting to smuggle cannabis.
4. **Physical impossibility** – where the defendant attempts to do something that is illegal, but the illegal result cannot be physically achieved.   [287]
   a. E.g. a defendant who shoots a corpse believing that he is murdering the deceased cannot be convicted of attempting to

kill that corpse because it is not physically possible to kill someone who is already dead.

b. **Method exception** – impossibility is *not* a good defence when it relates to the method used by the defendant. **[288]**

    (1) *R. v. White* [1908–10] All ER 340 – the defendant tried to kill his mother with poison, but the amount he used was not enough to kill her. His conviction for murder was upheld.

    (2) **Beware** – law lecturers love to pose questions concerning impossibility. If the victim is dead *before* the defendant tried to kill him or her, it is not attempted murder.

        (a) The *mens rea* for attempted murder is the intent to kill, but if the victim is already dead it is physically (as well as legally) impossible to kill the victim.

        (b) This is true regardless of the method the defendant used in his or her effort to kill the victim.

F. Abandonment [289]

1. Is where the defendant withdraws or attempts to withdraw from the criminal conduct.

  a. Does not appear to be a defence to attempts.

  b. Rationale: The offence of attempts is complete as long as the defendant's actions are sufficiently proximate to the completion of the full offence. If the defendant abandoned his or her plans prior to the proximate act there is no *actus reus*, and if he or she abandoned the plans after the proximate act he or she has committed an attempt.

III. Conspiracy [290]

A. Historically

1. Under the common law conspiracy is an agreement between two or more persons to commit a criminal act or acts or to accomplish a legal act by unlawful means.

2. Introduced as an inchoate offence by the infamous Star Chamber Court in 1611 in the *Poulterer's* Case 9 Co.Rep. 55b.

  a. Star Chamber Court was an administrative court that was outside the common law court system.

  b. It was a tool of the monarchy and was used to prosecute perceived enemies of the throne. Actions were arbitrary and without a jury.

    c. It was abolished in the eighteenth century.
3. Conspiracy has always been controversial. Many legal commentators have called for its abolition or reform.
    a. It is too vague and almost always defies definition.
    b. Conviction may result before any act is performed in furtherance of the substantive offence.
    c. Therefore, conspiracy may punish mere thoughts.

B. General Principles [291]

1. Distinguished from attempts – conspiracy does not require any act toward the commission of the substantive offence.
    a. Under Irish law there have been a number of types of conspiracy recognised.
       (1) To commit a crime.
       (2) To defraud.
       (3) To pervert the course of justice.
       (4) To effect a public mischief.
       (5) To corrupt public morals.
       (6) To commit a tort.
       (7) To outrage public decency.
    b. Conspiracy must fall within one of these categories. *DPP* v. *Withers* [1974] 3 All ER 984.
2. *Actus reus* **of conspiracy** – the agreement is the required *actus reus*. [292]
    a. The importance in conspiracy is what was agreed to be done by the parties, rather than what actually occurred. *R.* v. *Bolton* [1991] Crim LR 57.
3. *Mens rea* **of conspiracy** – [293]
    a. The conspirators must have intended to commit the substantive offence.
    b. The defendant conspirator must have known what the conspiracy was about.
       (1) However, the defendant conspirator need not know the exact or precise details or agreement.
       (2) E.g. *R.* v. *Porter* [1980] NI 18 – the defendant knew that the package he was asked to pick up contained something like weapons.
       (3) Intent is not motive, e.g. in *Wai Yu-tsang* v. *R.* [1991] 4 All ER 664, it was held that in a conspiracy to defraud, the defendant's motives for carrying out the fraud were not relevant.

C. *Agreement Required* [294]

1. Two or more persons are required.
   a. Note: Spouses cannot enter into a criminal conspiracy. Rationale: Traditionally the law has regarded a husband and wife as one.
   b. English statutory approach – Criminal Law Act 1977, section 2 endorsed the traditional rule regarding spouses to preserve the stability of marriage.
2. Was agreement made? [295]
   a. Negotiation or other preparatory measures is not an agreement.
      (1) E.g. the defendant discussed stealing a payroll with others. No conspiracy was found because there was no agreement. *R.* v. *Walker* [1962] Crim LR 458.
   b. Whether there is an agreement is a question of fact for the jury. [296]
      (1) *R.* v. *Porter* [1980] NI 18 – the defendant was charged with conspiring to make materials available which might be useful to terrorists. The defendant, a lorry driver, was asked to pick up a parcel in England and bring it back to Northern Ireland. The defendant asked if the parcel contained weapons. He was told not to make any comments if he knew what was good for him. The defendant tried to pick up the package but another driver had already done it. The appeals court held: No evidence of an agreement, but there was sufficient inferences that could be made that the defendant had joined the conspiracy.
3. The agreement need not be formal. [297]
   a. All that is required is that the parties pursue a common illegal aim or goal.
   b. Conspiracy need not be a secret.
      (1) E.g. *R.* v. *Parnell* (1881) 14 CCC 508 – an agreement was made in an open meeting of the Land League. The agreement need not be formal.
   c. Independent conduct toward a common goal is not acting in agreement.
      (1) If two or more persons are acting independently toward the same illegal goal, there is no conspiracy.
      (2) E.g. Al Capone and Ma Barker both have plans to kill Elliot Ness. They are not engaged in a conspiracy because they have not entered into an agreement and are acting

independently of each other. They simply share the same goal or target.

D. Impossibility – *see generally [283]*   [298]

1. The defence of impossibility only applies if the agreement is to engage in a specific course of criminal conduct that is impossible.
   a. *DPP* v. *Nock & Alsford* [1978] 2 All ER 654 – the defendant conspired to produce cocaine. They obtained powder that they thought contained cocaine and planned to separate cocaine from the powder. It was impossible, as the powder did not contain cocaine. The defendants could not be convicted of conspiracy.
2. Subsequent impossibility – if the impossibility arises after the agreement is made, the conspiracy was complete when the agreement was reached and the defence of impossibility will not apply.
   a. E.g. Fred and Ethel plan to murder Lucy. Before Fred and Ethel can kill Lucy, she dies of natural causes. The conspiracy was complete when the agreement was reached. Both Fred and Ethel can be convicted of conspiracy to commit murder.

E. The Trial of the Conspirators   [299]

1. Where conspirators are tried separately, the acquittal of one conspirator does not prejudice the conviction of the other. *DPP* v. *Shannon* [1974] 2 All ER 1009.
2. Where conspirators are tried jointly, the verdict should be the same for both.
3. English statutory approach – Criminal Law Act 1977, section 5 – the acquittal of one conspirator will not prejudice the conviction of the other conspirator, regardless of how they are tried.

IV. Incitement   [300]

A. Historically

1. At common law it was a misdemeanour to counsel, incite or induce another to commit or join in the commission of any offence. *R.* v. *Higgins*, 102 ER 269 (1801).
2. Incitement was late in developing under the common law.
3. Under the common law, the crime of incitement (or solicitation, as it is called in some jurisdictions) required:

a. *Mens rea* – that the defendant acted volitionally and with the intent of causing the person solicited to commit the crime, and

b. *Actus reus* – the defendant counselled, incited or induced another to commit the crime.

B. *Modern Incitement* [301]

1. Can be found in some statutes.
   a. Example: Prohibition of Incitement to Hatred Act 1989 makes it an offence to publish, distribute or broadcast any threatening, abusive or insulting materials that are intended to or are likely to incite hatred.
2. Modern Common Law Incitement –
   a. *Actus reus*:
      (1) The defendant must intentionally commit the *actus reus*, i.e. invite, request, command, hire, encourage, etc. another person to commit the substantive offence.
      (2) Requires more than a mere desire that a crime be committed.
         (a) Incitement requires steps toward recruiting another person to commit the crime.
         (b) Requires the persuasion of another person to commit a crime.
   b. *Mens rea*:
      (1) A specific intent offence – requires that the defendant must have intended the person incited to commit the substantive offence.

C. *Persuasion – could include:* [302]

1. Suggestion,
2. Proposal, or
3. Request, coupled with an implied promise of reward. *R.* v. *Fitzmaurice* [1983] 1 All ER 189.
4. Threats –
   a. Lord Denning suggested in *RRB* v. *Applin* [1974] 2 WLR 541 that incitement could be brought about through the use of threats or pressure.

D. Incitee Must Be Capable in Law of Committing the Complete Offence [303]

1. Where the defendant is aware that the person incited lacks the capacity to commit the substantive offence, there is no incitement.

   a. E.g. *R.* v. *Whitehouse* [1977] 3 All ER 737 – the defendant was accused of inciting his fifteen-year-old daughter to commit incest with him. Under the English Sexual Offences Act 1956 a female under the age of sixteen is presumed to be a victim and could not commit incest. The defendant could not be convicted of incitement.

E. The Idea of the Crime Need Not Originate with the Defendant, It Is Enough that the Defendant Encouraged Another to Commit a Crime [304]

1. Incitement can be made to the world at large.
2. E.g. *R.* v. *Most* (1881) 14 Cox CC 583 – publication of newspaper article urging revolutionaries around the world to assassinate all heads of state. Held to be sufficient communication to establish incitement to commit murder.

F. After Inciting No Further Act Required [305]

1. Neither the incitor nor the incitee need to perform any act in furtherance of the substantive offence.
2. Incitement is complete when it is communicated to the incitee, regardless if the incitee accepts or rejects it.

G. Attempted Incitement [306]

1. If the communication fails to reach the person to be incited or if it is intercepted by the police, the incitor can still be prosecuted for an attempted incitement. *Chelmsford Justices, ex parte Amos* [1973] Crim LR 437.

H. Impossibility [307]

1. If the crime incited is of a general nature, impossibility is not a defence.
2. However, if the crime incited is specific and the specific object is impossible, then impossibility is a defence.
3. E.g. *R.* v. *Fitzmaurice* [1983] 1 All ER 189 – the defendant was

asked by his father to recruit others for a robbery. The defendant approached and recruited others. Unknown to the defendant his father had no plans for a robbery, but instead the father intended to inform the authorities and claim a reward for preventing a robbery. The defendant was convicted of inciting a robbery. To commit a robbery was the general object of incitement and was not impossible.

I. Distinguished from Conspiracy [308]

1. Conspiracy is an agreement between two or more persons to commit a crime, while incitement is an attempted conspiracy.
2. However, incitement is not necessarily found in conspiracy.
   a. E.g. Larry and Curly both hate Moe. Together they jointly decide to murder Moe. Larry and Curly are guilty of conspiracy, but there was no incitement.

J. Criticism [309]

1. Incitement is a controversial offence.
2. Some commentators believe that incitement should not be an offence because it punishes conduct at too early a stage.
   a. Glanville Williams – purpose of offence is to enable police to 'nip criminal tendencies in the bud'.
   b. Some legal commentators see incitement as an attempted conspiracy, making it a double inchoate crime.

Table 6.1: Incohate Offences

	Attempts	Conspiracy	Incitement
Actus reus	Requires an act that progresses sufficiently toward the commission of the complete offence.	Requires an agreement to pursue a common illegal aim or goal.	Requires an intentional invitation, request, command, hiring, encouragement, etc. to another to commit any substantive offence.

	Attempts	**Conspiracy**	**Incitement**
Mens rea	1) Intention to commit substantive offence. 2) Must have required *mens rea* for the substantive offence.	1) Conspirators must have intended to commit the substantive offence. 2) The defendant conspirator must have known what the conspiracy was about.	1) A specific intent offence – requires that the defendant must have intended the person incited to commit the substantive offence.
Is impossibility a defence?	Generally yes, except beware of method exception [288].	Only applies if the agreement is to engage in a specific course of criminal conduct that is impossible.	No if the crime incited is of a general nature. Yes if the crime incited is specific and the specific object is impossible.

Review Questions

1. Bonnie and Clyde entered a creative writing contest for *Super Sleuth* magazine. In order to make details of planning a bank robbery as authentic as possible, Bonnie went to the local bank and timed the delivery of money. Clyde met with several people and discussed purchasing a gun.
   (a) Can Bonnie be convicted of conspiracy to commit robbery?
   (b) Can Bonnie be convicted of incitement?
   (c) Can Bonnie and Clyde be convicted of attempted robbery?
2. Sean is sick and tired of his wife Mary. 'Nag, nag, nag, that is all she does,' he thinks to himself. He goes down to the local pub and meets a few of his friends, including Moe and Larry. After a few drinks Sean starts telling everyone who will listen about how his wife is making his life a living hell. 'She complains if I go out with the lads, she complains if I work late for overtime, but she loves to spend all the money I bring home.' After several more drinks he slurs, 'My life would be so much better if some decent lad would take her off of my hands.' Moe and Larry hear these comments and knowing that Sean is a wealthy man, they agree privately to kill Mary.
   (a) Will Sean be convicted of incitement to commit the murder of his wife?

(b) Can Moe and Larry be convicted of attempted murder?

(c) Can Moe and Larry be convicted of conspiracy to commit murder?

3. Ken was angry at his girlfriend Barbie because she had been unfaithful. Ken asked Richard to rape Barbie to teach her a lesson. Richard agreed. Richard lay in wait for Barbie near her home. Richard saw a woman approach and, believing her to be Barbie, he attacked and raped the woman. In fact, the woman was not Barbie, but her friend Madge. Identify all the inchoate offences that may have been committed.

4. Starskey and Hutch decided to rob the ABC Bank on the quays. They bought shotguns, sawed off the shotguns and timed the security guards. On the appointed day, Starskey and Hutch went to the ABC Bank and found that it had burned down during the night.

(a) Can Starskey and Hutch be convicted of an attempted robbery?

(b) Have Starskey and Hutch entered into a conspiracy?

5. Troy and Paris both want to kill the president of the Republic of Ithaca. Are Troy and Paris co-conspirators?

6. Fred and Rosemary West spent hours planning the kidnapping of their victims. Are Fred and Rosemary co-conspirators?

7

CRIMINAL HOMICIDES

Chapter synopsis

I. General Principles
II. Murder
III. Manslaughter
IV. Aiding and Abetting a Suicide
V. Infanticide

I. General Principles   [311]

A. Homicide

1. Historically, homicide was defined as the killing of a human being by a human being.
   a. Suicide was included as a homicide.
   b. Suicide was a felony. See [352] below.
2. Today, homicide is the killing of a human being by another human being and excludes suicide.
3. Note: Not all homicides are unlawful, e.g. killing another in self-defence or killing without the required *mens rea*.

B. Common Requirements of Unlawful Homicides   [312]

1. Sound memory and age of discretion.
   a. The defendant must be legally sane. See insanity defence [179].
   b. The defendant must be over the age of criminal responsibility. See *doli incapax* [174].   [313]
2. Any reasonable creature in *rerum natura*.
   a. Requires that the defendant have killed a human being.
      (1) A corpse is not a human being.
      (2) A foetus is not a human being under the common law. However, since the decision of *AG* v. *X* (1992) some legal commentators argue that in Ireland a foetus may be recognised as a human being.

3. Within a year and a day – **[314]**
   a. Under the common law the victim must have died within a year and a day of the defendant's assault.
   b. This requirement developed due to causation difficulties caused by the medical and scientific standards of the time. See causation [110].
   c. Note: This requirement that the victim must die of his or her injuries within a year and a day of the assault has been abolished by section 38 of the Criminal Justice Act 1999.
4. *Actus reus* – requires an unlawful killing. **[315]**
   a. There must be a death.
      (1) There is no legal definition of when death occurs.
         (a) Traditionally, death occurred when there was a complete and permanent stoppage of the circulation of the blood.
         (b) The traditional definition has been rejected since the development of life-support machinery and procedures.
         (c) The heart and lungs can be maintained artificially to 'circulate the blood', e.g. *R.* v. *Malcherek & Steel* (1981) – due to injuries inflicted by the defendant the victim was placed on life support. When it became apparent that the victim would never recover, life support was removed. The defendant argued that withdrawing life support was the cause of the victim's death and it broke the chain of causation between the defendant's act(s) and the victim's death. The court rejected the defendant's argument. See *novus actus interveniens* [114 and 318 *et seq*].
         (d) Charleton – the accepted medical criterion for death is when 'there is irreversible brain damage, in the sense that none of the vital centres of the brain stem are still functioning'.
   b. No requirement that there must be a corpse to prove death of the victim. **[316]**
      (1) *People (AG)* v. *Ball* (1936) 70 ILTR 202 – the defendant was charged with murdering his mother. The defendant said that his mother had committed suicide and he threw her body into the sea to prevent embarrassment. However, the police found a blood-stained hatchet in his house and a large amount of blood splashed about the house.

(2) *People (AG)* v. *Cadden* (1957) 91 ILTR 97 – a conviction based on circumstantial evidence can only result where:
   (a) The circumstances of the incident were consistent with the defendant committing the act, and
   (b) The circumstances are inconsistent with any conclusion other than guilt.

5. Causation [317]

a. Unlawful homicides are *result* offences. See *actus reus* [52]. In other words, causation requires that the defendant must have done some act that led to the victim's death.

b. There must be proof that the defendant did some act that hastened the victim's death.
   (1) It is not a valid defence for the defendant to argue that the victim would have died anyway. *AG's Reference (No. 3 of 1994)* [1996] 2 All ER 10.
   (2) E.g. Faulty Towers is the highest building in town and recently a number of people have committed suicide by leaping from the roof. Colonel Potter, a retired army officer, is distressed to see people falling to their deaths as he sits on his balcony. To ease their suffering, Colonel Potter has begun shooting at the jumpers in an effort to kill them before they hit the pavement. If Colonel Potter successfully kills one of the jumpers, he has hastened the jumper's death and committed a murder.

c. *Novus actus intervenien* is when new forces join with the defendant's act(s) to kill the victim. See [114]. [318]
   (1) Such forces break the chain of causation and release the defendant from criminal liability for the victim's death.
      (a) E.g. *R.* v. *Jordan* (1956) 40 Cr App Rep 152 – the defendant stabbed the victim. While in the hospital the victim received inappropriate medical treatment and developed pneumonia from this treatment and died. Held: The medical treatment was wrong and the stab wound did not contribute to the victim's death. The medical treatment constituted a *novus actus interveniens.*
      (b) Note: For medical treatment due to an injury inflicted by the defendant to amount to a *novus actus interveniens*, the medical treatment must be extraordinary and unusual and a substantial cause of the death. See *R.* v. *Mellor* [1996] 2 Cr App R 245.

d. **Not** *Novus Actus interveniens.* [319]

(1) The victim is under no duty to mitigate his or her losses – if the defendant intentionally assaults the victim causing a serious injury and the victim refuses medical care for whatever reason and dies, the defendant is guilty of murder.

(a) *R. v. Blaue* [1975] 3 All ER 446 – the defendant attacked the victim with a knife because she refused to have sex with him. The victim was a Jehovah's Witness and refused a blood transfusion. When the victim died the defendant argued that her refusal was not reasonable and constituted a *novus actus interveniens.* Held: The policy of the law has always been that those who inflict violence upon others must take their victims as they find them, including religious and spiritual values, therefore the victim's refusal was not a *novus actus interveniens.*

(b) *R. v. Flynn* [1867] 16 WR 319 (IR) CCC – the defendant and the victim engaged in a fight. Afterward the defendant threw a stone and hit the victim in the head. The victim went to the pub, to the police station and rode home over four miles although he felt weak. Two days later he called for a doctor, but died on the third day after being injured. Held: The victim did not do anything that he would not ordinarily do, therefore he did not make his injury worse. The victim's conduct did not amount to a *novus actus interveniens.*

(2) **Eggshell skull rule** – requires that the defendant must accept his or her victim as he or she finds him. See [120]. [320]

(a) E.g. Mrs Hannibal despised her postman, Randy. She believed that Randy was slow, sloppy and rude. One day she observed Randy folding her copy of *Bon Appetite* as he stuffed it through the letterbox. In a rage, Mrs Hannibal bit Randy's nose in an effort to disfigure him. Randy died a few days later when he developed blood poisoning due to his compromised immune system. It is no defence for Mrs Hannibal to rightly claim that Randy would not have died had it not been for the fact that his immune system was compromised.

II. Murder

A. Common Law Murder   [321]

1. Beginning in 1512, the benefit of clergy was denied for killings done with 'malice aforethought'. See benefit of clergy [12].
2. Other unlawful homicides were called **manslaughter** and continued to attract the benefit of clergy.
3. Murder was defined by Chief Justice Coke in 1640 as occurring '…when any man of sound memory, and of the age of discretion, unlawfully killith within any country of the realm any reasonable creature in *rerum natura* under the king's peace with malice aforethought either expressed by the party or implied by law, so as the party wounded, or hurt…die of the wound or hurt…within a year and a day after the same.'
4. **Common law *mens rea* of murder** – required malice aforethought.   [322]
   a. **Malice** – originally required that the defendant had ill will or spite toward the victim.
   b. **Aforethought** – originally required that the defendant planned or had premeditation to kill the victim.
   c. The term 'malice aforethought' lost its original meaning and was broadly interpreted to punish defendants who were considered to be morally the same as an intentional killer. Thus, by the mid-seventeenth century malice aforethought included:
      (1) An intention to kill (express malice).
      (2) An intention to cause serious injury (implied malice).
      (3) Killing while resisting lawful arrest (constructive malice).
      (4) Killing in the course of committing a felony (constructive malice).
         (a) This was often referred to as the felony murder rule.
         (b) It was abolished in England by the Homicide Act 1957.
         (c) It was abolished in Ireland by section 4 of the Criminal Justice Act 1964.
         (d) It is retained in many jurisdictions in the US, but it is generally limited to violent or certain enumerated classes of felonies.
   d. **Constructive malice** was thought to have been abolished in England by the Homicide Act 1957.   [323]
      (1) *DPP* v. *Smith* (1961) – the defendant was attempting to evade arrest. When ordered to stop the defendant continued to drive, and the victim, a police officer, was

clinging to the front of the car. The defendant drove erratically for approximately 100 yards, where the victim was either thrown from the car or fell off of the car into the path of oncoming traffic and sustained fatal injuries. The defendant was convicted of capital murder. On appeal his conviction was overturned. The court found that a manslaughter conviction was appropriate. The House of Lords reversed and reinstated the capital murder conviction, rejecting any subjective test as to the defendant's intentions.

(2) The *Smith* decision was criticised. In *Smith*, the *mens rea* for murder only required a showing that the defendant intended to do some unlawful act which, whether the accused realised it or not, was likely to cause death or serious injury.

   (a) Legal commentators argued that the decision reintroduced constructive malice.

   (b) *Smith* case led to legislation to reverse its effect. In Ireland, section 4 of the Criminal Justice Act 1964 was introduced.

5. Punishment [324]

a. Historically, under common law a defendant convicted of murder received a mandatory death sentence and forfeited all of his or her property.

b. The forfeiture provision was removed by the Forfeiture Act 1870.

c. The Criminal Justice Act 1964 abolished the death sentence for common law murder except in cases of capital murder. See [334] below.

d. Section 2 of the Criminal Justice Act 1964 imposed a mandatory life sentence for common law murder.

B. *Modern Murder – Criminal Justice Act 1964* [325]

1. General Principles –

a. Defined: Section 4 CJA 1964.

b. *Actus reus* – requires the unlawful killing of another person.

c. *Mens rea* – section 4 – replaces 'with malice and aforethought'.

   (1) Section 4 – the defendant must have *intended to kill or to cause serious injury* to some person, whether the defendant actually killed that person or someone else.

(2) **Intention to kill** – the test of intention is subjective.
                                                                    [326]
   (a) The defendant's foresight of death as a natural and probable consequence of his or her conduct does not amount to an intention to kill per se, but it may be evidence from which intention can be drawn. *People (DPP)* v. *Douglas & Hayes* [1985] ILRM 25.
   (b) Note: Intention is not the same as motive. See *mens rea* [80].

2. Good motive – **euthanasia**   **[327]**
   a. An alleged good motive for an intentional killing is not a defence.
      (1) Euthanasia is killing another to end that person's suffering. Sometimes it is referred to as mercy killing.
         (a) Euthanasia is legal in some jurisdictions, but is not legal in England or Ireland.
         (b) Once the defendant has the intent to kill to end the victim's suffering and kills the victim, the defendant has committed a murder. See hastening death [317].
      (2) A person cannot consent to be murdered.   **[328]**
         (a) Therefore, a defendant will have no valid defence to murder, even if the victim begged the defendant to be killed.
         (b) This is true even if the victim was suicidal.

3. **Serious injury** – the Act does not define the term 'serious injury'.   **[329]**
   a. In England the term 'grievous bodily harm' has been held to mean serious bodily harm.
   b. Includes recognised psychiatric illness as grievous bodily harm.
      (1) *R.* v. *Burstow* [1997] 4 All ER 225 – eight months of silent phone calls and hate mail caused the victim to suffer severe depression. Held: To constitute grievous bodily harm.
      (2) Requires more than simple fears or problems with coping with everyday life.

4. **Presumption** – section 4 (2) – the defendant is presumed to have intended the natural and probable consequences of his or her conduct.   **[330]**
   a. Presumption may be rebutted by the defendant.
   b. Ultimately the jury must determine whether the defendant intended to cause death or serious injury. It is a two-step process:

(1) Jury should consider whether death or serious injury was a natural and probable consequence of the defendant's conduct.

(2) If so, is there an alternative explanation and has the prosecution proved beyond a reasonable doubt that the presumption has not been rebutted by the defence?

5. **Causation** – the defendant's act(s) must have led to the victim's death. See [317] above. **[331]**

6. **Penalty** – **[332]**

   a. Criminal Justice Act 1990, section 1 abolished the death penalty for any offence.

   b. Section 2 – penalty for murder is now a mandatory life sentence.

      (1) It is an indeterminate sentence.

      (2) Most murderers are released after approximately twelve years.

   c. Many legal commentators have argued for:

      (1) Determinate sentences for murder.

      (2) Allowing for judicial discretion in sentencing.

         (a) An indeterminate sentence makes it difficult to plan a programme of rehabilitation for the murderer.

         (b) Judicial discretion would allow judges to impose lighter sentences to killers who are seen as less of a risk to society, e.g. see euthanasia [327].

7. **Recommendations for changes** – Law Reform Commission's Consultation Paper on the Mental Element in Murder (March 2001) has recommended: **[333]**

   a. That the fault element of murder be broadened to include:

      (1) Reckless killing, i.e. killings that show an extreme indifference to human life.

      (2) Recklessness as to serious injury.

   b. A result is intended if:

      (1) It is the defendant's conscious object or purpose to cause it.

      (2) The defendant was aware that it was virtually certain that his or her conduct would cause it, or it was virtually certain to cause it if he or she were to succeed in his or her purpose of causing some result.

   c. Recklessly – a person acts recklessly when he or she consciously disregards a substantial and unjustifiable risk that death will occur. The disregard of the risk involves a gross deviation from the standard of conduct that a law-abiding person would observe in the defendant's situation.

C. *Capital or Aggravated Murder*   [334]

1. The offence of capital murder was created by the Criminal Justice Act 1964.
    a. Capital murder applied to the killing of:
        (1) A police officer or prison officer acting in the course of duty.
        (2) Foreign heads of state or diplomats in furtherance of political reasons.
    b. Rationale for creation of capital murder offence.
        (1) To protect people who are exposed to danger due to their public duties.
2. **Aggravated murder – Criminal Justice Act 1990**   [335]
    a. General principles –
        (1) Section 1 abolished the death penalty for all offences and thereby abolished capital murder.
        (2) Definition: Section 3 created a new form of murder with the same protected categories as under capital murder. This new form is generally called aggravated murder.
        (3) *Actus reus* –
            (a) Killing a police officer or prison officer acting in the course of duty.
            (b) Killing a foreign head of state or diplomats in furtherance of political reasons.
        (4) *Mens rea* –
            (a) Aggravated murder (section 3) is not committed unless it can be shown that the defendant knew of each ingredient of the offence or was reckless as to whether or not that ingredient existed.
            (b) Effect – *People (DPP)* v. *Noel & Marie Murray* (1977) has been placed on a statutory footing. See *Murray* [139].
        (5) Distinct from murder – section 3(2) (a) provides that this new form of murder is distinct from murder.
            (a) Note: Under section 6 a person accused under section 3 may be convicted of murder or manslaughter if there is not sufficient evidence for a conviction under section 3.
        (6) Penalties –
            (a) Section 4 provides a mandatory life sentence with a requirement that the defendant serve at least forty years.

(b) Section 5(1) – the power to commute or remit punishment cannot be exercised until after forty years.

(c) Section 5(2) allows remission for good behaviour.

D. Special Defences for Murder – *these defences are in addition to
the defences in Chapters 4 and 5.* **[336]**

1. **Provocation** is the sudden and temporary loss of self-control,
making the defendant incapable of refraining from acting. The
partial defence of provocation will reduce murder to manslaughter.

   a. **Historically**, by the eighteenth century the partial defence of
   provocation developed to mitigate the harshness of the death
   penalty, which originally applied to all unjustifiable homicides
   (Royal Commission on Capital Punishment Report, Cmd.
   8932, para 144 (1953)).

      (1) Lord Holt C. J. in *R.* v. *Mawgridge* (1706) Kel 119 stated
      that a physical attack or the discovery of a man commit-
      ting adultery with his wife would support a defence of
      provocation.

      (2) Legal commentators are divided over whether provocation
      is a partial justification defence (see [166]) or a partial
      excuse defence (see [165]).

      (3) McAuley and McCutcheon – defence has been shrouded
      in ambivalence and contains elements of both justification
      and excuse.

      (4) The continued existence and use of provocation has been
      questioned by many legal commentators.

         (a) England has no capital punishment, but retains
         provocation as a defence to murder.

         (b) Ireland has no capital punishment, but retains provo-
         cation as a defence to murder.

         (c) The US has no mandatory death penalty laws
         (unconstitutional per *Sumner* v. *Shuman*, 483 US 66
         (1977)), but many jurisdictions retain provocation as
         a defence to murder.

      (5) Under the common law, provocation was only available
      where the victim had done something to the defendant.
      R. v. *Duffy* [1949] 1 All ER 932.

   b. **Ireland employs a subjective test.** **[337]**

      (1) Leading case is *People (DPP)* v. *MacEoin* [1978] IR 27 –
      two men became friends in prison. The defendant moved

into the victim's flat. Both men drank heavily. One evening after drinking the defendant went to bed. The victim attacked the defendant with a hammer. The defendant took the hammer from the victim, but the victim kept hitting the defendant. The defendant lost control and struck the victim, knocked him down and hit him up to six times with the hammer. The court expressly rejected the objective reasonable person standard for provocation.

(2) *MacEoin* **subjective test** requires:

    (a) Some acts or conduct done by the deceased to the defendant which caused the defendant a sudden and temporary loss of self-control, and

    (b) Rendered the defendant subject to such passion as to make the defendant for that moment not the master of his or her mind.

(3) The force used by the defendant must be reasonable having regard to the provocation. Reasonable is *subjective*.

(4) A balance is required between the provocation generated and the amount of force used.

c. **Provocative conduct –**   **[338]**

(1) Unlawful acts – where the victim performs some unlawful act, causing the defendant to suffer a sudden and temporary loss of self-control – this is a sufficient provocation.

    (a) Note: Under the English Homicide Act 1957, provocation is no longer restricted to acts directed by the victim to the defendant.

    (b) E.g. *R. v. Pearson* [1992] Crim LR 193 – two teenage brothers struck and killed their father with a sledgehammer. One lived with the father, who was abusive, and the other brother lived with the mother. The brother who did not live with the abusive father was not allowed to plea provocation. Held: Jury should have been allowed to consider the effect of the deceased's conduct and words on both brothers.

    (c) It is not clear whether Ireland follows the common law rule.

(2) Lawful acts – where the victim performs some lawful act that causes the defendant to suffer a sudden and temporary loss of self-control, this may be sufficient provocation.   **[339]**

    (a) E.g. *People (DPP) v. Kehoe* [1992] ILRM 481 unrep.,

HC – the defendant and his former partner were drinking. He returned to her apartment to find his former best friend. The defendant grabbed a knife from the kitchen and killed his friend. The defendant was convicted of murder, but the court did not hold that a lawful act (friend being present) could not amount to provocation.

(3) **Words alone** can amount to a provocation in Ireland.
[340]

d. *Mens rea* – the defendant may have intended to kill or cause serious injury, but he or she may still avail of provocation.

(1) E.g. *People (DPP)* v. *Bambrick* (1999) unrep., HC – the defendant and the victim were drinking together when the victim made suggestive remarks and then sexual advances toward the defendant. The defendant suffered a flashback of memories of childhood abuse and lost control. He killed the victim with a wood stake.

(2) **Doctrine of transferred malice** – under the common law, so long as the defendant directed his or her act toward the victim, the defendant could avail of provocation defence regardless of who was killed. (Not clear if it applies in Ireland.)
[341]

(a) E.g. Christopher is blind in one eye. One day he observed one of his employees stealing from the till. When he confronted the employee, the employee spat in Christopher's good eye, causing him to suffer a sudden and temporary loss of self-control and sight. Christopher threw his letter opener at the employee. The letter opener killed a client. Christopher could avail of provocation.

e. **Cumulative provocation** – in some situations, such as long-term spousal abuse, the court will look at the most recent provoking act in the context of the long-term abuse. **[342]**

(1) Irish approach – *People (DPP)* v. *O'Donogue* (1992) unrep. CCC – the defendant was granted a barring order against her husband. The defendant allowed her husband to come home. He verbally abused the defendant, whereupon she lost control and killed him with a hammer. The defendant was convicted of manslaughter.

(2) English approach – cooling off inconsistent with defence of provocation.

    (a) *R.* v. *Ahluwalia* (1993) 4 All ER 889 – the defendant had a violent husband. One day he threatened to beat her the next morning. She waited until her husband fell asleep. She threw petrol into the room and set it afire. The defendant could not avail of the defence of provocation because she had not suffered a sudden loss of self-control.

    (b) *R.* v. *Thornton* (No. 2) [1996] 2 All ER 1023 – the defendant suffered physical abuse for years from her husband. She declared her intention to kill him at one point. After a new provocation she went to the kitchen, picked up a carving knife, sharpened it and went into another room and stabbed him. The defendant was convicted of murder. She could not avail of provocation because of the lapse of time between the provocation and the killing. The jury found that she had not suffered a sudden loss of self-control.

  f. **Self-induced provocation** – the defendant cannot rely on the defence of provocation where he or she has deliberately brought about the acts of provocation. **[343]**

2. **Imperfect or excessive self-defence** – will operate as a partial defence reducing murder to manslaughter. **[344]**

  a. A person is allowed under the common law to use reasonable force to defend oneself or another person.

  b. Note: Merely because the person acting in defence of self or another kills his or her attacker does not mean that the force used was unreasonable.

  c. Reasonable – force that was objectively necessary. *People (AG)* v. *Commane* (1975) 1 Frewen 400 – the deceased attacked the defendant and was knocked out and incapacitated by the defendant. The defendant then strangled the deceased. The defendant had used excessive force.

3. Debate – enactment of the Non-Fatal Offences Against the Person Act 1997.

  a. Legal commentators have noted that excessive self-defence may not have survived the enactment of the Non-Fatal Offences Against the Person Act 1997.

  b. Section 18 put common law self-defence on a statutory footing, but is silent on excessive self-defence.

  c. Section 22(2) abolished the common law defences regarding use of force in self-defence.

d. However, excessive self-defence is not addressed by the Act, and the defence is limited to murder. The Act only deals with non-fatal offences.

4. **Criticism of special defences** – gender biased. [345]
   a. Many feminists believe that the special defences of self-defence and provocation are male orientated.
      (1) Because of the imbalance of strength between men and women, women are less likely than men to react to an imminent threat or provocation.
      (2) E.g. for provocation the defendant is required to have suffered a temporary loss of self-control.
         (a) Lashing out in a sudden burst is seen as a male trait.
         (b) For battered women the loss of self-control is not sudden, but generally a long process.
   b. However, in jurisdictions where cumulative provocation, such as the 'battered woman's syndrome', has been recognised, some commentators have criticised the removal of the sudden loss of control requirement as giving one gender the license to kill.
   c. Proposed reform – a new defence of self-preservation for the killing of an abusive partner.
      (1) The new defence would be gender neutral (available to both genders).
      (2) It would still reduce murder to manslaughter, but treat both genders the same.

III. Manslaughter [346]

A. In General

1. Manslaughter covers all unlawful killings that do not constitute murder.
2. There are two types of manslaughter:
   a. Voluntary, and
   b. Involuntary.
3. Distinguishing murder from manslaughter.
   a. *Actus reus* – for murder and manslaughter it is the same, i.e. the defendant's act(s) must cause the death of another person.
   b. *Mens rea* is different for murder and manslaughter.
      (1) Manslaughter has a different and lower level of blameworthiness.
      (2) Conviction carries less stigma and punishment.

B. Voluntary Manslaughter *is a killing that arises out of:* **[347]**

1. Provocation (see [336] above), or
2. Where the defendant acted in self-defence and used unreasonable force, but no more force than he or she genuinely believed was necessary. (See [344] above.)

C. Involuntary Manslaughter *is a killing that does not constitute murder because the defendant did not have the* mens rea *for murder.*
[348]

1. Required *mens rea* for murder – see [325] above.
   a. The intention to kill, or
   b. The intention to cause serious injury.
2. Involuntary manslaughter generally arises in three different ways:
   a. The defendant killed while doing an unlawful and dangerous act.
   b. The defendant willfully refused to perform a legal duty and the victim died as a result.
   c. The defendant performed a lawful act with gross negligence and as a result the victim died.
3. **Unlawful and dangerous act** – requires that the action be both unlawful and dangerous, e.g. *R.* v. *Larkin* [1943] 1 All ER 217 – threatening a person with an open razor is unlawful and dangerous. **[349]**
   a. Dangerous means a danger of causing physical harm.
      (1) Whether the act is dangerous is an objective question for the jury.
      (2) Note: Dangerous does *not* mean a danger of causing *serious* harm.
         (a) If an act may cause serious harm, murder may apply. See [329].
   b. An act that is not unlawful or dangerous will not support a manslaughter conviction, e.g. *R.* v. *Arobieke* [1988] Crim LR 314.
   c. Causation – the unlawful and dangerous act must cause the death.
4. **Willful refusal to perform a legal duty** – requires that where a person is under a positive duty to act and he or she fails to do so, if another dies as a result a manslaughter charge may be brought. **[350]**
   a. Duty can arise in a number of ways (see [68–73]):
      (1) Special relationship between the defendant and victim.

(2) Voluntary assumption of the duty – the defendant assumed responsibility for the victim.

(3) Contractual duty – requiring the defendant to act.

(4) Statutory duty – requiring the defendant to act.

(5) Prior conduct – where the defendant's prior conduct put the victim in peril, the defendant may have a duty to act to help the victim.

5. **Lawful act performed negligently** – provides that lawful acts performed with a high degree of negligence that lead to a death can result in a manslaughter conviction.   **[351]**

   a. English approach – *R. v. Adomako* [1994] 3 All ER 79 employs a three-step process:

   (1) Was the defendant negligent? (Applying ordinary principles.)

   (2) Did the negligence cause the death?

   (3) Was the negligence so great as to constitute gross negligence?

   b. Irish approach – the defendant may be convicted of manslaughter where he or she acts in a way that a reasonable person would realise would run a very high degree of risk of causing substantial injury to another. *People (AG) v. Dunleavy* [1948] IR 95 – the defendant killed a cyclist while driving without lights on the wrong side of a busy road.

   (1) Objective test – a reasonable person would realise that the defendant's act(s) pose a very high degree of risk of causing substantial injury to another person.

   (2) Issue of fact – whether the defendant's act(s) pose the required risk is a question of fact for the jury to decide.

IV. Aiding and Abetting a Suicide   [352]

A. Historically

1. Under the common law suicide was a felony as it was considered self-murder.

2. Blackstone (1783) wrote:

   a. No one has the power to destroy life.

   b. Suicide is a double offence: against God (spiritual) and against the king (temporal).

3. Transferred intent applied – if a person attempted to kill himself or herself but accidentally killed someone else, he or she was guilty of murder.

4. The punishment for a successful suicide was:

   a. The person was buried in the public road (unconsecrated ground) with a stake through his or her body.

b. All the deceased's possessions were forfeit to the Crown.

c. These punishments remained until 1882 and 1870, when they were repealed.

d. After the repeal of the historical punishments for suicide, it remained a crime without a punishment in Ireland until 1993.

B. *Modern Law on Suicide*   [353]

1. **Criminal Law (Suicide) Act 1993** – section 2(1) provides that suicide is not a criminal offence in Ireland.

    a. Attempted suicide is no longer a criminal offence.

    b. The doctrine of transferred intent no longer applies.

    c. However, it is still an offence under the 1993 Act to aid and abet a suicide.

2. **Criminal Law (Suicide) Act 1993 – section 2(2) – aiding and abetting –**   [354]

    a. Any person who aids, abets, counsels or procures a suicide or an attempted suicide by another person is guilty of an offence.

        (1) *Dunbar* v. *Plant* (1997) (civil case). Held: A woman aided and abetted the suicide of her fiancé where they simultaneously hanged themselves and the woman survived.

        (2) *AG* v. *Able* [1984] 1 All ER 277 – an injunction was sought to restrain publication by the Voluntary Euthanasia Society. The publication provided advice on committing suicide.

    b. **Suicide pacts –**   [355]

        (1) Irish approach – if two friends decide to kill themselves and shoot each other at the same moment but one of them survives, the survivor is guilty of murdering his or her friend.

        (2) English approach – section 4(1) of the Homicide Act 1957 provides that if two people enter into a suicide pact a survivor may only be guilty of manslaughter.

    c. Punishment – up to fourteen years' imprisonment for the aiding and abetting of a suicide.

3. **Criticism –**

    a. The prohibition against assisted suicide by persons terminally ill and suffering has been challenged on numerous grounds.

        (1) For example, it is argued that assisted suicide is intended to stop suffering and the intent is not to murder.

b. Recently the European Court of Human Rights in *R. (Pretty)* v. *DPP* [2001] UKHL 61, [2001] W.L.R. 1598 refused to overturn the House of Lords' decision that there is no right to assisted suicide.

V. Infanticide [356]

A. Historically

1. At common law no allowance was made for a mother who killed her young child due to some mental condition such as post-natal depression.
2. If a mother was convicted of murder the mandatory death sentence was generally always commuted to life imprisonment.
3. England – Infanticide Act 1922 was introduced due to the impossibility of convicting a mother due to public opinion (Smith and Hogan).
   a. 1922 Act limited the offence of infanticide to newly born children, e.g. a baby killed thirty-two days after birth was not a newly born child and the mother was convicted of murder.
   b. 1938 Act was introduced to enlarge the definition of 'new born'.
4. Irish approach – the English Infanticide Act 1938 is the basis of the 1949 Irish Infanticide Act.

B. Infanticide Act 1949 [357]

1. General principles
   a. Definition: Section 1(3) provides that the offence of infanticide is committed where a mother causes the death of her child within twelve months of its birth in circumstances that would otherwise have made her guilty of murder, providing that the balance of her mind was disturbed as a result of the effects of childbirth or lactation.
   b. *Actus reus* –
      (1) The mother of a child under the age of twelve months,
      (2) Intentionally killed the child, or
      (3) Intentionally caused serious injuries to the child, killing the child
      (4) While her mind was disturbed as a result of the effects of childbirth or lactation.
   c. *Mens rea* – the mother must have intended to kill the child or to cause serious injury to the child.

2. The offence is tried and punished in the same way as manslaughter.
3. Burden of proof is on the prosecution to prove beyond a reasonable doubt that the defendant's actions do not fit within the definition of infanticide.
4. Criticism – some legal commentators object to this female-orientated defence, saying there is little basis in science to support the idea of a link between childbirth and mental illness. **[358]**
   a. Charleton – the Irish test is wide and allows for a variety of conditions and causes, such as:
      (1) Stress of greater burden on poor family of another child.
      (2) Failure of bonding between the mother and child.
      (3) Stress where the mother is not able to cope with the child.
      (4) Lactation – is no longer valid as psychiatrists now agree that it does not cause temporary insanity.
   b. Clarkson:
      (1) Notes there is some evidence suggesting a link between childbirth and mental illness.
      (2) However, most young babies are killed as a result of 'battered baby syndrome'.
         (a) Baby killers suffer from environmental stress with various personality disorders unrelated to the effects of childbirth and lactation.
         (b) Questions why fathers are treated differently. An infant can cause enormous stresses for both parents.
      (3) Criminal justice system medicalises women.
         (a) Homicide rate for children under the age of one is almost four times higher than the general population, with nearly one half of these babies killed by their mothers. Generally, women only commit ten per cent of homicides.
         (b) Society sees mothers as nurturing and caring and therefore they must be crazy to kill their own children.
      (4) Advocates abolition of this gender-biased special offence, with mentally unbalanced parents able to plead diminished responsibility.
      (5) Note: Ireland does not recognise the defence of diminished responsibility. See [199].

Review Questions

1. 'Man commits suicide after sex with hen', 28 May 2004, Lusaka (Reuters) – 'A fifty-year-old Zambian man has hanged himself after his wife found him having sex with a hen, police say. The woman caught him in the act when she rushed into their house to investigate a noise. "He attempted to kill her but she managed to escape," a police spokesman said on Friday. The man from the town of Chongwe, about thirty miles east of Lusaka, killed himself after being admonished by other villagers. The hen was slaughtered after the incident.'
   (a) Assume that the man did not kill himself, but his wife killed him after he attacked her. Would the wife be able to avail of the defence of provocation?
   (b) Assume that the man did not kill himself, but he killed his wife. Would he be able to avail of the defence of provocation?

2. Tony was tired of his girlfriend Susan. While crossing the bridge in Waterford he picked her up and threw her into the river during high tide.
   (a) After Susan's body was recovered Tony said that he did not intend to kill Susan. He said that he knew that she was a very good swimmer. What offence, if any, can Tony be convicted of for killing Susan?
   (b) Assume that Susan's body is never found. Can Tony be convicted of any offence concerning her death?

3. Rose's mother was elderly and slowly dying from a painful disease. As the disease became unbearable, Rose's mother asked Rose to end her suffering. One evening after a particularly bad day Rose decided that her mother should not suffer any more. Knowing that it is a criminal offence, Rose still grabbed a pillow and placed it over her mother's face to smother her. After several minutes Rose went to the police station and told the officers that she had killed her mother. A post mortem revealed that the mother died of the disease prior to Rose placing the pillow on her face.
   (a) Can Rose be convicted of murder?
   (b) Can Rose be convicted of manslaughter?
   (c) Can Rose be convicted of attempted murder?

4. Elizabeth went to the local disco and saw her old boyfriend Frank. Frank wanted to dance with Elizabeth, but Elizabeth politely told him that she did not want to talk to him. Frank persisted in following Elizabeth around the disco trying to get her to change her mind.

After nearly an hour of being polite, Elizabeth finally became angry and told Frank to stop harassing her. When Frank expressed his undying love for her, Elizabeth laughed and told him that he was as 'thick as a plank'. Frank did not handle the rejection well and after a few pints he followed Elizabeth into the ladies' room, where he strangled her to death.

   (a) If Frank is charged with murder, will he be able to avail of the defence of provocation?

   (b) If Frank is charged with murder, will he be able to avail of the defence of intoxication?

5. Leopold Ratcliff was a member of the Purple Plague, the terrorist wing of a large international environmental organisation. Recently, when workers prepared to widen a road in Kilkenny, Leopold defended a tree with a shotgun, shooting over the workers' heads. None of the workers were seriously injured, although one sprained an ankle running from Leopold. The police were summoned. Over forty officers arrived on the scene. Thirty-five officers were in uniform, but five detectives were not. After the police attempted to convince Leopold to climb out of the tree and put down his shotgun, Leopold took careful aim and shot one of the plain-clothed detectives, killing him.

   (a) Will Leopold be convicted of attempting to murder the workers?

   (b) What charge or charges might be brought against Leopold for shooting the detective?

6. Sally gave birth to here first child on 1 November 2000. On 1 March 2001, Sally's husband came home and announced that he was leaving Sally for a younger woman. Sally became depressed and one week later, unable to cope with the baby screaming at three a.m., Sally suffocated her baby. Will infanticide apply?

7. Spencer saw his old enemy, Louis, walking down the street. Spencer grabbed a steel rod and began to hit Louis in the knees, trying to cripple him. A taxi driver stopped Spencer and rushed Louis to the hospital. Unfortunately, Louis developed a blood clot on his injured knee and almost died when it went into his lung. If Louis makes a full recovery, can Spencer be convicted of attempted murder?

8. Thelma and Louise decided to rob a pizza delivery person. Unfortunately, the person delivering the pizza refused to hand over his money, even when Thelma pointed her gun at him. In frustration, Thelma hit the pizza delivery person with her gun, but the pistol discharged and killed Louise. Can Thelma be held criminally liable for her friend Louise's death?

Figure 7.1

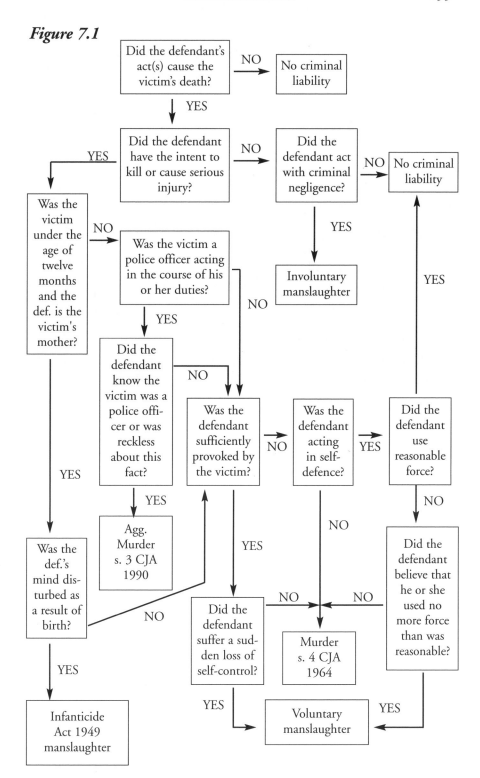

8

NON-SEXUAL OFFENCES
AGAINST THE PERSON

Chapter synopsis

I.   Assault
II. Aggravated Assault
III. Threats and Coercion
IV. Kidnapping and Abduction

I. Assault [359]

A. Historically

1. Under the common law there were separate offences for assault, battery and false imprisonment.
2. The law treated all non-fatal offences as misdemeanours punishable with imprisonment and fines.
3. Offences Against Person Act 1861 was the first real attempt to codify the non-fatal offences.
4. Non-Fatal Offences Against the Person Act 1997 –
   a. Generally codifies the common law with regard to non-fatal offences.
   b. Repealed virtually all of the substantive provisions of the OAPA 1861, except those provisions dealing with abortion.
   c. Common law offences of assault, battery and false imprisonment were abolished.
   d. Much of the pre-1997 case law is still relevant in interpreting areas where common law was codified or reformed by NFOAPA 1997.

B. Non-Fatal Offences Against the Person Act 1997 [360]

1. Definition: NFOAPA 1997, section 2(1) provides that an assault occurs where the defendant, without lawful excuse, intentionally or recklessly and without consent:

a. Section 2(1)(a) – directly or indirectly applies force to or causes an impact on the body of another, or
   (1) Under the common law – defined common law offence of battery.
b. Section 2(1)(b) – causes another to believe on reasonable ground that he or she is likely to be immediately subjected to the direct or indirect force or impact.
   (1) Under the common law – defined common law offence of assault.

2. *Actus reus*
   a. Directly or indirectly applying force to or causing an impact to the body of another, or
   b. Causing another to believe objectively that he or she will be immediately subjected to a direct or indirect force or impact.

3. *Mens rea* – intention or recklessness.
   a. Act does not define recklessness.
   b. Common law rule of subjective test will probably continue. See *R. v. Cunningham* [88].

C. Force [361]

1. Definition: NFOAPA 1997, section 2(2) provides that force includes:
   a. Application of heat, light, electric current, noise or any other form of energy, and
   b. Application of matter in solid, liquid or gaseous form.
2. No minimum force requirement in the Act.
   a. Common law rule – any degree of force, no matter how slight, is sufficient to constitute the offence.
   b. Example: If Blanche kisses Fred without his consent, she has committed an assault under section 2.
   c. *R. v. Thomas* [1985] Crim LR 677 – the defendant touched the bottom of a woman's skirt and rubbed it. This was held to constitute a battery, despite the fact that the woman did not feel the contact. It was held that touching another's clothing while the clothing is being worn is the equivalent of touching the person.

D. Mere Words [362]

1. It is not clear whether mere words can amount to a criminal assault under the NFOAPA 1997.

    a. Under the common law mere words, no matter how threatening or harsh, could not amount to a criminal assault.

      (1) It was required that there be some threatening act of any kind that would create an apprehension of immediate violence in the victim.

      (2) Example: *R. v. Byrne* [1968] 3 CCC 179 (Canadian) – the defendant went to the ticket office at a theatre with a coat over his arm. He said, 'I've got a gun, give me all of your money or I'll shoot.' It was held that no assault had been committed.

    b. Law Reform Commission and legal commentators –

      (1) Condemned the common law rule that mere words, no matter how threatening or harsh, could not amount to a criminal assault.

    c. There is no reason why words that would cause a person to reasonably apprehend the infliction of immediate force cannot come within the second form of the offence, i.e. section 2(1)(b).

  2. Negating acts –

    a. Under the common law mere words could negate acts that would otherwise be a criminal assault.

    b. Classic case – *Tuberville* v. *Savage* (1669) – the defendant put his hand on his sword and said: 'If it were not assize time, I would not take such language.' It was held that the act of the defendant placing his hand on his sword was an assault, but his words negated any apprehension the other man would have had of receiving an immediate battery, i.e. contact or impact.

E. Immediacy [363]

  1. Under the common law, for an assault to occur the threatened battery (contact or impact) had to be immediate.

    a. In other words, to amount to an assault it could not be a threat of a future battery.

    b. Example: The next time I see you I'm going to thump you (no assault).

  2. NFOAPA 1997, section 2(1)(b) retains the common law requirement of immediacy.

    a. Immediacy – not defined in the Act.

    b. Under the common law, immediacy developed into a flexible proximity test.

(1) *R.* v. *Horseferry Road Magistrates' Court, ex parte Saidatan* [1991] 1 All ER 324 – it was held that immediacy required proximity in time and causation; that violence will result within a reasonably short period of time.

3. Stalking – English approach.   **[364]**
   a. In order to deal with stalking cases the definition of immediacy was extended.
      (1) *R.* v. *Ireland* [1997] 4 All ER 225 – the defendant made repeated phone calls to three women; most of the calls were silent and sometimes he resorted to having breathing. It was held that the immediacy requirement was satisfied because of the fear that the caller's arrival at her door may be imminent. The victim may fear the possibility of immediate personal violence.
      (2) *R.* v. *Constanza* [1997] 2 Cr.App.R. 492 – the defendant made repeated silent phone calls and sent 800 letters to the victim. The victim interpreted the last two letters as clear threats. It was held that there had been an assault when the victim read these latter letters, as there was a fear of violence at some time which did not exclude the immediate future.
   b. Clarkson – one can understand this judicial response to the appalling plight of the victims, but this is surely stretching the immediacy requirement too far.
      (1) Protection from Harassment Act 1997 created two criminal offences of harassment.

4. Stalking – Irish approach – no need to extend scope of immediacy requirement.   **[365]**
   a. NFOAPA, section 10(1) – see [389].
      (1) Created new offence of harassment by any means, including the telephone.
      (2) Makes it an offence for any person without lawful authority or reasonable excuse to harass another by any means, including use of the telephone.

F. Apprehension   [366]

1. Common law assault required the reasonable apprehension of an immediate infliction of force.
   a. No contact of any type was required.
   b. Apprehension does not require fear.
      (1) Merely requires that the victim perceive or recognise that he or she may receive an immediate battery (contact or impact).

(2) Example: Tyrone swings a golf club over Kirk's head. Kirk is seated in Tyrone's favorite chair. Tyrone has committed an assault. However, if Kirk is asleep and cannot perceive Tyrone's conduct, there is no assault.
   c. Reasonable apprehension is an objective requirement.
      (1) A reasonable person would have believed that force was imminent.
2. NFOAPA 1997, section 2(1)(b):
   a. Requires reasonable apprehension of the immediate infliction of force.
   b. Follows the old common law.

G. Consent   [367]

1. NFOAPA 1997, sections 2(1)(a) and 2(1)(b) –
   a. Both require that the defendant's conduct must be committed without the consent of the victim.
   b. Restates common law – that consent was a valid defence to assault so long as no bodily harm was caused.
      (1) Fact that consent was given does not of itself mean that the defendant will be found not guilty.
      (2) There are public policy considerations that might override the victim's consent.
         (a) *AG's Ref. (No. 6 of 1980)* (1981) – the defendant had engaged in a fist fight with another man in order to settle a disagreement. The other man sustained bruising to his face and a bloody nose. The Court of Appeal recognised that while consent may be a defence in minor cases, it is contrary to public policy to allow people to inflict actual bodily harm on each other. Not material whether the fight took place in a public or a private place.
         (b) *R. v. Brown* [1993] 2 All ER 75 – see [425] for facts. House of Lords held that while consent was a defence to violent sports like boxing, it should not be expanded to include sadomasochistic behaviour leading to grievous bodily harm.

H. *Incidents of Ordinary Daily Life* [368]

1. Common law – doctrine of implied consent.
    a. Because any contact could amount to a common law battery, the law recognised that contact in some circumstances was lawful.
        (1) Example: Bumping into someone on a crowded street.
        (2) Example: The contact between players in a match played according to the rules of the game.
        (3) Seizing someone's hand while at a party – not a common law battery. *Collins* v. *Wilcock* [1984] 3 All ER 374.
2. NFOAPA 1997, section 2(3) provides:
    a. For a defence that the force or impact was not intended or likely to cause injury and
    b. Occurred in circumstances that would be considered to be generally acceptable in ordinary daily life,
    c. Providing that the defendant does not know or believe that the victim finds the particular force or impact unacceptable.

I. *Discipline* [369]

1. Common law
    a. It was well recognised that lawful discipline existed. For example:
        (1) A man was allowed to physically discipline his wife so long as he used a stick that was no larger in circumference than his thumb (Rule of Thumb).
        (2) A master had the right to administer discipline to servants and apprentices.
        (3) The captain of a ship could inflict corporal punishment on the sailors under his command.
        (4) Teachers could inflict corporal punishment on students.
    b. All have fallen into disuse, except parents (and those *in loco parentis*), who are still allowed to physically discipline children, but the discipline must be reasonable.
        (1) *A.* v. *UK* (1998) unrep. ECHR – an English jury found that a stepfather who used a garden cane on his stepson's buttocks as discipline to be reasonable. The child's father took the issue to the European Court of Human Rights. It was found that the punishment inflicted violated the child's rights under Article 3 of the European Convention of Human Rights, which prohibits torture or inhuman or degrading treatment.

2. Non-Fatal Offences Against the Person Act 1997
   a. Section 24 – the common law exemption for teachers regarding corporal punishment was abolished.
   b. The Law Reform Commission was clearly unhappy that any person has the power to inflict corporal punishment on children; however, it recognised the right of parental discipline is widely accepted in Irish society. Accordingly, it suggested that parents continue to be allowed to inflict reasonable physical discipline, but that parents be 're-educated'.

J. Penalties   [370]

1. A defendant guilty of an assault under section 2 shall be liable on summary conviction to a fine not exceeding £1,500 or
2. To a term of imprisonment not exceeding six months or
3. To both.

II. Aggravated Assault   [371]

A. Common Law

1. The Offences Against the Person Act 1861 contained a wide variety of aggravated assault offences, all of which have now been abolished.
   a. Section 18 prohibited the unlawful and malicious causing of a wound or grievous bodily harm (GBH) or shooting at another with the intent to maim, disfigure or disable any person, or to do some other GBH to any person, or to resist the arrest of any person.
   b. Section 20 was a slightly less serious form of aggravated assault. It prohibited the unlawful and malicious wounding of or infliction of GBH upon any other person with or without a weapon.
   c. Section 47 was the least serious form of aggravated assault. It provided that any assault that occasioned actual bodily harm was an offence that could be punished by up to five years' penal servitude.
2. Law Reform Commission recommended the abolition of the aggravated assault offences under the OAPA 1861.
   a. Advocated simpler scheme that penalised assaults causing harm or serious harm.
   b. Term 'harm' preferred to 'injury', largely because it more easily includes mental harm.
   c. LRC recommendations were accepted and enacted in the NFOAPA 1997.

B. NFOAPA 1997 [372]

1. **General Principles of Aggravated Assault –**
   a. Definition:
      (1) Under section 3, an aggravated assault occurs where the defendant assaults another, causing the victim harm.
      (2) Under section 4, an aggravated assault occurs where the defendant intentionally or recklessly causes serious harm to another.
   b. *Actus reus –*
      (1) Under section 3, assaulting another and causing harm.
         (a) Assault, see [360] above.
            i. Directly or indirectly applying force to or causing an impact to the body of another, or
            ii. Causing another to believe objectively that he or she will be immediately subjected to a direct or indirect force or impact (section 2).
         (b) Harm is defined in section 1.
            i. Harm to body or mind that includes pain and unconsciousness.
      (2) Under section 4, causing another serious harm.
         (a) Note: No requirement that an assault take place.
         (b) Serious harm is defined in section 1.
            i. An injury that causes a substantial risk of death, serious disfigurement, the substantial loss or impairment of the function of any organ or body member.
   c. *Mens rea –* [373]
      (1) Under section 3, intentionally or recklessly.
         (a) Implied in the statute.
         (b) Subjective recklessness – see *R.* v. *Cunningham* [88].
      (2) Under section 4, intentionally or recklessly.
         (a) Expressed in statute.
         (b) Subjective recklessness – see *R.* v. *Cunningham* [88].
2. Penalties – [374]
   a. Under section 3:
      (1) On summary conviction, to imprisonment for a term not exceeding twelve months or to a fine not exceeding £1,500 or both.
      (2) On conviction on indictment, imprisonment for a term not exceeding five years, a fine or both.

b. Under section 4:
   (1) A person guilty of an offence under this section shall be liable on conviction on indictment to a fine or to imprisonment for life or to both.

C. Syringe Offences [375]

1. General Principles –
   a. Syringe definition: Section 1 – any part of a syringe or needle or any sharp instrument capable of piercing skin and passing on to another person blood or a blood-like substance.
   b. Section 6 has four main provisions.
2. **Section 6(1) – Stabbing or Threatening to Stab** [376]
   a. Definition: It is an offence to:
      (1) Injure another by piercing the skin of that other person with a syringe, or
      (2) Threaten to pierce the skin of another with a syringe,
      (3) With the intention of, or
      (4) Where there is a likelihood of causing that person to believe that he or she may be infected with a disease as a result of the injury caused or threatened.
   b. *Actus reus* –
      (1) Piercing the skin of another with a syringe, or
      (2) Threatening to pierce the skin of another with a syringe.
         (a) Note: There is no requirement that the syringe be filled with anything including blood or a blood-like substance.
   c. *Mens rea* – in two parts –
      (1) Intention or recklessness regarding the piercing or threatening to pierce.
         (a) Likely to be subjective recklessness – required under previous aggravated offences under the OAPA 1861. See subjective recklessness [91].
      (2) And either:
         (a) Intention to cause a belief in the victim that he or she may have been infected with a disease, or
         (b) Objective recklessness – the circumstances are such that a victim would believe that he or she may have been infected with a disease.
   d. Penalty –
      (1) On summary conviction – to a fine not exceeding £1,500 or to a term of imprisonment not exceeding twelve months or to both.

(2) On conviction on indictment – to a fine or to a term of imprisonment for a term not exceeding ten years or to both.

3. **Section 6(2) – Spraying or Threats to Spray** [377]
   a. Definition: It is an offence to:
   (1) Spray, pour or put blood or a blood-like substance onto another person,
   (2) Or to threaten to do so,
   (3) With an intention to cause a belief of infection in the victim,
   (4) Or where there is a likelihood of causing such a belief.
   b. *Actus reus* –
   (1) Spraying, pouring or putting blood or a blood-like substance on another.
   (2) Threatening to spray, pour or place blood or a blood-like substance on another.
   c. *Mens rea* – in two parts –
   (1) Intention or recklessness regarding spraying, pouring, putting blood or a blood-like substance on another.
      (a) Likely to be subjective recklessness – required under previous aggravated offences under the OAPA 1861. See subjective recklessness [91].
   (2) And either:
      (a) Intention to cause a belief in the victim that he or she may have been infected with a disease, or
      (b) Objective recklessness – the circumstances are such that a victim would believe that he or she may have been infected with a disease.
   d. Penalty –
   (1) On summary conviction – to a fine not exceeding £1,500 or to a term of imprisonment not exceeding twelve months or to both.
   (2) On conviction on indictment – to a fine or to a term of imprisonment for a term not exceeding ten years or to both.

4. **Section 6(3) – Transferred Intent** [378]
   a. Definition: It is an offence to commit or attempt to commit any offence under 6(1) and 6(2) and
   (1) Injure a third person with a syringe by piercing that person's skin, or
   (2) Spraying, pouring or putting onto a third person blood or a blood-like substance.

(3) Resulting in the third person believing that he or she may become infected with a disease as a result of the injury or conduct.

b. *Actus reus* –
  (1) Under 6(1):
    (a) Piercing the skin of another with a syringe, or
    (b) Threatening to pierce the skin of another with a syringe.
  (2) OR under 6(2):
    (a) Spraying, pouring or putting blood or a blood-like substance on another.
    (b) Threatening to spray, pour or place blood or a blood-like substance on another.
  (3) AND while attempting to pierce, threaten, spray, pour, etc., a third party is:
    (a) Pierced by the syringe, or
    (b) Sprayed, or had blood or a blood-like substance put on him or her.
    (c) Resulting in the third person believing that he or she may become infected with a disease.

c. *Mens rea* –
  (1) The defendant must have the *mens rea* required under either 6(1) [376] or 6(2) [377].
  (2) Section 6(3) itself requires no additional *mens rea*.
    (a) Therefore, once *mens rea* for underlying attempt under 6(2) or 6(3) is shown, that *mens rea* is transferred to the third party.
    (b) While attempting to rob Mary, Peter threatens Mary with a syringe filled with red dye. While swinging the syringe around the syringe slips from Peter's hand and stabs Paul in the back. Although Peter did not intend to threaten or injure Paul, Peter's intent toward Mary is transferred to Paul.

d. Penalty –
  (1) On summary conviction – to a fine not exceeding £1,500 or to a term of imprisonment not exceeding twelve months or to both.
  (2) On conviction on indictment – to a fine or to a term of imprisonment for a term not exceeding ten years or to both.

5. **Section 7(1) – Possession of Syringe/Blood Container in a Public Place**   [379]
   a. Definition: It is an offence to be found in possession in a public place of a syringe or a blood container with intent to cause or threaten to cause an injury to or to intimidate another person.
      (1) Public place is defined in section 1 as including any street, seashore, park, land or field, highway and any other premises or place to which the public have or are permitted to have access, whether on payment or not, and includes any train, vessel, aircraft or vehicle used for the carriage of persons for reward.
   b. *Actus reus* –
      (1) Having possession of a syringe or blood container in a public place.
   c. *Mens rea* – intention to cause or threaten to cause an injury to or to intimidate another.
   d. Penalty –
      (1) On summary conviction – to a fine not exceeding £1,500 or to a maximum term of imprisonment of twelve months or to both.
      (2) On conviction on indictment – to a fine or to imprisonment for a term not exceeding seven years or to both.

6. **Section 8(1) – Placing or Abandoning a Syringe**   [380]
   a. Definition: It is an offence to place or abandon a syringe in any place in such a manner that it is likely to injure another and does in fact injure another person, or where it is likely to injure, cause a threat or frighten another person.
   b. *Actus reus* –
      (1) Placing or abandoning a syringe in any place where it is likely to injure another and it does injure another, or
      (2) Placing or abandoning a syringe in any place where it is likely to injure another, cause a threat or frighten another person.
   c. *Mens rea* – objective recklessness (see [88]).
   d. Defences –
      (1) Anyone administering or assisting in lawful medical, dental or veterinary procedures is not liable to prosecution under this section.
      (2) Where the syringe was placed in the defendant's normal residence and the defendant did not intentionally place

the syringe in such a manner that it injured or was likely
to injure or cause a threat or to frighten another person.

   e. Penalty –

      (1) On summary conviction – to a fine not exceeding £1,500
or to a term of imprisonment not exceeding twelve
months or to both.

      (2) On conviction on indictment – to a fine or to imprison-
ment for a term not exceeding seven years or to both.

D. Aggravated Syringe Offences   [381]

  1. **Section 6(5)(a) – Stabbing with a Contaminated Syringe**

    a. Definition: It is an offence to intentionally injure another by
piercing his or her skin with a contaminated syringe.

      (1) Contaminated syringe is defined in section 1 as a syringe
which has in it or on it contaminated blood or contaminated fluid.

    b. *Actus reus* – stabbing another with a contaminated syringe.

    c. *Mens rea* – intention.

      (1) To stab or pierce the skin

      (2) With a contaminated syringe.

    d. Penalty – on conviction on indictment, up to imprisonment
for life.

  2. **Section 6(5)(b) – Intentionally Spraying with Contaminated
Blood**   [382]

    a. Definition: It is an offence to intentionally spray, pour or put
contaminated blood onto another person.

      (1) Contaminated blood is defined in section 1 as blood
which is contaminated with any disease, virus, agent or
organism which if passed into the bloodstream of another
could infect the other with a life-threatening or potentially life-threatening disease.

    b. *Actus reus* – spraying, pouring or placing contaminated blood
onto another person.

    c. *Mens rea* – intention.

    d. Penalty – on conviction on indictment, up to imprisonment
for life.

  3. **Section 6(5)(c) – Transferred Intent**   [383]

    a. Definition: It is an offence to attempt or commit an offence
under section 6(5)(a) or 6(5)(b) and

      (1) Injure a third person with a contaminated syringe by
piercing his or her skin or

(2) Spray, pour or put contaminated blood onto a third party.
b. *Actus reus* –
   (1) While attempting to stab or while stabbing another with a contaminated syringe, piercing the skin of a third person. OR
   (2) While attempting to spray or pour contaminated blood onto another or while spraying or pouring contaminated blood on another, a third person is sprayed, etc. with the contaminated blood.
c. *Mens rea* – intention to commit offence under 6(5)(a) or 6(5)(b) is transferred to third party.

4. **Section 8(2) – Intentionally Placing a Contaminated Syringe** [384]
   a. Definition: It is an offence for a person to intentionally place a contaminated syringe in any place in such a manner that it injures another.
   b. *Actus reus* – placing a contaminated syringe in any place in such a manner than it injures another person.
   c. *Mens rea* – intention. See [81].
   d. Penalty upon conviction on indictment – up to life imprisonment.

III. Threats and Coercion [385]

A. Under the Common Law

1. Threats –
   a. A threat to kill or cause injury at some point in the future was generally not a crime.
      (1) Not an assault because the threat was not of immediate violence.
   b. Exception – section 16 of the OAPA 1861 – it was an offence to maliciously send written death threats to any person.
   c. Law Reform Commission:
      (1) Found this to be too limited as it only applied to:
         (a) Written threats, and
         (b) Threats to kill.
      (2) Recommended the repeal of section 16 OAPA 1861 and proposed:
         (a) Expanding to include any threat to kill or to cause serious harm to any person.
         (b) Unnecessary to show that recipient of threat was the intended target of threat.

      (c) Recommendations – enacted into section 5 of the NFOAPA 1997.

2. Coercion –   **[386]**

    a. Coercion was unknown to Irish law.

    b. Exception – section 7 of the Conspiracy and Protection of Property Act 1875.

      (1) Prohibited the:

          (a) Use of violence or intimidation against any person or their family.

          (b) Following that person alone or with others while acting in a disorderly manner.

          (c) Watching his or her house or place of business.

          (d) Hiding his or her property with a view to forcing that person to do something or to restrain from doing something.

      (2) Intimidation included any conduct for which a court would bind the defendant to the peace.

    c. Law Reform Commission:

      (1) Was generally happy with this provision, but proposed that the punishment be increased.

      (2) Recommended that other types of harassment be criminalised.

          (a) Any act that seriously interfered with another person's peace and privacy should be an offence.

      (3) Recommendations – enacted into sections 9 and 10 of the NFOAPA 1997.

B. Non-Fatal Offences Against the Person Act 1997   **[387]**

1. **Section 5 – Threats –**

    a. Definition: It is an offence to make a threat to kill or to cause serious harm to any person and to communicate the threat by any means to any person providing that the defendant intended that the recipient believe the threat.

      (1) Serious harm – see [372].

    b. *Actus reus* –

      (1) Threatening to kill, or to cause serious harm to another.

      (2) Communicating the threat by any means to any person.

    c. *Mens rea* – intention.

      (1) To make the threat.

      (2) To communicate the threat.

      (3) That the recipient of the threat believes it.

(a) It does not matter if the recipient did or did not believe the threat.

(b) Requires only that the defendant intended for the recipient to believe it.

   d. Penalty –

     (1) On summary conviction – a fine up to £1,500, a term of imprisonment not exceeding twelve months or to both.

     (2) On a conviction on indictment – to a fine or to imprisonment for a term not exceeding ten years or to both.

2. **Section 9 – Coercion –**   **[388]**

   a. Definition: It is an offence to compel, without lawful authority, a person to refrain from doing something that he or she is legally entitled to do, or alternatively, to do something that he or she is legally entitled not to do by:

     (1) Using violence or intimidation to that person or his or her family.

     (2) Injuring or damaging his or her property.

        (a) Property is defined in section 1 as limited to tangible property, whether real or person, but includes money and animals that are capable of being stolen.

     (3) Persistently following him or her from place to place.

     (4) Watching or besetting his or her place of residence or business, or the approaches to the residence or business, or any other place where that person happens to be.

     (5) Following him or her with others in a disorderly fashion.

   b. *Actus reus* – points (1)–(4) listed above.

   c. *Mens rea* – intention.

   d. Penalty –

     (1) On summary conviction – to a fine not exceeding £1,500 or to a term of imprisonment not exceeding twelve months or to both.

     (2) On conviction on indictment – to a fine or to a term of imprisonment not exceeding five years or to both.

3. **Section 10 – Harassment –**   **[389]**

   a. Definition: It is an offence to harass another without lawful authority or reasonable excuse, seriously interfering with that person's peace and privacy or causing alarm, distress or harm by any means, including:

     (1) Persistently following.

     (2) Watching.

     (3) Pestering.

(4) Besetting.
(5) Communicating with the victim.
    (a) Harm is defined in section 1 as harm to body or mind and includes pain and unconsciousness.
b. *Actus reus* –
  (1) Seriously interfering with a person's peace or privacy, or
  (2) Causing that person alarm, distress or harm, by
  (3) Performing any conduct including those outlined in points (1)–(5) above.
c. *Mens rea* – section 10(2) requires that the conduct be carried out either intentionally or recklessly.
  (1) Objective standard – conduct must be such that any reasonable person would realise that such serious interference or alarm, etc. could result.
d. Penalty –
  (1) Section 10(3) – the court may issue what amounts to an injunction to prohibit any further contact between the victim and the defendant, either in addition to or instead of penalties under section 10(6).
  (2) Section 10(6).
    (a) On summary conviction – a fine not exceeding £1,500 or to a term of imprisonment not exceeding twelve months or to both.
    (b) On conviction on indictment – to a fine or to imprisonment for a term not exceeding seven years or to both.

IV. Kidnapping and Abduction [390]

A. Historically

1. Under the common law, the deprivation of liberty could have been punished in a variety of ways.
  a. Common law false imprisonment.
  b. Kidnapping.
2. False imprisonment occurred where a defendant intentionally or recklessly deprived another person totally of his or her liberty for any amount of time.
  a. False imprisonment could take place anywhere as long as it was total.
    (1) Driving a car so fast that a passenger was afraid to get out could amount to a false imprisonment. *McDaniel* v. *State* (1942) 15 Tex Crim 115.

(2) Possible to falsely imprison another in the middle of a public street. *Ludlow* v. *Burgess* [1971] Crim LR 238.
  b. Words alone could amount to a false imprisonment.
3. Kidnapping was a more serious form of false imprisonment that involved an element of abduction. **[391]**
  a. In *R.* v. *D.* [1984] 2 All ER 449 the House of Lords found four distinct ingredients in the offence:
    (1) The taking and carrying away of one person by another.
    (2) Force or fraud on the part of the kidnapper.
    (3) The absence of consent by the victim.
    (4) The absence of a lawful authority.
  b. *People (AG)* v. *Edge* [1943] IR 115 – a majority of the Supreme Court found that kidnapping was a colloquial term only. It was not an offence known to the law. It was a term that referred to a type of false imprisonment.
4. Child stealing was an offence under section 56 of the OAPA 1861. **[392]**
  a. Definition: It was an offence to unlawfully, with force or fraud, take a child under fourteen away from its guardian with intent either to deprive the guardian of possession of the child or to steal any article from the child, whether owned by the child or not.
    (1) Offence did not apply to any person who claimed a right of possession of the child, e.g. the mother of the child, the father of an illegitimate child, etc.
  b. Related offences.
    (1) It was an offence under section 55 to take an unmarried girl under the age of sixteen away from her mother or father without their consent.
    (2) It was an offence under section 54 (and section 7 of the Criminal Law Amendment Act 1885 as amended by section 20 of the Criminal Law Amendment Act 1935) to abduct women and unmarried girls under the age of eighteen for the purpose of marrying or having intercourse with them.

B. Non-Fatal Offences Against the Person Act 1997 [393]

1. Section 15(1) – False Imprisonment
  a. Definition: It is an offence for a person to intentionally or recklessly:
    (1) Take or detain,

(2) Cause to be taken or detained, or

(3) Otherwise restrict the personal liberty of another person without that person's consent.

b. *Actus reus* –

(1) Without the victim's consent,

    (a) Taking or causing the victim to be taken,

    (b) Detaining or causing the victim to be detained,

    (c) Otherwise restricting the personal liberty of the victim.

(2) Note: It is not required that the victim be totally detained.

(3) Note: Consent must be real and freely given. See [406].

c. *Mens rea* – intentional and recklessness.

(1) Probably subjective – see [88].

d. Penalty –

(1) On summary conviction – to a fine not exceeding £1,500 or to a term of imprisonment not exceeding twelve months or to both.

(2) On conviction on indictment – up to life imprisonment.

2. **Section 16(1) – Abduction of a Child by a Parent   [394]**

a. Definition: It is an offence for a parent, guardian or a person who has custody of a child under the age of sixteen to take the child out of the State or causes the child to be taken, sent or kept:

(1) In defiance of a court order, or

(2) Without the consent of each person who is a parent or guardian or any person who has custody of the child granted by a court,

(3) Unless the consent of the court was obtained.

    (a) Section 16(2) provides that the offence applies to a parent, guardian or a person who has custody of the child granted by a court, but it does not apply to a parent who is not a guardian of the child.

(4) Section 16(3) provides a defence where:

    (a) The defendant has not been able to communicate with the person who is a parent or guardian or any person who has custody of the child granted by a court, but believes that they would consent if they were aware of the relevant circumstances, or

    (b) The defendant did not intend to deprive others having rights of guardianship or custody of the child of those rights.

b. *Actus reus* –
   (1) A parent (guardian or legal custodian) of a child under sixteen taking, sending or keeping the child out of the State.
   (2) In defiance of a court order, or
   (3) Without the consent of the child's parent (guardian or legal custodian) or the court.
c. *Mens rea* – intention.
d. Penalty –
   (1) On summary conviction – to a fine not exceeding £1,500 or to a term of imprisonment not exceeding twelve months or to both.
   (2) On conviction on indictment – to a fine or to imprisonment for a term not exceeding seven years or to both.

3. **Section 17(1) – Abduction of a Child by Others**   **[395]**
   a. Definition: It is an offence to intentionally take, detain or cause a child under the age of sixteen without lawful authority or reasonable excuse to be taken or detained, so as to:
      (1) Remove the child from the lawful control of any person having the lawful control of the child, or
      (2) To keep the child out of the lawful control of any person having the lawful control of the child.
      (3) Does not apply to person subject to section 16.
         (a) Section 16 applies to a parent, guardian or a person who has custody of a child under the age of sixteen.
   b. *Actus reus* –
      (1) The defendant must not be a parent, guardian or a person with custody of the child who is under sixteen years of age.
      (2) The defendant must:
         (a) Take or detain the child without lawful authority or reasonable excuse, or
         (b) Cause the child to be taken or detained without lawful authority or reasonable excuse.
      (3) The defendant must deprive the person having lawful control of the child from having lawful control.
   c. *Mens rea* – intention.
   d. Defence – Section 17(2) provides that it shall be a defence that the defendant believed that the child had attained the age of sixteen.

e. Penalty –
(1) On summary conviction – to a fine not exceeding £1,500 or to a term of imprisonment not exceeding twelve months or to both.
(2) On conviction on indictment – to a fine or to a term of imprisonment for a term not exceeding seven years or to both.

Review Questions

1. Howard has been in treatment for a number of years due to his phobias concerning germs. For the first time in more than a decade Howard is convinced to attend a family function. His cousin Lenny, knowing that Howard cannot abide kissing, grabs Howard and plants a kiss on his mouth.
   (a) Can Lenny be convicted of assault?
   (b) Can Lenny be convicted of aggravated assault?
2. Shane tells Mags that the next time he sees Walter he is going to give Walter a fat lip for flirting with his partner.
   (a) Can Shane be convicted of assaulting Walter? Why or why not?
   (b) Can Shane be convicted of threatening Walter? Why or why not?
3. Shane wants Walter to stop flirting with his partner, so Shane blocks the right of way where Walter walks his dog and flirts with Shane's partner.
   (a) Can Shane be convicted of coercion?
   (b) Can Shane be convicted of false imprisonment?
4. Rodney was walking down the street minding his own business. He was just at the dentist and had a painful tooth pulled. His gum was still bleeding, so he spit the blood into the gutter near the bus stop. Unfortunately, the wind blew some of his bloody spit onto Paula, who was waiting for a bus. Paula took one look at Rodney and concluded that he probably had some contagious disease. She began to wail that she was probably going to die. Paula's brother Peter rushed to her side as Rodney walked over to apologise. Peter ordered Rodney to leave. Rodney got angry because he realised that both Paula and Peter believed that he was a drug abuser with an infectious disease. Rodney also didn't like Peter ordering him to leave. In a rage Rodney told Paula and Peter to leave or he would spit blood on them. They fled in terror and contacted the police.
   (a) Can Peter be convicted of assault?
   (b) Can Rodney be convicted of assault?

5. Brenda is blind. One afternoon while she was sitting in an empty café enjoying a cup of coffee a man entered the café waving a gun. Can the gunman be convicted of assaulting Brenda?

Table 8.1: Non-Fatal Offences Against the Person Act 1997

Assault	s. 2(1)	It is an offence, without lawful excuse, to intentionally and without consent apply force to or cause an impact on the body of another, or cause another to reasonably believe that he or she is likely to be immediately subjected to a force or impact. **See [360].**
Aggravated assault	s. 3	It is an offence to assault another and cause the victim harm. **See [372].**
Aggravated assault	s. 4	It is an offence to assault another and cause the victim serious harm. **See [372].**
Threats	s. 5	It is an offence to make a threat to kill or to cause serious harm to any person and to communicate the threat by any means to any person providing that the defendant intended that the recipient believed the threat. **See [387].**
Coercion	s. 9	It is an offence to compel, without lawful authority, a person to refrain from doing something that he or she is legally entitled to do, or alternatively, to do something that he or she is legally entitled not to do by: using violence or intimidation to that person or his or her family; injuring or damaging his or her property; persistently following him or her from place to place; or watching or besetting his or her place of residence or business, or the approaches to the residence or business, or any other place where that person happens to be or following him or her in a disorderly fashion. **See [388].**
Stabbing with a syringe	s. 6 (1)	It is an offence to injure another by piercing the skin with a syringe, or threaten to pierce the skin of another with a syringe, with the intention of or where there is a likelihood of causing that person to believe that he or she may be infected with a disease as a result of the injury caused or threatened. **See [376].**

Spraying blood	s. 6(2)	It is an offence to pour, spray or put blood or a blood-like substance on another or threaten to do so, with an intention to cause a belief of infecting the victim, or where there is a likelihood of causing such a belief. **See [377]**.
Transferred intent	s. 6(3)	It is an offence to commit any offence under sections 6(1) and 6(2)and injure a third person with a syringe by piercing that person's skin, or spraying, pouring or putting blood or a blood-like substance on a third party, resulting in that third person believing that he or she may become infected with a disease as a result of the injury or conduct. **See [378]**.
Possession of syringe/blood container	s. 7(1)	It is an offence to be found in possession in a public place of a syringe or a blood container with the intent to cause, or threaten to cause, an injury to, or to intimidate, another person. **See [379]**.
Placing or abandoning a syringe	s. 8(1)	It is an offence to place or abandon a syringe in any place in such a manner that it is likely to injure another and does in fact injure another person, or where it is likely to injure, cause a threat or to frighten another. **See [380]**.
Stabbing with a contaminated syringe	s. 6(5)(a)	It is an offence to intentionally injure another by piercing his or her skin with a contaminated syringe. **See [381]**.
Contaminated blood	s. 6(5)(b)	It is an offence to intentionally spray, pour or put contaminated blood onto another person. **See [382]**.
Transferred intent	s. 6(5)(c)	It is an offence to commit an offence under sections 6(5)(a) or 6(5)(b) and injure a third person. **See [383]**.
Placing a contaminated syringe	s. 8(2)	It is an offence for a person to intentionally place a contaminated syringe in any place in such a manner that it injures another. **See [384]**.

9

SEXUAL OFFENCES

Chapter synopsis

I. General Principles [396]

A. Seriousness of Sexual Offences

1. Sexual offences are some of the most serious offences known to Irish law.
2. However, area is beset with ideological conflicts.

B. Changing Social Values – Effect on Sexual Offences

1. O'Malley notes that the study of sexual offences is a study in social values.
2. Most sexual offences under Irish law are still heavily influenced by nineteenth-century legislation.
3. Feminists: [397]
   a. Argue that law, particularly in this area, reflects male values and concerns.
   b. Have challenged many areas, effecting legal and social change in views, e.g. rape is now accepted as a crime of violence rather than a crime of passion.
      (1) How a woman was dressed, what time of day she was attacked, where she was when attacked, her past sexual conduct and whether she immediately reported the attack were all used to determine whether the woman had consented to the sexual conduct.
      (2) Section 7, Criminal Law (Rape) (Amendment) Act 1990 – a judge now has discretion whether to warn juries of

dangers involved in convicting a defendant on the basis of the uncorroborated evidence of the complainant.

(3) Sex Offenders Act 2001 – provides that upon conviction sex offenders must be registered and this Act enables certain complainants to be heard and legally represented.

(4) Criminal Evidence Act 1992 –

    (a) Section 27(2) provides that it is no longer necessary for warnings to be given about convicting on the uncorroborated evidence of children in trials on indictment, but warnings may be given if the trial court deems it necessary to do so in the interest of justice.

    (b) Section 27(1) abolished the requirement that unsworn testimony of children must be corroborated.

c. Proposed changes include: **[398]**

(1) A complete overhaul of the area of sexual offences to make all offences gender neutral to reduce victim blaming, which women fear, and the main fear of men of being falsely accused.

    (a) Either gender could commit or be the victim of a sexual offence.

    (b) Currently, rape can only be committed by a man against a woman.

(2) If consent is raised at trial the burden of proof should be on the defendant to prove the victim's consent.

(3) Rape shield laws that would not allow the admission of any evidence concerning the victim's past sexual history. Feminists have argued that otherwise the juries are not deciding whether the victim was raped, but rather whether the victim deserves or is entitled to the protection of the law.

C. Law Reform Commission   [399]

1. Report on Vagrancy and Related Offences (1985) recommended the abolition of all existing indecency offences and their replacement with a new offence of intentionally committing indecent conduct in a public place or where the conduct is seen by another person without that other person's consent.

D. Statute of Limitations – *there is no statute of limitations on the trial of sexual offences.*   **[400]**

1. However, there is a constitutional requirement that trials take place as soon as possible. See [27].
2. *D. v. DPP* [1994] 2 IR 465 for an order of prohibition to be granted by the High Court to prohibit a lesser court from proceeding to hear a case, the defendant must show that on a balance of probabilities there is a real risk that he or she could not receive a fair trial.
3. *B. v. DPP* [1997] 2 ILRM 118 – the defendant was charged in 1993 for offences committed against his children between 1962 and 1974. The defendant sought an Order of Prohibition on the grounds that delay in bringing the complaint prejudiced his right to a fair trial. His daughters stated they could not make a complaint to the police because they had wanted to spare their mother from further pain. Court found that the defendant's own abusive behaviour constituted a continuing psychological dominion over the daughters.
   a. Special factors for the court to consider when examining a delay.   **[401]**
      (1) Relationship between defendant and victim – did the defendant owe the victim trust and duty?
      (2) Dominion – was the defendant in a position to exercise control over the victim, thus keeping a complaint from being made?
      (3) Who caused the delay – was it the State or police? If so, it might be unreasonable for a trial to proceed.
      (4) Nature of abuse – each case must be viewed on its own merit.
      (5) Alibi destroyed by delay?
      (6) Witnesses unavailable due to delay?
      (7) Admission of guilt by the defendant must always be considered by the courts.

E. Multiple Sexual Offences – *may occur from the same conduct or incident.*   **[402]**

1. *O'B v. Pattwell & the DPP* [1994] 2 ILRM 465 – the defendant was charged with indecent assault, unlawful carnal knowledge, rape and buggery, all arising from the same incident.
   a. Supreme Court held that prosecution could and should insist upon the greater charge, notwithstanding the effect the charge might have on the victim.

b. Supreme Court has held that a defendant may be charged with different offences arising from the same incident, but only one conviction and sentence can be imposed.

c. Supreme Court agreed with general principle in *People (AG) v. Coughlan* (1968) where the Court of Criminal Appeal held that the prosecution should, when deciding on which charges to bring, remember the effect upon the victim of having to testify.

II. Penetration Offences

A. Rape   [403]

1. **Historically**
   a. Rooted in ancient concept of property.
      (1) Under most ancient societies only men could own property.
      (2) Women and dependent children were treated as chattels.
      (3) A daughter remained a chattel of her father or brother until she married and became the chattel of her husband.
      (4) The rape of a woman was viewed as damaging the property of the man who owned her, e.g. Deuteronomy 22:28–29 – the punishment for the rape of a virgin daughter was payment of fifty shekels to the girl's father and forced marriage to the victim.
      (5) Under Brehon law, two types of rape were recognised:
         (a) Forcible rape.
         (b) Intercourse with a woman without her consent.
         (c) Where rape was established, Brehon law emphasised compensation for the victim, which went to the man who had authority over the woman (her father or husband). A failure to pay compensation gave the victim the right to choose between killing the offender or selling him into slavery.
   b. **Common Law**
      (1) Blackstone defined rape as carnal knowledge of a woman forcibly and against her will.
         (a) Carnal knowledge = sexual intercourse.
      (2) Hale noted that sexual penetration by the penis of a vulva was necessary while sexual emission by the man was not.
      (3) **Marital immunity rule** – long after wives were no longer considered the chattels of their husbands under the

common law, a husband was not legally capable of raping his wife.

   (a) Marriage vows = consent. By consenting to the marriage the wife was deemed to have consented to intercourse with her husband.

   (b) Marital immunity rule was abolished by section 5 of the Criminal (Rape) (Amendment) Act 1990.

2. **Modern Rape** [404]

   a. General principles – still a common law offence, but with statutory amendments.

      (1) Definition: Section 2(1) Criminal Law (Rape) Act 1981 – a man commits rape if:

         (a) He has sexual intercourse with a woman who at the time of the intercourse does not consent to it.

         (b) At the time of the intercourse he knows that she does not consent or he is reckless as to whether she does or does not consent to the intercourse.

      (2) *Actus reus* – man has sexual intercourse with a woman who at the time does not consent to the intercourse.

         (a) Note: Rape is not gender neutral, it can only be committed by a male against a female.

      (3) *Mens rea* – at the time of the intercourse the man knows that the woman does not consent or he is reckless as to whether she does or does not.

   b. *Actus reus* – man has sexual intercourse with a woman who at the time does not consent to the intercourse. [405]

      (1) **Sexual intercourse** under section 1 of the CLRA 1981 is vaginal intercourse.

         (a) Anal intercourse without consent is not rape. *R.* v. *Easton* (1981).

         (b) Section 63 of the Offences Against the Person Act 1861 – for sexual intercourse, emission is not necessary, just penetration.

         (c) Slightest penetration is sufficient, e.g. *People (AG)* v. *Dermody* [1956] IR 307 – young victim testified that the defendant had 'put his private part a wee bit into mine'. Girl's hymen was intact, court held that sexual intercourse had occurred.

      (2) **Consent** – the woman's consent to intercourse must be real and not induced by fraud. [406]

(a) Prosecution must prove that woman did not consent.

(b) Fraud – consent must not be induced by fraud, e.g. defendant lying about the nature of the intercourse.

   i.   *R.* v. *Flattery* (1877) 13 Cox CC 388 – man told victim that he was performing a medical operation.

   ii.   *R.* v. *Williams* [1922] All ER 433 – singing teacher told student that he was opening a new passage to improve her singing voice.

(c) Contrast – not lying about the nature of the act. *R.* v. *Linekar* [1995] 3 All ER 69 – a prostitute agreed to accept £25 for sex. Afterwards, the man refused to pay. Court found that the prostitute's consent was not obtained by fraud. The lie to secure consent did not go to the nature of the act.

(d) However, impersonating the woman's husband is rape under section 4 of the Criminal Law Amendment Act 1885. The Act codified the Irish court's rejection of the English approach of treating impersonators to be guilty of assault only. *R.* v. *Dee* (1884) 15 Cox CC 579 – a man entered the bedroom of a woman who had been sleeping and had intercourse with her. She thought the defendant was her husband.

(e) Woman must be able to give consent, i.e. if a woman cannot exercise judgment she cannot give consent to intercourse. *R.* v. *Lang* (1975) 62 Cr App Rep 50. **[407]**

   i.   E.g. sleeping woman could not give consent. *R.* v. *Mayers* and *R.* v. *Larter & Castleton* [1995] Crim LR 75 (CA).

   ii.   E.g. intoxicated (not merely drunk) woman could not give consent. *R.* v. *Camplin* (1845) 1 Cox CC 220 and *R.* v. *Malone* [1998] 2 Crim LR 834.

(f) Submission by the victim does not indicate her consent. **[408]**

   i.   O'Malley notes that there is a significant difference between consent and submission. A woman may submit out of fear and not consent to the intercourse.

   ii.   *R.* v. *Olugboja* [1981] 3 All ER 443 – every consent involves submission, but not every submission involves consent. Jury should take into account the complainant's state of mind and the events leading up to sexual intercourse. In this case the victim was sixteen and raped by a friend of the defendant. The victim asked to be left alone. The defendant told the police that while the victim had not initially consented to intercourse, he had persuaded her. The victim had removed her own trousers out of fear and she did not physically resist the defendant.

   iii. Resistance by victim – under section 9 of the Criminal Law (Rape) (Amendment) Act 1990, if the woman does not resist physically, this failure to rest does not constitute consent.

c. *Mens rea* **of rape** – section 2(1)(b) 1981 CLRA 1981. **[409]**

   (1) At the time of the intercourse the defendant must know that the woman is not consenting or he is reckless as to her consent.

   (2) Recklessness – not clear if recklessness is subjective or objective under Irish law.

   (a) *People (DPP)* v. *Creigton* (1994 C.C.A.) – equated reckless conduct with heedless conduct.

   (b) English approach – subjective test, *R.* v. *Satnam & Kewal* [1985] Crim LR 236. Court of appeal held that if the jury comes to the conclusion that the defendant did not care whether the woman was consenting but carried on anyway, the defendant was reckless.

   i. Subjective test – it is the defendant's actual state of mind that is important, not what a reasonable person would have thought.

   (c) Irish approach is likely to follow English subjective approach. Section 2(2) CLRA 1981 provides that where the jury is considering whether the defendant believed that the woman was consenting it should have regard to the presence or absence of reasonable grounds for such a belief.

   (3) Mistake – the law accepts that a defendant might mistake a woman's interest and believe that she is consenting when in fact she is not = no rape. **[410]**

   (a) After penetration – if the defendant becomes aware that the woman is not consenting he must withdraw immediately. *Kaitmaki* v. *R.* [1984] 2 All ER 435 – the defendant argued that rape was complete upon penetration. He did not have the required *mens rea* at penetration, therefore no rape. Privy Counsel held that while all elements were established at time of penetration the offence was not complete until the defendant withdrew.

(b) Unreasonable belief of consent – a genuine but mistaken belief that the woman was consenting is found in the controversial case of *R.* v. *Morgan* [1975] 2 All ER 347. A husband invited three friends to have sex with his wife. He told the men that if she struggled and fought she was pretending in order to heighten her pleasure and fun. The three men had sex with the wife, although she attempted to fight them off. Convictions for rape were upheld on other grounds, but Law Lords held that where a man genuinely believes that a woman is consenting no rape occurs, even if the belief is not reasonable.

(c) *Morgan* controversy led to the English Sexual Offences (Amendment) Act 1976, which is reflected in section 2 of the CLRA 1981.

(d) English approach to consent and *mens rea* – under the Sexual Offences Act 2003, section 76 an irrebuttable presumption that the victim did not consent and the defendant had *mens rea*. The irrebuttable presumption applies where:

   i. The defendant intentionally deceived the victim as to the nature or purpose of the sexual act.

   ii. Section 74 – a person consents if she agrees by choice and has the freedom and capacity to make that choice.

   iii. The defendant intentionally induced the victim to consent to the sexual act by impersonating a person known personally to the victim.

3. **Penalties** – see [47–49] regarding factors in aggravation and mitigation. **[411]**

  a. Section 5, Criminal Justice Act 1993 provides that the victim of a sexual or violent offence has a statutory right to give evidence at sentencing regarding the effect of the offence on the victim.

b. Section 48, Offences Against the Person Act 1861 allows for a penalty of up to life imprisonment for conviction of rape.

c. *People (DPP)* v. *Tiernan* [1988] IR 250 – Supreme Court noted that rape is one of the most serious offences known to Irish law causing long-term emotional damage as well as physical harm. Court noted that any attempt to view it as a minor offence would be unconstitutional as it represents an attack on human dignity.

    (1) Feminists argue that sentences imposed by judges do not reflect the seriousness of crime.

B. Rape under Section 4 of the Criminal Law (Rape) (Amendment) Act 1990 – *created a new category of rape.* [412]

1. General Principles

    a. Definition: A sexual assault that involves either penetration of the anus or mouth by a penis or the penetration of the vagina by any hand-held object.

        (1) Gender neutral – either a man or woman can be a perpetrator with a hand-held object and either a man or woman can be the victim of non-consensual anal intercourse.

    b. *Actus reus* –

        (1) Penetration of the anus or mouth by a penis, or

        (2) The penetration of the vagina by any hand-held object without consent.

    c. *Mens rea* – the Act does not specifically address:

        (1) Intention to assault under indecent circumstances – requires intention.

            (a) Indecent circumstances – see *R.* v. *Court* [1988] 2 All ER 221 [423].

        (2) Prosecution must prove that the defendant intended to assault the victim in a way that right-minded persons would think indecent.

2. **Special consent issues –**

    a. The Act does not address the issue of consent.

    b. Because rape under section 4 is a sexual assault it would appear that the position adopted with regard to sexual assaults would apply here. See [424].

        (1) Consent to the acts by a person over the minimum age causes no harm or minor harm is a defence. See assaults [360] and sexual assaults [423].

C. Statutory Rape – Criminal Law Amendment Act 1935 – *refers to unlawful carnal knowledge of girls.* [413]

1. General Principles
   a. Definition: When a male has sexual intercourse with a female who is under the age of consent.
      (1) Section 1 CLAA 1935 – it is a felony offence to have sexual intercourse with a girl under the age of fifteen.
      (2) Section 2 – it is a misdemeanour to have sexual intercourse with a girl under the age of seventeen but over fifteen.
         (a) Criminal Law Act 1997 – see [39].
         (b) Note: Both sections of 1935 Act are now arrestable offences.
   b. *Actus reus* – sexual intercourse with a girl under the age of seventeen.
      (1) Slightest penetration is sufficient. See rape [405].
      (2) Once it is shown that the defendant has sexual intercourse with a girl under the age of consent, the offence has been committed. *People (AG)* v. *O'Connor* [1949] 15 Ir Jur Rep 25.
   c. *Mens rea* – strict liability. See [149].
      (1) Consent by the girl is not a defence.
   d. **Theory behind offence** – enacted to protect young girls, not alone against lustful men, but against themselves. Maguire CJ in *AG (Shaughnessy)* v. *Ryan* (1960).
2. **Consent** is no defence, but is presumed in statutory rape cases. [414]
   a. *AG (Shaughnessy)* v. *Ryan* (1960) – the defendant was charged with attempted unlawful carnal knowledge of the victim. He alleged that she consented. It was held that the girl's consent was not relevant.
   b. If the girl did not consent to the sexual intercourse the charge should be rape.
3. Penalties –
   a. Conviction under section 1 (sexual intercourse with a girl under fifteen) – up to life imprisonment.
   b. Conviction under section 2 (sexual intercourse with a girl over fifteen but under seventeen) – up to five years for first offence and up to ten years for second offence.
4. LRC Recommendations 1990 – report on child abuse. [415]
   a. Reduce age for section 1 to thirteen.

b. Not an offence to have intercourse with a girl over fifteen unless the male is more than five years older or he is in a position of authority, i.e. person having even temporary responsibility for the girl.

c. If the girl is over thirteen, strict liability should not apply if the defendant genuinely and reasonably believed her to between thirteen and fifteen. The defendant should be charged with a less serious offence.

d. If the man genuinely and reasonably believed the girl to be over seventeen he should have a full defence. Whether the belief was genuine should be looked at as with rape.

5. Other legal commentators –
   a. Statutory rape should be gender neutral – it should protect boys as well as girls.
      (1) In the news in recent years there has been an increase in reporting of women engaging in sexual relations with teenage boys. The most infamous case involved an American teacher, Pamela Smart, who exploited her young paramour into killing her husband.
   b. Statutory rape should continue to be a strict liability offence to protect young people from exploitation by adults.

D. Incest – Punishment of Incest Act 1908   [416]

1. General Principles
   a. Definition: Sexual intercourse with a defined blood relative.
   b. *Actus reus* –
      (1) Section 1 PIA 1908 – where a man has intercourse with a female who is to his knowledge his granddaughter, daughter, sister or mother.
      (2) Section 2 PIA 1908 – where a female over the age of seventeen allows sexual intercourse with a male who is to her knowledge her grandfather, father, brother or son.
         (a) Note: The family terms include both full and half relationships, i.e. half brothers, etc.
   c. *Mens rea* –
      (1) Intention.
      (2) Specifically, knowledge of the relationship is required. Note: Reckless is not sufficient, knowledge is required.   [417]
         (a) *R. v. Carmichael* [1940] 2 All Er 165 – the defendant was charged with three counts of incest with his youngest daughter, S., when they began to live

together and have three children. The defendant had been married to S.'s mother, but the marriage broke up about the time S. was born. The defendant did not believe that S. was his child because S.'s mother said she was not. The defendant wanted to bring this information out at trial and the fact that he told his second wife that S. was not his child. Trial judge refused to admit and the defendant was convicted. The Court of Appeal held that the evidence went to the heart of the case and the conviction was quashed.

(b) *R.* v. *Baille-Smith* [1977] Crim Lr – the defendant had sex with a female who was lying beside him in his bed. He claimed that he thought that it was his wife, but it was in fact his thirteen-year-old daughter. This evidence was excluded from the directions to the jury and the trial court wrongly indicated that the defendant had admitted knowledge of the female's relationship to him. The Court of Appeal quashed the conviction.

2. Penalties – Criminal Law (Incest Proceedings) Act 1995 – now an arrestable offence.

a. Maximum penalty for male incest is life imprisonment.

3. Criticisms – **[418]**

a. Reflects the traditional view of the male as the sexual aggressor and the female as the passive victim.

b. Also fails to address other familial relationships, such as aunts, nieces, uncles and nephews.

E. Intercourse with Mentally Ill Person [419]

1. General Principles

a. Section 5 of the Criminal Law (Sexual Offences) Act 1993 created three offences.

(1) Intercourse or attempted intercourse with a mentally impaired person.

(2) Buggery or attempted buggery with a mentally impaired person. See buggery [420].

(3) Acts or attempted acts of gross indecency by a male with someone who is mentally impaired. See gross indecency [427].

b. *Actus reus* – engaging in the defined sexual activity with a mentally impaired person.

c. *Mens rea* – intention to carry out one of the defined sexual activities knowing that the person was mentally impaired or subjective recklessness.
2. Mental impairment – disorder of the mind that renders the person incapable of living an independent life or preventing serious exploitation.
3. Defences –
    a. Marriage – if the defendant is married to the mentally impaired person.
    b. If the defendant did not and had no reason to suspect that the person was suffering from a mental impairment.
        (1) *R.* v. *Hudson* [1965] 1 All ER 721 – in considering an identical English statute it was held that subjective test was required.
        (2) Note that if the defendant is also mentally impaired the defendant may not be able to form the required *mens rea*.
4. Penalties –
    a. Intercourse or buggery with a mentally impaired person – up to ten years' imprisonment.
    b. Attempted intercourse or buggery with a mentally impaired person – up to three years for first conviction and five years for a conviction for second attempt.
    c. Acts or attempted acts of gross indecency by a male with another who is mentally impaired – up to two years' imprisonment.

F. Buggery [420]

1. Historically
    a. Under section 61 of the Offences against the Person Act 1861 buggery was described as an abominable crime punishable by penal servitude for life.
    b. Generic terms that covered:
        (1) Sodomy (anal intercourse).
            (a) Between males.
            (b) Between male and female.
            (c) Note: Consent was not a defence.
        (2) Sexual intercourse between people and animals (bestiality).
    c. Law successfully challenged.
        (1) Supreme Court in *Norris* v. *AG* [1984] IR 36 upheld the prohibition on sodomy between consenting adult couples.

(2) European Court on Human Rights in *Norris* v. *Ireland* (1991) found a breach of Article 8 of the European Convention on Human Rights, which guarantees a right to personal and marital privacy.

(3) Criminal Law (Sexual Offences) Act 1993.

   (a) Section 2 abolished the offence of buggery between consenting persons aged seventeen or over.

   (b) Act did not alter the existing law on intercourse between people and animals.

2. **Modern Buggery** [421]

a. Criminal Law (Sexual Offences) Act 1993, section 3 created a new class of buggery similar to statutory rape.

b. *Actus reus* – where the defendant:

   (1) Has anal intercourse with a person under fifteen.

   (2) Has anal intercourse with a person under seventeen but over fifteen.

   (3) Attempted anal intercourse with a person under fifteen.

   (4) Attempted anal intercourse with a person under seventeen but over fifteen.

   (5) From common law – intercourse with an animal.

      (a) *R.* v. *Bourne* (1952) 36 Cr App R 125 – the husband was convicted of aiding and abetting his wife to commit the offence by compelling her on two occasions to submit to the insertion of the male organ of a dog which he had excited into her vagina. The husband's conviction was upheld although the wife was never charged or convicted of buggery due to her lack of consent to the conduct.

c. *Mens rea* – strict liability [422]

   (1) It does not matter if the defendant genuinely believed and reasonably believed that the person was over seventeen.

   (2) It is also not relevant if the person consented to the intercourse with the defendant.

d. Defences –

   (1) If the defendant was married to the other person at the time of the intercourse.

   (2) Or the defendant reasonably believed that he was married to the other person.

e. Sentencing –

   (1) Anal intercourse with a person under fifteen is punishable up to life imprisonment.

(2) Anal intercourse with a person under seventeen but over fifteen is punishable:
(a) Up to five years for first offence.
(b) Up to ten years for subsequent offences.
(3) Attempted anal intercourse with a person under fifteen is punishable:
(a) Up to five years for first offence.
(b) Up to ten years for subsequent offences.
(4) Attempted anal intercourse with a person under seventeen but over fifteen is punishable:
(a) Up to two years for first offence.
(b) Up to five years for subsequent offences.

III. Sexual Assaults [423]

A. Sexual Assault – section 2 of the Criminal Law (Rape) (Amendment) Act 1990 *placed the common law offences of indecent assault against women and indecent assault against men on a statutory footing.*

1. General Principles
a. Definition: The defendant intentionally assaulted the victim and the surrounding circumstances are capable of being considered by right-minded persons as indecent.
b. *Actus reus* – requires an assault that is sexual, i.e. involving indecency. See assault [360].
(1) Non-Fatal Offences Against the Person Act 1997, section 2 – where the defendant intentionally or recklessly:
(a) Directly or indirectly applies force to or causes impact upon the victim's body, or
(b) Causes the victim to reasonably fear or appreciate the infliction of the force or impact. [424]
(2) **Indecent** – precise definition is difficult. *R.* v. *Court* [1989] AC 28 – three categories of behaviour examined.
(a) Inherently not indecent acts, i.e. shaking hands even if the defendant became sexually excited by the contact. (Not a sexual assault.)
(b) Inherently indecent acts, i.e. a man running after young schoolgirls 'flashing' his genitals. (Always a sexual assault.)
(c) Acts that may or may not be indecent depending on the surrounding circumstances, i.e. one person patting

another person on the bottom. These acts should be
judged according to the view of right-minded people
looking at:

   i.   Relationship between the parties.

   ii. How and why the defendant started this course
of action or conduct.

  c. *Mens rea* – intention –

    (1) The defendant must intend to commit an assault that is
indecent.

    (2) Note that the *mens rea* for assault is intention or subjec-
tive recklessness. Sexual assault appears to allow only
proof of intention.

2. Defence of consent –

  a. Consent to the *actus reus* activity may be a defence depending
upon:

    (1) The age of the victim.

    (2) The nature of the assault and its consequences.

  b. Age of victim –   **[425]**

    (1) Criminal Law Amendment Act 1935, section 14 – the
minimum age at which a person can consent to a sexual
assault is fifteen.

    (2) Note: A sexual assault is not the same thing as sexual
intercourse and thus the age of consent for sexual intercourse is not fifteen. See statutory rape [413].

  c. Nature of assault and consequences – follows general rules
regarding consent, see [367].

    (1) Generally, so long as there is valid consent and no serious
harm results, consent is a defence.

      (a) Section 3 of the NFOAPA 1997 seems to allow
defence of consent where the assault causes harm. See
[372].

      (b) Section 4 of the NFOAPA 1997 does not allow the
defence of consent where the defendant intentionally
or recklessly inflicted serious harm on the victim.

      (c) *R.* v. *Brown* (1993) 2 All ER 75; affirmed by ECHR
as *Laskey, Saggard & Brown* v. *UK* (1997) EHRR 39.
The appellants were convicted of a number of counts
of assault. They had engaged in various consensual
homosexual sadomasochistic activities that involved
inserting nails and other items into various sensitive
parts of their bodies. Due to their activities, injuries

were sustained requiring medical attention. It was accepted by all parties that consent was a defence to minor assaults, but not to assaults involving grievous bodily harm. The House of Lords decided that there was no basis for allowing a defence of consent to assaults causing actual bodily harm. See [367].

B. *Aggravated Sexual Assault – section 3 CLRAA 1990* *created the offence.* **[426]**

1. General Principles
   a. Definition: A sexual assault, together with serious violence or threats of serious violence, grave humiliation, degradation or injury.
   b. *Actus reus* –
      (1) The defendant intentionally assaulted the victim and the surrounding circumstances are capable of being considered by right-minded persons as indecent.
      (2) The defendant, while performing the sexual assault, used serious violence or threats of serious violence, grave humiliation, degradation or injury.
   c. *Mens rea* – two parts.
      (1) An intention to commit an assault that is indecent.
      (2) An intention to subject the victim to serious violence, to serious violence or threats thereof, grave humiliation, degradation or injuries.
2. Penalties – section 3(2) provides that a person guilty of an aggravated sexual assault shall be liable on conviction to imprisonment for life.

C. *Gross Indecency with Males under Seventeen* **[427]**

1. Historically, gross indecency – Criminal Law Amendment Act 1885, section 11.
   a. Prohibited gross indecency between men of any age whether consensual or not.
      (1) Act prohibited the commission or attempted commission of any conduct of gross indecency between males, whether in public or in private.
      (2) Act does not define what conduct is illegal, but taken to mean any sexual act between males that did not constitute buggery. See buggery [420].
   b. Sentence – punishable by up to two years' imprisonment.

2. **Modern gross indecency with males under seventeen** – Criminal Law (Sexual Offences) Act 1993, section 4 repealed section 11 of the 1885 Act and replaced it with the new offence of gross indecency with males under the age of seventeen.   **[428]**
   a. Lacks definition of prohibited activities, but still taken to mean any sexual act between a man and male under the age of seventeen that does not constitute buggery. See buggery [421].
      (1) *Actus reus* requires concerted behaviour, i.e. the indecent conduct by the defendant must be with the other male rather than merely towards him.
      (2) E.g. *R.* v. *Preece & Howells* [1976] Crim LR 392 – the defendants were masturbating in two public toilet cubicles. There was a hole in the wall between the cubicles. One defendant admitted watching the other, but the second defendant denied watching the first. For gross indecency with another man to be established, there had to be participation and co-operation between the two. Conviction upheld on other grounds.
   b. Attempts to commit gross indecency with a male under seventeen is also prohibited.   **[429]**
      (1) *Actus reus* of attempted gross indecency with a male under seventeen requires more than a mere description of the intended activity, i.e. requires some form of solid invitation from the defendant to the young male to participate in grossly indecent conduct.
         (a) E.g. *People (AG)* v. *England* (1947) 1 Frewen 81 – the defendant told another man where homosexual acts were committed and the best time to visit the house. His conviction was overturned that the conversation was not an attempt because there was no proximate act. See attempts [271].

IV. Indecency Offences   [430]

A. Indecent Exposure

1. Offence is criminalised under:
   a. Common law,
   b. Section 4 of the Vagrancy Act 1824, and
   c. Section 18 of the Criminal Law Amendment Act 1935.
2. Definition: Where a man exposes his penis to a female in a public place.

a. Examples – flashing, streaking or urinating in public.
3. *Actus reus* –
    a. A man intentionally exposing his penis,
    b. To a female in a public place.
4. *Mens rea* – intention.
    a. Note: No sexual motive is required or even an intention to insult or annoy.
5. Biggest issue – definition of a public place.
    a. The defendant must be capable of being seen by more than one person for it to be considered public. *R. v. Farrell* (1862) 9 Cox CC 446.
    b. So long as either the offender or the victim was in a public place the offence can be committed. *McCabe* v. *Donnelly* [1982] NI 153 – in this Northern Ireland case a similar indecent exposure statute required that the conduct occur in a public place. In this case the defendant stood in front of his window and masturbated in front of a young woman who was standing on the pavement.

B. Outraging Public Decency – *Common Law Offence*   [431]

1. Definition: Performing a lewd, obscene or disgusting act, which is performed in public and that is an outrage to public decency.
2. *Actus reus* – performing a lewd, obscene or disgusting act in public that is capable of being an outrage to public decency.
    a. What is lewd, obscene or disgusting? This is a matter of fact for the jury to decide.
    b. What is an outrage to public decency? This is a matter of fact for the jury to decide.
        (1) *Knuller* v. *DPP* [1972] 2 All ER 898 held that outrage goes beyond merely offending or even shocking reasonable people and will depend upon the circumstances of the incident.
3. *Mens rea* – conduct must be done deliberately, but it is not necessary to prove an intention to outrage public decency. *R. v. Gibson & Sylveire* [1991] 1 All ER 439.

Review Questions

1. George Daffy has no training as a doctor, but he loves to watch *ER* on television. George bought a couple of medical books and began to pass himself off as a doctor. For over two years he worked as a

doctor in an elderly ill doctor's surgery practice. It was only after he gave a patient a contraindicated drug that killed the patient that it was discovered that George is not a doctor. One of the patients that George saw on several occasions was Nancy. She is very upset because George Daffy performed various breast and gynecological exams on her.

(a) Will George be convicted of any offence for allegedly physically examining Nancy for tumors by performing an extensive breast exam on Nancy?

(b) Will George be convicted of any offence for performing alleged gynecological exams on Nancy by placing various medical instruments in her vagina?

2. Homer came into the pub and told his friend, Billy, that his wife, Marge, wanted to have a baby, but Homer was unable to father a child due to a case of mumps as a teenager. Homer said that Marge wanted Homer to ask Billy if he would donate sperm so Marge could have a baby. Billy asked Homer three or four times if it was true. Excited, Billy left the pub and went to Homer and Marge's house. When Marge saw Billy she invited him in. Billy told Marge exactly what Homer had said to him, and when Marge agreed that she would like Billy to donate sperm so she could have a baby, Billy pushed the surprised Marge down onto the couch and began to have sexual intercourse with her. Billy was not aware that there was any other way to donate sperm. Will Billy be convicted of raping Marge?

3. Susan is fourteen years of age. She borrowed her older sister's driver's license and went to a disco in town. Susan had several pints and met Adam, who bought her several more pints. Susan fancied Adam and readily agreed to go back to his apartment to spend the night. When Susan got back to Adam's apartment she became violently ill and passed out on the floor of the toilet. Adam removed her soiled clothes and put her on the couch, clothed only in her undergarments.

(a) What sexual offence, if any, can Adam be charged with for removing Susan's clothing?

(b) If Adam has sexual intercourse with Susan, what offence will he have committed?

(c) Would your answers be different if Susan was a fourteen-year-old male named Neal who fancied Adam and agreed to go home with Adam?

4. If a person performed lewd, obscene or disgusting acts in a public toilet in Phoenix Park, that person would have committed what criminal offence?

5. Tim and Tina are fifteen-year-old twins. Tina talks Tim into engaging in sexual intercourse with her. If the police learn of their sexual activities, what criminal offence, if any, will they each be charged with?

6. 'Guard sues Marilyn Manson, Minneapolis', 5 December 2001 (AP) – 'A security guard at a Marilyn Manson concert…claims that Manson grabbed his head, held it against his hips and proceeded to gyrate his hips at the October 27, 2000 concert…The security guard asked 32-year-old Manson to stop but he did not.' Assume that the event took place in Dublin. What offences, if any, has Marilyn Manson committed if the allegations are true?

7. Kevin and Sally have been married for fifteen years and have one daughter, Rosie, aged twelve. Kevin came home late one night and fell into bed. He felt someone get into bed beside him. He didn't know who it was and didn't really care. He rolled over and had sex with the person, who turned out to be Rosie. Will Kevin be convicted of incest?

8. Cavendish is young man of nineteen and he has always had fantasies about his mother's older sister, Bertha. Cavendish succeeds in seducing Bertha. They have consensual sexual intercourse several times before they are caught in the act by Cavendish's mother.
    (a) What criminal offences, if any, has Cavendish committed?
    (b) What criminal offences, if any, has Bertha committed?

9. Wayne and Fred live beside a convent, from which a soup kitchen for the homeless is run every day. For the fun of it, Wayne dares Fred to drop his trousers in front of the nuns. Fred accepts the dare, goes to the living room window and drops his trousers in full view of Sister Robustica, who is napping. Fred dances around outside the window for a full five minutes before Sister Robustica awakes and puts on her eye glasses and bursts out laughing. Disappointed, Fred goes home to watch television.
    (a) What criminal offences, if any, has Fred committed?
    (b) What criminal offences, if any, has Wayne committed?

10. 'Man commits suicide after sex with hen', 28 May 2004, Lusaka (Reuters) – 'A fifty-year-old Zambian man has hanged himself after his wife found him having sex with a hen, police say. The woman caught him in the act when she rushed into their house to investigate a noise. "He attempted to kill her but she managed to escape," a police spokesman said on Friday. The man, from the town of Chongwe, about thirty miles east of Lusaka, killed himself after being admonished by other villagers. The hen was slaughtered after the incident.' What sexual offence, if any, has the husband committed?

Table 9.1: Sexual Offences

Rape	Common law offence with statutory amendments	A man commits rape if he has sexual intercourse with a woman who at the time of the intercourse does not consent to it, and at the time of the intercourse the man knows that she does not consent or he is reckless as to whether she does or does not consent to the intercourse. **See [404]**.
Rape under s. 4	Criminal Law (Rape) (Amend.) Act 1990	A sexual assault that involves either penetration of the anus or mouth by a penis, or the penetration of the vagina by any hand-held object. **See [412]**.
Statutory rape	Criminal Law Amend. Act 1935	A statutory rape occurs when a man has sexual intercourse with a girl under the age of consent. Under s. 1 it is a felony to have sexual intercourse with a girl under the age of fifteen. Under s. 2 it is a misdemeanour to have sexual intercourse with a girl over fifteen, but under seventeen. **See [413]**.
Incest	Punishment of Incest Act 1908	It is an offence for defined blood relatives to engage in sexual intercourse. S. 1 prohibits a man from having intercourse with a female who is to his knowledge his granddaughter, daughter, sister or mother. S. 2 prohibits a woman over the age of seventeen to allow sexual intercourse with a male who is to her knowledge her grandfather, father, brother or son. **See [416]**.
Intercourse with a mentally ill person	Criminal Law (Sexual Offences) Act 1993	S. 5 created three offences. (1)Intercourse or attempted intercourse with a mentally impaired person. (2) Buggery or attempted buggery of a mentally impaired person. (3) Acts or attempted acts of gross indecency by a male with someone who is mentally impaired. **See [419]**.

Buggery	Common law and Criminal Law (Sexual Offences) Act 1993	S. 3 of the CLSOA 1993 provides that it is an offence to have anal intercourse with a person under the age of seventeen, and it is a more serious offence to do so with a person under the age of fifteen. From the common law it is still an offence to engage in sexual intercourse with an animal. **See [421].**
Gross indecency with males under seventeen	Criminal Law (Sexual Offences) Act 1993	S. 4 prohibits gross indecency between a man and a boy under the age of seventeen, or attempted gross indecency. This is thought to include any sexual acts that do not constitute buggery. **See [428].**
Sexual assault	Criminal Law (Rape) (Amend.) Act 1990	S. 2 provides that it is a sexual assault to intentionally assault another and the surrounding circumstances are capable of being considered by right-minded persons as indecent. **See [423].**
Aggravated sexual assault	Criminal Law (Rape) (Amend.) Act 1990	S. 3 provides that it is an aggravated sexual assault to sexually assault another together with serious violence or threats of serious violence, grave humiliation, degradation or injury. **See [426].**
Indecent exposure	Common law, Vagrancy Act 1824 and Criminal Law Amendment Act 1935	It is an offence for a man to expose his penis to a female in a public place. **See [430].**
Outraging public decency	Common law	It is an offence to perform a lewd, obscene or disgusting act in public that is an outrage to public decency. **See [431].**

10

PROPERTY OFFENCES

Chapter synopsis

I. General Principles   [432]

A. Historically

1. In the early common law only forcible appropriation of property was punished. (Today a forcible appropriation would be a robbery.)
2. By the middle ages the common law expanded to criminalise non-violent taking of personal property, i.e. larceny.
   a. Larceny did not develop in a rational fashion.
      (1) Economic problems placed pressure on the common law courts to expand the scope of larceny to deter new types of property taking.
         (a) Hall notes that fifteenth-century England was a time of economic chaos.
         (b) England was changing from a feudal, agricultural society into one with manufacturing in towns and a merchant class.
      (2) The judiciary manipulated the elements of larceny to encompass the new types of property taking.
      (3) Law became riddled with technicalities, legal fictions and anomalies.
3. Until the enactment of the Criminal Justice (Theft and Fraud Offences) Act 2001, the property offences were found in a number of Acts, such as:

a. The Larceny Acts 1861, 1916, 1990.
b. Forgery Acts 1861 and 1913.
c. Criminal Damage Act 1991.

B. Criminal Justice (Theft and Fraud Offences) Act 2001 (CJTFOA 2001) [433]

1. Repealed the Larceny Acts 1916, 1990.
   a. Abolished numerous specific offences of larceny created by the 1916 Act.
   b. Introduced a smaller range of more general offences.
2. Repealed the Forgers Acts 1861, 1913.
3. Consolidated law relating to dishonesty.
4. Modern problems of computer and white-collar crime are addressed.
   a. Act gives force to the Convention on Protection of European Communities' Financial Interests.
      (1) Designed to address corruption by or of national and European Community officials.
      (2) Measures to deal with money laundering, fraud and protection of the euro.
5. Provisions include:
   a. Section 4 – theft.
   b. Section 6 – making gain or causing loss by deception.
   c. Section 7 – obtaining services by deception.
   d. Section 8 – making off without payment.
   e. Section 9 – unlawful use of computer.
   f. Section 10 – false accounting.
   g. Section 11 – suppression of documents.
   h. Section 12 – burglary.
   i. Section 13 – aggravated burglary.
   j. Section 14 – robbery.
   k. Section 15 – possession of implements for theft, burglary, blackmail, extortion or unauthorised taking of a vehicle.
   l. Section 17 – handling stolen property and other proceeds of crime.
   m. Section 18 – possession of stolen property.
   n. Section 19 – withholding information regarding stolen property.
   o. Section 21 – money laundering.
   p. Section 25 – forgery.
   q. Section 32 – counterfeiting.

C. Theory – Why Protect Personal Property?   [434]

1. Clarkson notes that the political and economic structure of society depends upon the concept of personal property.
   a. Ownership and possession are protected and thereby encouraged.
   b. Unauthorised interferences with property rights and interests are viewed as threatening the socio-economic foundations of the State.
2. Two types of harm occur:
   a. The owner or possessor is deprived or threatened with deprivation of his or her interest in property.
   b. Society is harmed:
      (1) Because of the threat to the economic base of the social system.
      (2) Large costs are spent on the prevention and apprehension of offenders.
         (a) E.g. shoplifting – costs to retailer passed on to consumers.

D. Exam Hint: Make certain the victim has a protected property interest.

II. Theft   [435]

A. General Principles

1. Definition: Section 4 CJTFOA 2001 provides:
   a. A person is guilty of theft if he or she dishonestly appropriates property without the consent of its owner and with the intention of depriving its owner of the property.
      (1) Broad definition: It is no longer a requirement that the defendant takes and carries away property. See appropriation below [436].
2. *Actus reus*: Appropriation of property without the consent of its owner.
3. *Mens rea*: Intention to deprive the owner of his or her property.

B. Property – *section 2(1) defined as money and all other property, real or personal, including things in actions and other intangible property. See [437].*

C. Dishonesty – *section 2(1) defines as without a claim or right made in good faith.*

1. Similar phrase was used in the Larceny Act 1916, i.e. fraudulently and without a claim or right made in good faith.
    a. Held to be a subjective test. *People (DPP)* v. *O'Loughlin* [1979] IR 85.
    b. In other words, did the defendant genuinely believe that he or she had a valid claim to the property?
        (1) *People (AG)* v. *O'Loughlin* – machinery that was reported stolen was found on the defendant's land. He claimed that he bought it from a dealer, but the dealer denied it. At trial, the defendant wanted to introduce evidence of a claim of right, that he had been owed a debt and thought that he had a right to take the machinery in lieu of payment of the debt. Court of Criminal Appeal held that the evidence should have been admitted. Held: A claim of right established if the defendant had honestly believed that he was entitled to take the good although his claim was not well-founded in law or fact.
2. Section 4(4) – the trier of fact when considering whether the defendant believed that he or she had acted dishonestly should have regard to the presence or absence of reasonable grounds for such a belief in conjunction with any other relevant matters.

D. Appropriation – *Section 4(5)CJTFOA 2001*   **[436]**

1. Defined as usurping or adversely interfering with the proprietary rights of the owner of the property.
    a. Larceny Act 1916 required the physical taking and carrying away of property.
        (1) Now an individual already in possession of the property can steal it.
            (a) Formerly such conduct was covered by various criminal offences.
            (b) E.g. embezzlement, fraudulent conversion and obtaining by false pretences.

E. Property   **[437]**

1. Generally, only personal property or chattels can be stolen.
2. Section 5(2) – a person cannot steal land.
    a. Land is generally regarded as *quicquid plantatur solo solo cedit.*

    (1) Translated: Whatever affixed to the land belongs to the owner of that land is regarded as land.

    (2) Examples: Walls, trees, buildings, growing crops, etc.

b. Section 5(3) – land does not include incorporeal hereditaments, thus they can be stolen.

    (1) Incorporeal hereditaments – confer rights against the land of another.

    (2) Principle types of incorporeal hereditaments.

        (a) Rent charges – a recurring obligation to pay a sum of money which is attached to or charged on land, i.e. rent payments.

        (b) Profits *a prendre* – an entitlement to derive a benefit from the land of another, which may include the right to appropriate and remove items which formerly constituted part of the land, e.g. right to cut and remove timber, shoot game or fish.

        (c) Easements, e.g. rights of way, etc.

c. Wild mushrooms, flowers, fruit or foliage are all considered land until picked, then they become chattels or personal property capable of being stolen. **[438]**

    (1) Act of picking is a severance of reality.

    (2) Section 5(4) provides that a person who picks:

        (a) Mushrooms or any other fungus growing wild on any land, or

        (b) Who picks flowers, fruit or foliage from a plant (including any shrub or tree) growing wild on any land,

        (c) Does not steal what is picked.

    (2) Exception – unless the picker does it for reward or for sale or other commercial purpose.

3. Section 5(2) – there are three exceptions to the general rule that a defendant cannot steal land or things forming part of land and severed from it by or under the direction of the defendant, except where the defendant: **[439]**

a. Is a trustee, personal representative or is authorised by power of attorney or as a liquidator of a company to sell or dispose of land owned by another, appropriates the land or anything forming part of it by dealing with it in breach of the trust placed on him or her, or

    (1) E.g. Frazier gave his brother Niles a power of attorney to sell his holiday home in Killarney. Niles enjoyed the

holiday home, but could not afford to pay a fair market value for it. In violation of the confidence placed in him Niles sold the holiday home to himself far below the market value and placed the deeds in a close friend's name.

b. Is not in possession of the land, appropriates anything forming part of the land by severing it or causing it to be severed, or after it has been severed.

   (1) E.g. Tyrone was tired and decided to take a shortcut through Farmer Finbar's apple orchard. Noticing that the apples were ripe, Tyrone picked an apple and ate it. He then picked a number of apples to take home. In picking the apples Tyrone has severed realty. When severed the apples become personal property or chattels and are stolen when appropriated or eaten.

c. Is in possession of the land under a tenancy or license, and appropriates the whole or part of any fixture or structure let or licensed to be used with the land.

4. **Animals –**   [440]

   a. Domestic animals may be stolen, e.g. farm livestock.

   b. Wild creatures – section 5(5) provides that wild creatures, whether tamed or untamed, are regarded as property.

   (1) However, wild creatures (alive or dead) cannot be stolen unless the wild creatures have been reduced to possession by or on behalf of another, and

   (2) The possession has not been lost or abandoned.

F. *No Consent*   [441]

1. Section 4(2) provides that property is not appropriated without the consent of the owner if:

   a. The defendant believes that he or she had the owner's consent or would have the owner's consent if the owner knew of the appropriation of the property and the circumstances in which it was appropriated.

   b. The defendant appropriates the property in the belief that the owner cannot be discovered by taking reasonable steps.

2. Consent obtained as a result of deception or intimidation is not valid consent.

3. Section 4(4) – when considering whether the owner had consented to or would have consented to its appropriation, or that the owner could not be discovered, the trier of fact should have

regard to the presence or absence of reasonable grounds for such a belief in conjunction with any other relevant matters.

G. *Intent to Deprive the Owner of the Property*   [442]

1. Depriving – defined as temporarily or permanently depriving the owner of his or her property.
2. Much broader than under Larceny Acts, where the prosecution was required to prove that the defendant, at the time he or she took the property, intended to permanently deprive the owner of his or her property.
3. E.g. under Larceny Acts, joyriding or the taking of a car with the intention to make use of it then abandon it was not a theft. However, under the CJTFOA 2001 it is a theft.

H. *Penalties – section 4(6) provides that a person convicted on indictment of theft may be fined or imprisoned for a term not exceeding ten years or both.*

III. *Robbery*   [443]

A. *General Principles*

1. Definition: Section 14 CJTFOA 2001 provides:
   a. A person who steals is guilty of robbery if, at the time or immediately before the stealing and in order to do so, he or she uses force or puts or seeks to put any person in fear of being then and there subjected to force.
2. *Actus reus*:
   a. Stealing, and
   b. At the time or immediately before, the defendant used force, or
   c. Puts or tried to put the owner of the property or any other person in fear of being subjected to imminent force.
3. *Mens rea*: Two parts –
   a. It must be shown that the defendant intended to steal, i.e. deprive the owner of his or her property.
   b. That the defendant intended to use force or threats of force to steal the property.

B. *Force*   [444]

1. Does not mean violence, slightest degree would be sufficient.
2. Defendant puts or seeks to put the victim in fear for the purpose of stealing the property.

a. The victim need not be afraid, just must perceive imminent force to himself or another, e.g. if Les put a knife to Dougie's throat and demanded Dougie's wallet, Les has committed a robbery. Likewise, if Les put a knife to Dougie's throat and ordered Mike to hand over his wallet or he would cut Dougie, this too would be a robbery.

3. Force must be used at the time of the stealing or just immediately prior to the stealing.

a. Unusual case – *R.* v. *Donaghy* [1986] Crim LR 625 – the defendants threatened a taxi driver in order to make him drive them to London. Once they arrived the defendants stole the driver's money. The defendants were acquitted of robbery, apparently on the grounds that the threats were not used in order to steal, but simply to get a ride to London.

C. Penalties – *section 14 (2) – a person guilty of robbery is liable on conviction on indictment to imprisonment for life.*   **[445]**

IV. Burglary   [446]

A. General Principles

1. Definition: Section 12 provides that a person is guilty of burglary if he or she enters a building as a trespasser intending to commit an arrestable offence, or being present as a trespasser, commits or attempts to commit such an offence.

2. *Actus reus*: Two parts –

a. Entering as a trespasser to commit an arrestable offence, or

b. Being present as a trespasser and committing or attempting to commit an arrestable offence.

3. *Mens rea*: Has two parts –

a. The defendant must have the *mens rea* to enter the building as a trespasser.

(1) Must be shown that the defendant was aware that his or her entry was a trespass, or that he or she was reckless as to this fact.

(2) Therefore, if the defendant entered accidentally, negligently or against his or her will, his or her entry would not be sufficient for burglary.

b. The defendant must have the *mens rea* for the arrestable offence.

(1) E.g. the *mens rea* for rape is where, at the time of sexual intercourse, the man knows that the woman does not

consent or he is reckless as to whether she does or does not consent. See [409].

(2) E.g. the *mens rea* for murder is that the defendant intended to kill or to cause serious injury to some person – section 4, Criminal Justice Act 1964. See [325].

B. *Trespassing*   [447]

1. A trespass is committed if a defendant enters another person's land without the consent of that person.
    a. Land includes buildings.
2. A trespass is committed if a defendant enters another person's land with the consent of that person, then exceeds the consent.
    a. E.g. Scrutton LJ. *In the Calgarth* (1927): 'When you invite a person into your house to use the staircase you do not invite him to slide down the banister.'
    b. *R.* v. *Jones & Smith* [1976] 3 All ER 54 – the defendants entered a house belonging to the second defendant's father with the intention to steal. The second defendant had his father's permission to enter the house, but he was not allowed to remove anything from the house. The Court of Appeal upheld the defendant's burglary conviction on the grounds that the owner's permission had been exceeded.
    c. *People (DPP)* v. *McMahon* [1987] ILRM 87 – members of the Gardaí entered a licensed premises, believing that they had the authority to do so under the Gaming and Lotteries Act 1956. In fact, the Acts relied upon did not give them the authority to enter the premises. The court concluded that they had exceeded their authority and had therefore entered as trespassers.
3. A trespass is committed if a defendant innocently enters the land of another and then realises his or her mistake that his or her entry was a trespass. From the moment of his realisation he or she is a trespasser.   [448]
    a. Applied: Tom moved to a new home in a housing estate where all the houses were identical. Tom walked into number 35, believing it to be his own home. After he walked through the front door he realised that he had entered the wrong home. At that moment Tom became a trespasser. If Tom commits an arrestable offence or attempts to commit an arrestable offence he may be charged with burglary.

C. Arrestable Offences – *section 12(4) provides that an arrestable offence is an offence for which a person of full age and not previously convicted may be punished by imprisonment for a term of five years or by a more severe penalty.*

D. Building or Part of a Building – section 12(2) provides: [449]

1. Inhabited vehicles, vessels or other inhabited temporary moveable structures are buildings.
    a. Section 12(1) applies to these temporary moveable structures whether or not the inhabitant is present at the time of the defendant's entry.
    b. Examples: Mobile homes, caravans, boats.
2. Building defined: A structure of considerable size and intended to be permanent or at least to endure for a considerable time. *Stevens* v. *Gouley* (1859) 7 CBNS 99.
    a. Examples:
        (1) A freezer container resting on sleepers rather than its chassis and used to store frozen food was a building. *B. & S.* v. *Leathley* [1979] Crim LR 321.
        (2) However, similar structures used for a similar purpose but still on their chassis were considered vehicles rather than buildings. *Norfolk Constabulary* v. *Seekings & Gould* (1986) Crim LR 167.
3. Question for jury to decide – whether the structure is a building.
4. Part of a building – if a person enters a building lawfully, then with the intent to steal enters another part of the building, he or she has committed a burglary.
    a. Example: While on holiday in Galway, Joyce visited the Curl-up-n-Dye Beauty Salon. When the owner was called away to an emergency phone call, Joyce opened a door clearly marked 'Employees Only'. She saw the owner's handbag on a desk and went into the room to remove money from the handbag. Joyce lawfully entered the salon, but entering the private office was an entry into a part of the building with the intention to steal.
    b. *R.* v. *Walkington* [1979] 2 All ER 716 – the defendant entered a department store and paid particular attention to the tills. He approached a till at a counter which was partially open, but found nothing in it and closed it. Held: The Court of Appeal held that the counter area could constitute a different

part of the building which the defendant did not have permission to enter. It was up to the jury to decide whether the defendant had entered a part of the building as a trespasser, and did so with the intent to steal.

E. Entry [450]

1. Common law – under the common law there were very technical rules regarding entry.
   a. Prosecution was required to show that some part of the defendant's body had entered the building.
      (1) Even a finger inside of the building was deemed to be enough for entry.
   b. Effective and substantial entry –
      (1) *R. v. Collins* [1972] 2 All ER 1105 – the defendant, dressed only in his socks, climbed a ladder to the window, intending to commit a rape. The victim mistook him for her boyfriend and invited him in. To what extent he had entered the room prior to the invitation was not clear. Held: The prosecution required to show that he had made an 'effective and substantial' entry.
2. Recent cases have endorsed the common law:
   a. *R. v. Brown* [1985] Crim LR 212 – the defendant had inserted his top half of his body through a broken shop window. Held: The defendant's whole body did not need to be inside the building and that proof that an effective entry had been made was sufficient.
   b. *R. v. Ryan* [1996] Crim LR 320 – the defendant's head and right arm were trapped inside the building. Held: The fact that his entry was not sufficient to complete his purpose was not relevant.
3. Issue of entry has not been decided by the Irish courts, but common law rule that the insertion of any part of the defendant's body into a building should continue to be taken as an entry.

F. Penalties – *section 12 (3) – a person guilty of burglary is liable on conviction on indictment to a fine or imprisonment for a term not exceeding fourteen years or both.*

V. *Aggravated Burglary* [451]

A. *General Principles*

1. Definition: Section 13 provides that aggravated burglary is where a burglary is committed in circumstances where the defendant has with him or her at the time a firearm, imitation firearm, weapon of offence or explosive.
2. *Actus reus*: Burglary with a weapon (two parts).
   a. Entering as a trespasser armed with a weapon to commit an arrestable offence, or
   b. Being present as a trespasser armed with a weapon and committing or attempting to commit an arrestable offence.
3. *Mens rea*: Requires *mens rea* of ordinary burglary, plus the defendant must be aware that he or she had the article in his or her possession at the material time.
   a. Ordinary burglary – the defendant must have the *mens rea* to enter the building as a trespasser, and
      (1) Must be shown that the defendant was aware that his or her entry was a trespass, or that he or she was reckless as to this fact.
      (2) Therefore, if the defendant entered accidentally, negligently or against his or her will, his or her entry would not be sufficient for burglary.
   b. The defendant was aware that he or she had the weapon in his or her possession when he or she entered as a trespasser, or when he or she committed or attempted to commit the arrestable offence.

B. *Armed* [452]

1. Under the first type of *actus reus* the defendant must be armed when he or she enters as a trespasser.
2. Under the second type of *actus reus* the defendant must be armed when he or she commits or attempts to commit the arrestable offence.

C. *Firearms – section 13 (2) provides that a firearm is:* [453]

1. A lethal firearm or other lethal weapon of any description from which any shot, bullet or other missile can be discharged.
2. An air gun (both rifle or pistol) or any other weapon incorporating a barrel from which metal or other slugs can be discharged.

3. A crossbow.
4. Any type of stun gun or other weapon for causing any shock or other disablement to a person by means of electricity or any other kind of energy emission.

D. Weapon of Offence – *section 13(2) provides that a weapon of offence is:* **[454]**

1. Any article which has a blade or sharp point, or
2. Any other article made or adapted for use for causing injury to or incapacitating a person, or intended by the person having it with him or her for such use or for threatening such use, or
3. Any weapon of whatever description designed for the discharge of any noxious liquid, noxious gas or other noxious thing.

E. Explosives – *section 13(2) provides that explosive means any article manufactured for the purpose of producing an explosion, or intended by that person having it with him or her for that purpose.* **[455]**

F. Penalties – *section 13(3) provides that a person guilty of aggravated burglary is liable on conviction on indictment to imprisonment for life.*

VI. Handling Stolen Property   [456]

A. General Principles

1. Handling stolen property –
   a. Definition: Section 17(1) provides that a person commits the offence of handling stolen property when a person who, knowing or being reckless as to whether property is stolen, receives it or undertakes to assist in its retention, removal, disposal or realisation.
2. *Actus reus*: Two parts –
   a. The defendant receives stolen property, or
   b. The defendant assists in the retention, removal, disposal or realisation of stolen property.
3. *Mens rea*: knowing or being reckless as to whether property is stolen.
   a. Reckless – defined in section 16(2) as occurring where a person disregards a substantial risk that the property handled is stolen.

b. Substantial risk – defined in section 16(2) as meaning a risk of such a nature and degree that, having regard to the circumstances in which the person acquired the property and the extent of the information then available to him or her, its disregard involves culpability of a high degree.

B. *Stolen Property* [457]

1. Includes property obtained by stealing.
2. Includes property unlawfully obtained.
    a. E.g. proceeds of the disposal of stolen property.
    b. Example: Shadrick stole Emily's diamond engagement ring and sold it to Henry. Fearing that the police were about to search his room, Shadrick gave the money (proceeds from the disposal of the stolen ring) to his nephew Cain and bragged about where he obtained the money. Cain has handled stolen property, although he never came into possession of the stolen engagement ring.
3. Prosecution must prove that the property handled by the defendant was in fact stolen at the time it was handled.
    a. Generally, it is not necessary to show exact ownership of property – *Attorney General* v. *Conway* (1925) 60 ILTR 41 – it is sufficient that the defendant knew that the property had been stolen from someone.

C. *Conviction* – *under section 17 (3) it is not dependent on whether the principal offender has or has not been previously convicted or is or is not amenable to justice.* [458]

1. Principal offender – under section 16(1) for purposes of sections 17 and 18, the person who has stolen or otherwise unlawfully obtained the property alleged to have been handled or possessed, and cognate words shall be construed accordingly.

D. *Receiving* [459]

1. The most common form of handling.
2. Central element is possession.
    a. It must be shown that the defendant took actual possession of the stolen property, or
    b. That the defendant took possession constructively.
3. Defendant knew of the existence of the stolen property.
    a. *People (AG)* v. *Nugent & Byrne* (1964) 89 ILTR 139 – a sum of stolen money was found in a car belonging to the first

defendant and in which the second defendant was traveling as a passenger. There was no evidence that either defendant knew that the money was there. In relation to the second defendant, the Court of Criminal Appeal held that a passenger could not be presumed to have knowledge of the contents of another person's car.

E. Retention – *the defendant kept or continued to have possession.*

F. Removal – *the defendant moved the stolen property.*

G. Disposal and Realisation – *the defendant sold, gave away, bartered, destroyed, etc. the stolen property.*

H. Note: Under section 19 it is an offence to withhold information regarding stolen property – [460]

1. Any person may be required by the police to account for property in his or her possession where:
   a. There are reasonable grounds for believing that an offence of theft or handling stolen property has been committed, and
   b. Where the person is found in possession of such property, and
   c. The police inform him or her of their belief concerning the property.
      (1) Ordinary language required – section 19(3) requires the police to use ordinary language or an offence under section 19 cannot be brought.
      (2) Inadmissible for other offences – under section 19(4) any information given in compliance with a requirement to divulge information is not admissible in evidence against that person or his or her spouse in any criminal proceedings other than an offence under section 19(2).
2. Section 19(2) – if the person fails or refuses without reasonable excuse to give an account or gives false or misleading information, he or she is guilty of an offence and is liable on summary conviction to a fine not exceeding £1,500 or imprisonment for a term not exceeding twelve months or both. [461]

I. Penalties – *section 17(4) provides that a person guilty of handling stolen property is liable on conviction on indictment to a fine or imprisonment for a term not exceeding ten years or both, but is not* *liable to a higher fine or longer term of imprisonment than that which applies to the principal offence.*

VII. Possession of Stolen Property [462]

A. General Principles

1. Definition: Section 18 provides that possession of stolen property occurs where a person, without lawful authority or excuse, possesses, but does not steal, the stolen property, knowing or being reckless as to whether it was stolen.
2. *Actus reus* – being in possession of stolen property.
3. *Mens rea* – knowing or being reckless as to whether property is stolen.
   a. Presumption – section 18(2) provides that where a person has in his or her possession stolen property in such circumstances (including purchase of the property at a price below its market value) that it is reasonable to conclude that either the person:
   (1) Knew that the property was stolen, or
   (2) Was reckless as to whether it was stolen.
   b. Rebut presumption – unless the court or the jury is satisfied having regard to all the evidence that there is a reasonable doubt as to whether he or she knew the property was stolen or was reckless as to whether it was stolen.

B. Conviction *of the defendant under section 18(3) is not dependent on whether the principal offender has or has not been previously convicted or is or is not amenable to justice. See principal offender [458].* **[463]**

C. Sentencing *– under section 18(4) a person convicted of this offence is liable on conviction on indictment to a fine or imprisonment for a term not exceeding five years or both, but is not liable to a higher fine or longer term of imprisonment than that which applies to the principal offence.*

D. Note: Under section 19 it is an offence to withhold information regarding stolen property. *See [460] above.*

Review Questions

1. Samantha practises witchcraft and searches the nearby countryside for various plants and animals to put into her homeopathic potions. Samantha produces everything from beauty aids to poultices for bronchitis and removing skin cancers. Samantha sells her homeopathic potions to locals. Last week Samantha was observed by Farmer Finbar collecting the following items from one of his apple orchards. Identify which, if any, of the items could be deemed to have been stolen.
   (a) The flowers of the wild digitalis plant.
   (b) Three apples that had fallen from one of the trees.
   (c) A crow shot and killed by Farmer Finbar and hung in the orchard to ward off other crows who ruin the ripening apples and nearby corn.
   (d) Cow dung.

2. Ted awoke at three a.m. when he heard someone banging on his front door. He answered the door to find his cousin George crouching in the shadows of the shrubs near the front door. George jumped through the open door, turned off the hall light and thrust a briefcase into Ted's hands and told Ted to hide it well. George then ran out the back door and jumped over the neighbour's garden wall. Without opening the briefcase Ted put it in his freezer, then went back to sleep. The following morning the police arrived with a search warrant and found the briefcase, and to Ted's shock he discovered that it was filled with diamonds and emeralds.
   (a) Did Ted have the required *mens rea* for the offence of handling stolen property?
   (b) Did Ted have the required *mens rea* for the offence of possessing stolen property?
   (c) Did Ted's conduct of placing the briefcase in his freezer meet the *actus reus* requirements of *handling* stolen property?
   (d) Did Ted's conduct of placing the briefcase in his freezer meet the *actus reus* requirements of *possessing* stolen property?
   (e) Assume that when the police first arrived at his door with a search warrant they asked him where he hid the diamonds and emeralds, and Ted responded that he did not know what they were talking about. Is his response enough for him to be charged with withholding information regarding stolen property under section 19 of the CJTFOA 2001?

3. Tony and his friends Pauly and Christopher decided that they were going to climb down the shaft of the exhaust fan of the Giovase Family Sausage Company to retrieve a love letter that Tony had

hidden above the broken exhaust fan. Tony hid the letter the previous day when a meeting he was having with the head of the Giovase family had been interrupted by the arrival of the police. While climbing down the exhaust shaft Tony became stuck. He could not climb back up to the roof, nor could he descend to the broken exhaust fan. After Tony was rescued from the exhaust shaft by the fire brigade the police found the embarrassing letter.

(a) Can Tony be charged and convicted of burglary? Why or why not?

(b) Assume that instead of hiding a letter Tony hid an illegal handgun. Can Tony be charged and convicted of aggravated burglary? Why or why not?

4. Noreen wants to audition for a new girl group. Unfortunately, she does not have any decent clothes for the audition. In desperation, Noreen decides to steal some clothes from the A-B-C Boutique. While trying to exit the shop with two outfits, Noreen is stopped by the manager. Without thinking Noreen tells the manager that she has AIDS and she will bite him if he doesn't let her leave the shop. Noreen does not have AIDS.

(a) Noreen could not escape from the manager, thus she never left the shop with the clothes. Has Noreen committed a theft?

(b) Has Noreen committed a robbery?

5. After leaving the pub late one night, Patrick noticed that the window to his friend's flat was open. Patrick did not want to walk home and did not think that his friend George would mind if he spent the night on George's sofa. Patrick climbed into the window and promptly fell asleep on the sofa. Later, Patrick awoke when he heard a scream. He stumbled into the kitchen and grabbed a knife to protect himself. Within minutes the police burst into the house and arrested Patrick. Patrick had climbed into the wrong window and the female occupant was terror stricken to find a strange man sleeping on her sofa.

(a) Can Patrick be convicted of burglary?

(b) Can Patrick be convicted of aggravated burglary?

6. David took Archie's dog, Hamish. David hoped that Archie would think that Hamish had strayed and that Archie would offer a large reward for Hamish's safe return. David intended to return Hamish to Archie after a few days, even if no reward was offered. Has David committed a criminal offence?

7. Alexander saw a mobile phone in a locked parked car. Alexander broke the window of the car and ran away with the mobile. If Alexander is apprehended, will he be successfully convicted of robbing the car?

Table 10.1: Property Offences

Theft	S. 4 Criminal Justice (Theft and Fraud Offences) Act 2001	A person is guilty of theft if he or she appropriates property without the consent of its owner and with the intention of depriving its owner of the property. **See [435]**.
Robbery	S. 14 CJTFOA 2001	A person is guilty of robbery if, at the time or immediately before the stealing and in order to do so, he or she uses force or puts or seeks to put any person in fear of being then and there subjected to force. **See [443]**.
Burglary	S. 12 CJTFOA 2001	A person is guilty of burglary if he or she enters a building as a trespasser intending to commit an arrestable offence, or being present as a trespasser commits or attemps to commit an arrestable offence. **See [446]**.
Aggravated burglary	S. 13 CJTFOA 2001	A person is guilty of aggravated burglary if while committing a burglary the person has with him or her a firearm, imitation firearm, weapon of offence or explosive. **See [451]**.
Handling stolen property	S. 17 CJTFOA 2001	A person is guilty of handing stolen property where he or she knowingly or recklessly as to whether property is stolen, receives it or undertakes to assist in its retention, removal, disposal or realisation. **See [456]**.
Possession of stolen property	S. 18 CJTFOA 2001	A person is guilty of possession of stolen property where without lawful authority or excuse he or she possesses, but does not steal, stolen property, knowing or being reckless as to whether the property was stolen. **See [462]**.

11

PUBLIC WELFARE OFFENCES

Chapter synopsis

I.   Public Order Offences
II. Offences under the Criminal Justice (Public Order) Act 1994
III. Offences under the Intoxicating Liquor Act 2003
IV. Misuse of Drugs

I. Public Order Offences [464]

A. General Principles

1. Public order offences relate to conduct that causes annoyance, distress or alarm to general members of the public.
2. Until recently public order offences were governed by common law.
   a. Common law public order offences include:
      (1) Riot,
      (2) Violent disorder,
      (3) Affray,
      (4) Public intoxication, and
      (5) Abusive conduct in a public place.
   b. Until recently minor offences were prohibited by the Vagrancy Acts, especially the Act of 1824.
      (1) Supreme Court in *King* v. *Attorney General* [1981] IR 233 declared that much of section 4 of the 1824 Act, dealing with loitering with intent, was unconstitutional due to its inherent arbitrariness and ambiguity.
3. More serious public order offences were abolished and replaced by the Criminal Justice (Public Order) Act 1994.
   a. Also introduced a new offence of the display of offensive material.

II. Offences under the Criminal Justice (Public Order) Act 1994   [465]

A. Intoxication in a Public Place

1. General Principles
    a. Definition: Section 4(1) of the CJPOA 1994 provides that it is an offence for any person to be in any public place while intoxicated such that there is a reasonable apprehension that the person is a danger to himself or herself or others in his or her vicinity.
    b. *Actus reus* –
        (1) Being intoxicated in a public place.
        (2) Because of the intoxicated state objectively being a risk to oneself or to others.
    c. *Mens rea* – none, it is a state of affairs offence. See [65].
2. **Intoxicated** – section 4(4) provides that intoxicated means under the intoxicating influence of any alcoholic drink, drug, solvent or other substance or a combination of substances.   **[466]**
3. **Public place** – section 3 provides that a public place includes:
    a. Any highway;
    b. Outdoor area to which at the material time members of the public are permitted access;
    c. Cemeteries and churchyards;
    d. Any premises or other place to which at the material time members of the public have access whether by payment or not; and
    e. Any train, vessel or vehicle used for the carriage of persons for reward.
4. **Material time** means the time when the defendant is found to be intoxicated.
5. **Penalties** – section 4(2) provides that a summary conviction results in a fine not exceeding £100.

B. Disorderly Conduct in a Public Place   [467]

1. General Principles
    a. Definition: Section 5(1) of the CJPOA 1994 provides that it is an offence for any person in a public place to engage in offensive conduct:
        (1) Between midnight and seven a.m., or
        (2) At any other time, after having been requested by the police to stop.

b. *Actus reus* –
   (1) Being in a public place, and
   (2) Engaging in offensive conduct,
   (3) Between the hours of midnight to seven a.m., or at any other time after having been requested by the police to stop the offending conduct.
   c. *Mens rea* – intention or objective recklessness.
2. Offensive conduct – section 5(3) defines offensive conduct as unreasonable behaviour which, having regard to all the circumstances, is likely to cause serious offence or serious annoyance to any person who is or might reasonably be aware of the behaviour.
3. Penalties – on summary conviction a fine not to exceed £500.

C. Threatening, Abusive or Insulting Behaviour in a Public Place [468]

1. General Principles
   a. Definition: Section 6(1) of the CJPOA 1994 provides that it is an offence for any person in a public place to use or engage in any threatening, abusive or insulting words or behaviour with intent to provoke a breach of the peace or being reckless as to whether a breach of the peace may occur.
   b. *Actus reus* –
      (1) While in a public place to use or engage in any threatening, abusive or insulting words or conduct.
      (2) To provoke a breach of the peace.
   c. *Mens rea* – intention or objective recklessness.
2. Breach of the peace.
   a. Note: There is no requirement that an actual breach of the peace take place.
   b. Breach of the peace occurs whenever harm is or is likely to be done to a person or to his or her property, or creates a fear in that person of being harmed through an assault, an affray, a riot or other disturbance.
3. Penalties – on summary conviction to a fine not exceeding £500 or to a term of imprisonment not exceeding three months or to both.

D. Riot [469]

1. General Principles
   a. Definition: Under section 14(1) of the CJPOA 1994 it is an offence for any person to use unlawful violence:

(1) In the presence of at least twelve people in any place (public or private).

(2) Where unlawful violence to effect a common purpose is used or threatened.

(3) The conduct of the group is such that a person of reasonable firmness present at that place to fear for his or her safety or the safety of another.

  b. *Actus reus* –

(1) Where a person with at least eleven others in any place,

(2) Uses unlawful violence, and

(3) The conduct is capable of causing a person of reasonable firmness present to fear for his or her safety or the safety of another.

  c. *Mens rea* – intention or objective recklessness.

2. Violence – not clear from Act what conduct it includes.   **[470]**

  a. *O'Faolain* v. *Lord Mayor of Dublin* (1996) unrep. HC – under the common law offence of riot a man involved in a riot stared at a woman in such a way that she left the scene. It was held that it was reasonable to assume that had she not left the man would have resorted to violence. Therefore, his stare constituted force under the common law offence.

(1) Section 14(4) CJPOA 1994 abolished the common law offence of riot.

3. Section 14(2) provides:

  a. It does not matter whether the group of twelve or more persons uses or threatens to use unlawful violence simultaneously.

  b. The required common purpose may be inferred from conduct.

  c. No person of reasonable firmness need actually be, or be likely to be, present at that place.

4. Penalties – on conviction on indictment to a fine or to a term of imprisonment not exceeding ten years or to both.

E. Violent Disorder   [471]

1. General Principles

  a. Definition: Section 15(1) of the CJPOA 1994 provides that where a person is present with at least two others uses or threatens to use unlawful violence, and the conduct of these persons, taken together, would cause a person of reasonable firmness present at that place to fear for his or her or another person's safety.

b. *Actus reus* –
   (1) Being present with at least two others (in a public or private place),
   (2) Using unlawful violence, or threatening to use unlawful violence,
   (3) The conduct of the group, taken together, would cause a person of reasonable firmness to fear for his or her or another person's safety.
   c. *Mens rea* – intention or subjective recklessness (see section 15(3) below [472]).
2. Violence – not clear from Act what conduct it includes.   **[472]**
   a. *O'Faolain* v. *Lord Mayor of Dublin* (1996) unrep. HC – under the common law offence of riot a man involved in a riot stared at a woman in such a way that she left the scene. It was held that it was reasonable to assume that had she not left the man would have resorted to violence. Therefore, his stare constituted force under the common law offence.
   (1) Section 15(6) CJPOA 1994 abolished the common law offence of riot and unlawful assembly.
3. Section 15(2) provides:
   a. It does not matter whether the group of three or more persons uses or threatens to use unlawful violence simultaneously.
   b. No person of reasonable firmness need actually be, or be likely to be, present at that place.
   c. Section 15(3) provides that a person shall not be convicted unless the person intends to use or threaten to use violence, or is aware that his or her conduct may be violent or threaten violence.
4. Penalties – on a conviction on indictment to a fine or to a term of imprisonment for a term not exceeding ten years or to both.

F. Affray   [473]

1. General Principles
   a. Definition: Section 16(1) CJPOA 1994 provides that where a person in the company of at least one other person at any place uses or threatens to use, by more than words, violence towards each other, and the violence so used or threatened by one of those persons is unlawful and the conduct of this group taken together is such that a person of reasonable firmness present at that place to fear for his or her or another person's safety.

    b. *Actus reus* –
- (1) Being with at least one other person at any place,
- (2) Using violence, or threatening to use, by more than mere words, violence toward other members of the group.
- (3) The conduct of the group, taken together, is such that a person of reasonable firmness present at that place to fear for his or her or another person's safety.

    c. *Mens rea* – intention or subjective recklessness (see section 16(3) below).

2. Violence is not defined in the Act.
3. Section 16(5) CJPOA 1994 abolished the common law offence of affray.
4. Section 16(2) provides:
   - a. A threat cannot be made by words alone.
     - (1) In other words, a threat must include an act or acts, e.g. shaking of a fist, etc.
   - b. No person of reasonable firmness need actually be, or be likely to be, present at that place.
   - c. Section 16(3) provides that a person shall not be convicted unless the person intends to use or threaten to use violence, or is aware that his or her conduct may be violent or threaten violence.
5. Penalties –
   - a. On summary conviction – to a fine not exceeding £500 or to a term of imprisonment for a term not exceeding twelve months or to both.
   - b. On a conviction on indictment – to a fine or to a term of imprisonment for a term not exceeding five years or to both.

III. Offences under the Intoxicating Liquor Act 2003   [474]

A. Supply of Intoxicating Liquor to Drunken Persons by Non-licensees

1. General Principles
   - a. Definition: Section 5(1) provides that it is an offence for a person (not a licensee) to purchase alcohol for supply to, or consumption by, a drunken person on licensed premises, or to simply supply intoxicating liquor to a drunken person on licensed premises.
   - b. *Actus reus* –
     - (1) Where a person not a licensee on licensed premises

(2) Purchases alcohol for supply to, or consumption by, a drunken person or

(3) Supplies intoxicating liquor to a drunken person.

   c. *Mens rea* – strict liability.

     (1) Section 6(3) provides that a person who contravenes section 5(1)is guilty of an offence under this section.

2. Drunken person – section 2 provides that a drunken person is a person who is intoxicated to such an extent as would give rise to a reasonable apprehension that the person might endanger himself or herself or any other person.

3. Penalties – on summary conviction to a fine not exceeding:

   a. On the first offence to €1,500.

   b. For a second or any subsequent offence to €2,000.

B. Offences by Drunken Person on Licensed Premises [475]

1. General Principles

   a. Definition: Under sections 6(1) and 6(2) of the ILA 2003 it is an offence for a drunken person to seek entry to a licensed premises or to fail to leave a licensed premises after being told to do so by the licensee or a police officer.

   b. *Actus reus* –

     (1) Being drunk and

     (2) Seeking entry to a licensed premises, or

     (3) Failing to leave the licensed premises after being told to leave by the licensee or a police officer.

   c. *Mens rea* – strict liability.

     (1) Section 6(3) – a person who contravenes sections (1) and (2) is guilty of an offence under this section.

2. Penalties – on summary conviction to a fine not exceeding:

   a. For a first offence €300.

   b. For a second or subsequent offence €500.

C. Disorderly Conduct on Licensed Premises [476]

1. General Principles

   a. Definition: Pursuant to section 8(1) of the ILA 2003 a person shall not engage in disorderly conduct on licensed premises and shall leave the licensed premises on being told to do so by the licensee or a police officer, and shall not re-enter the bar of the licensed premises within a twenty-four-hour period.

   b. *Actus reus* –

     (1) Engaging in disorderly conduct on licensed premises.

(2) Or engaging in disorderly conduct on licensed premises and failing to leave the licensed premises when told to leave by the licensee or the police, or

(3) After being told to leave, re-entering the bar of the licensed premises within a period of twenty-four hours.

    c. *Mens rea* – strict liability.

      (1) Section 8(3) provides that a person who contravenes is guilty of an offence.

2. Disorderly conduct is defined in section 2 as being unreasonable behaviour by a person on licensed premises which having regard to all the circumstances is likely to cause injury, fear or distress to any other person on the premises and includes, but is not limited to:

    a. Violent, threatening, abusive, quarrelsome or insulting behaviour,

    b. Conduct causing damage to property,

    c. Conduct constituting an offence under the Firearms Acts 1925 to 2000, or the Non-Fatal Offences Against the Person Act 1997,

    d. Conduct in breach of the duty imposed under the Fire Services Act 1981, or

    e. Conduct likely to constitute a risk to the health, safety or welfare of any person.

3. Penalties – on summary conviction to a fine not exceeding:

    a. For the first offence €300.

    b. For a second or any subsequent offence €500.

IV. *Misuse of Drugs* [477]

A. *General Principles*

1. Misuse of Drugs Act 1977 as amended by the Misuse of Drugs Act 1984 are the main statutes.

2. Purpose of acts is to control the possession of certain drugs which are specified in the Schedule to the 1977 Act.

    a. Possession is crucial – note that it is not generally an offence to use prohibited drugs.

      (1) Exception – it is an offence to use opium under section 16.

    b. Possession is easier and less intrusive to penalise than use.

      (1) If use were an offence, the police would need greater powers to demand urine and blood samples, etc.

      (2) Possession merely requires the power to search a suspect.

3. Controlled drug is defined in section 2(1) of the 1977 Act as being any substance, product or preparations specified in the Schedule to the Act, or declared to be a controlled drug by the government using powers granted by section 2(2).
   a. **Section 4** allows the Minister for Justice to make regulations legalising the possession of drugs among certain named categories of people. **[478]**
      (1) Article 11 of the Misuse of Drugs Regulations 1988 lists groups allowed to be in possession of controlled drugs:
         (a) Police, customs and excise officers, postal employees, forensic scientists and carriers acting bona fide in the course of their employment.
         (b) Anyone else carrying controlled drugs to an exempted person or authorised by the Minister for Justice.
   b. **Section 5** empowers the Minister to make regulations to prevent misuse of controlled drugs by regulating: **[479]**
      (1) The manufacture, production or preparation of controlled drugs.
      (2) The importation or exportation of controlled drugs.
      (3) The supply and distribution of controlled drugs.
      (4) The transportation of controlled drugs.
      (5) The packaging and labelling of controlled drugs.

B. Possession [480]

1. General Principles
   a. Definition: Section 3 makes it an offence to be in possession of a controlled substance.
   b. *Actus reus* – being in possession of a controlled substance.
   c. *Mens rea* – knowledge of the drugs.
2. Possession is defined in section 1(2) as being in control of any controlled drug and includes constructive possession.
   a. In other words, a defendant need not be in actual possession so long as he or she has control over the drugs.
   b. It appears that possession of a drug in its natural state is not an offence.
      (1) However, any interference with the natural state will render the defendant liable to conviction.
      (2) *R. v. Stevens* [1981] Crim LR 568 – the defendant had dried out some magic mushrooms. It was held that the process of drying out the mushrooms constituted processing.

c. **Joint possession** – it is possible for drugs to be in the possession of more than one person at the same time, even where they are in the physical custody of only one person. *R.* v. *Whelan* (1972).   **[481]**

d. Knowledge of:

(1) The prosecution is required to prove that the defendant had knowledge of the existence of the drugs. *People (DPP)* v. *O'Shea (No. 2)* (1983) – the defendant was transferring boxes of drugs, but was not aware of the contents of the boxes. He was aware that something was wrong and that one of his fellow workers was carrying a gun. He thought that the boxes contained explosives. It was held that his conviction should be quashed.

3. Penalties – section 27 –

a. Where the relevant controlled drug is cannabis or cannabis resin and the court is satisfied that it was for the defendant's personal use:

(1) On summary conviction for a first offence a fine not exceeding £300.

(2) On conviction on an indictment for a first offence a fine not exceeding £500.

(3) On summary conviction for a second offence a fine not exceeding £400.

(4) On conviction on an indictment for a second offence a fine not exceeding £1,000.

(5) On summary conviction for a third or more offence to a fine not exceeding £1,000 or to a term of imprisonment not exceeding twelve months or to both.

(6) On conviction on an indictment for a third or more offence to a fine or to a term of imprisonment not to exceed three years or to both.

b. All other controlled drugs other than cannabis or cannabis resin for personal use:

(1) On summary conviction to a fine not exceeding £1,000 or to a term of imprisonment not exceeding twelve months or to both.

(2) On conviction on an indictment to a fine or to a term of imprisonment not exceeding seven years or to both.

C. Possession for the Purpose of Supply   [482]

1. General Principles

a. Definition: Section 15(1) provides that it is an offence for any person who has in his or her possession, whether lawfully or not, a controlled drug for the purpose of selling or otherwise supplying it in contravention of section 5.

b. *Actus reus.*

(1) Being in possession of a controlled drug

(2) For the purpose of selling or supplying it to another.

c. *Mens rea.*

(1) Knowledge of the drugs.

(2) Intention to sell or supply the drugs to another.

2. **Rebuttable presumption** – section 15(2) provides that where it is proved that a defendant was in possession of a controlled drug and the quantity was such or the circumstances were such that it is reasonable to assume that the drug was not intended for the immediate personal use of the defendant, it is presumed that the defendant was in possession with the intent to supply. **[483]**

a. Packaging may indicate an intention to supply. *People (DPP)* v. *Lawless* (1985) 3 Frewen 30 – during a raid the police recovered seventeen separate packets containing heroin. The presumption under section 15(2) was raised because the total amount of heroin was less than a lethal dose and was probably less than a day's intake for an addict. On appeal it was argued that the presumption should not have been raised. This was rejected, as there was no evidence that the defendant was an addict and the fact that the heroin was packaged into seventeen portions indicted an intention to supply.

3. Penalties – section 27(3) provides:

a. On summary conviction to a fine not exceeding £1,000 or to a term of imprisonment not exceeding twelve months or to both.

b. On conviction on indictment a fine or up to life imprisonment or to both.

D. Possession Defences – section 29 provides three defences. [484]

1. Section 29(2)(a) – where the defendant did not know nor had reasonable grounds for suspecting that he or she was in possession of a drug.

2. Section 29(2)(b) allows a defence where the defendant knew that he or she had possession of a drug, but believed it to be another drug that he or she could possess without committing an offence.

3. Section 29(2)(c) provides a defence to be in possession of a drug where the defendant had taken possession in order to prevent

someone else from committing an offence, or to hand it over to the police, and had taken all reasonable steps to destroy the drugs or to hand them over to the police.

4. Section 29(3) provides that a defendant charged under section 15 may rebut the presumption under section 15(2) by showing that at the time of the offence he or she was permitted under the regulations to be in possession of the controlled drugs.

E. Supplying   [485]

1. General Principles
   a. Definition: Supplying includes giving away the drugs for no payment. Under section 4 of the 1988 Regulations a person is prohibited from supplying controlled drugs to another. Under section 21(2) of the Act it an offence to contravene the Regulations.
   b. *Actus reus* – supplying a controlled drug to another.
   c. *Mens rea* – intention.
2. Defence – under section 29(5) the defendant has a defence if he or she can prove that the defendant did not know or suspect, nor had reason to suspect, of the existence of any element of the offence.
3. Penalties – section 27(6) provides that on conviction on an indictment to a term of imprisonment not to exceed fourteen years.

F. Offer to Supply   [486]

1. General Principles
   a. Definition: Offering to supply drugs includes giving away the drugs for no payment. Under section 4 of the 1988 Regulations a person is prohibited from supplying or offering to supply controlled drugs to another. Under section 21(2) of the Act it an offence to contravene the Regulations.
   b. *Actus reus* – offering to supply a controlled drug to another. Offer can be communicated by words or acts.
   c. *Mens rea* – intention to communicate offer.
      (1) Note: All that must be shown is that an offer was made. It does not matter whether it was a joke or not genuine.
      (2) An intention to actually supply the controlled drugs is not required. *R. v. Gill* (1992) – the defendant admitted offering to supply ecstasy, but was trying to cheat his

customers by selling vitamins to them. He argued that as his intent was to cheat his customers by supplying vitamins he could not be convicted of offering to supply a controlled drug. It was held that his intention to go through with the offer was not an element of the offence.

2. Penalties – section 27(10)(b) provides:
   a. On summary conviction to a fine not exceeding £100 or to a term of imprisonment not exceeding six months or to both, or
   b. On conviction on an indictment to a fine not exceeding £500, to a term of imprisonment not exceeding two years or to both.

G. Production [487]

1. Under section 5 of the 1977 Act the Minister may prohibit the manufacturing, production or preparation of controlled drugs.
   a. *Actus reus* –
      (1) Mere growing of a plant from which a drug may be extracted is not of itself a form of production unless it is accompanied by a process to make the drug more usable. *R. v. Goodchild (No. 2)* (1978).
      (2) *R. v. Harris* (1995) Cr App R 369 – the defendant was stripping cannabis plants prior to the separation of those parts which would be used for smoking. It was held that by preparing to discard the non-usable parts of the plant, the defendant had produced a drug by 'any other method'.
   b. *Mens rea* – an intention to produce a controlled drug.
      (1) Therefore, if Scott wants to produce cocaine but instead produces heroin, he cannot be convicted of production of a controlled drug.

2. **Cultivation** – [488]
   a. Section 17 of the Act also prohibits the cultivation of three kinds of plant:
      (1) The cannabis plant.
      (2) Opium poppies.
      (3) Coca plants.
   b. Cultivation is not defined in the Act and should be given its ordinary meaning.
   c. Defence – under section 29(5) the defendant has a defence if he or she can prove that the defendant neither knew of, or suspected, nor had reasonable grounds for suspecting the existence of any element of the offence.

Review Questions

1. Tony is a student and cannot afford to purchase the cannabis he likes to smoke. Tony decided to grow his own cannabis and went out and purchased a pot, soil and fertiliser. Unfortunately, Tony does not have a green thumb and his efforts are not rewarded – not one seed sprouts. What offence(s) has Tony committed, if any?

2. Tony took a few seeds to his eighty-four-year-old granny, Blanche, who does have a green thumb. Before long Blanche had grown a magnificent six-foot plant and decided to take it to the local flower show because Tony told her that it was an exotic Australian palm. What offence(s), if any, has Blanche committed?

3. The judge at the local flower show was amazed that his friend Blanche had grown a huge cannabis plant. He informed her of the true nature of her plant and agreed to take and destroy the plant in his huge composter. Unfortunately, on his way to his garden centre to destroy the plant, the flower judge was stopped by the police for speeding. The officers were amazed to see that the driver had a huge cannabis plant in his vehicle in plain view. What offence(s), if any, has the flower judge committed?

4. Fred and Ginger are university students and madly in love. Last Saturday night, while walking home at three in the morning, they decided to dance at the crossroads. They went into the middle of a busy intersection and began to sing and dance. Soon several other university students joined the pair. Unfortunately, several drivers objected to sharing the intersection with dancers and began to honk and yell at the dancers as they slowly drove by. Residents in the area awoke to all the noise and called the police. A lone police officer appeared and told the students that they had to stop dancing in the street. Fred, Ginger and the others ignored the police officer.
   (a) Will Fred and Ginger be convicted of disorderly conduct?
   (b) Will Fred and Ginger be convicted of being intoxicated in a public place?
   (c) Will Fred and Ginger be convicted of an affray?

5. Jackie Chong and her children have been allocated a house by the county council in a housing estate. Unfortunately, soon after the family moved into their new home several neighbours gathered to protest a house being given to 'foreign blow-ins' when so many local families had languished on the housing list for years. Twenty pro-testors picketed on the footpath in front of the Chong home, and when Jackie attempted to take her young son to school, she was

greeted with jeering and racial comments by two of the protestors. The other eighteen protesters remained silent, but stared with hostility at Jackie.

(a) Can the protestors all be convicted of disorderly conduct?

(b) Can the protestors all be convicted of engaging in threatening, abusive or insulting behaviour in a public place?

(c) Can the two protestors making racial comments be convicted of affray?

6. Betty and Wilma both fancied Fred. Last Friday night, Fred brought Betty into the local pub on a date, and on Saturday night he brought Wilma into the same pub on a date. On Sunday Betty and Wilma met on the public footpath outside the pub, and after exchanging insults, a fight ensued. When Fred arrived he found Betty and Wilma rolling on the ground, scratching and pulling each other's hair. When Fred attempted to separate the fighting women, Barney, the publican, pushed Fred away because Barney was enjoying watching the women fight. Soon Fred and Barney were fighting too.

(a) Can Betty, Wilma, Fred and Barney be convicted of disorderly conduct on a licensed premise?

(b) Can Betty, Wilma, Fred and Barney be convicted of disorderly conduct in a public place?

(c) Can Betty, Wilma, Fred and Barney be convicted of riot?

7. Shadrick has been having a bad week. On Monday at three in the afternoon he fell in the middle of a busy intersection while trying to stagger home from the pub. He merely curled up and went to sleep. On Tuesday at four in the afternoon the publican told him to leave the pub, as he was visibly intoxicated. Shadrick left the pub and returned one hour later and argued with the publican, then left again. On Wednesday at noon he again re-entered the pub. Advise Shadrick of any offences he may have committed under the Intoxicating Liquor Act 2003.

SECTION 4:
APPROACHING THE EXAM

12

APPROACHING THE EXAM

I. *Highlighting Where to Concentrate Your Revision*

A. *Be Prepared Early*

1. **Step 1:** Make certain that you have all the:
   a. Class notes.
   b. Assigned readings.
   c. Past exam papers.
      (1) **Note:** Past exam papers are useful for answer practice. Do *not* attempt to guess what areas will come up on the exam by reviewing past exam papers.
2. **Step 2:** Assess the materials.
   a. What areas did the lecturer *stress*?
      (1) What areas took up the most amount of time?
      (2) What areas appear year after year on exams?
      (3) What areas did the lecturer state were interesting, unusual, in need of change?
   b. Identify the grey areas – legal questions that are not resolved or are in need of an update.
      (1) Examiners often ask questions regarding the grey areas.
   c. Identify recent changes in the law.
      (1) Cases.
      (2) Statutes.
   d. Identify recent recommendations for change.
      (1) Reports of the law reform commission.
      (2) Law review articles.
      (3) Newspaper articles.
   e. Do *not* neglect the settled areas of the law.
      (1) Without a good knowledge of these areas a student will be unable to make a proper analysis or necessary comparisons.

B. Conquering Cases

1. The points that you make in your answers must be backed up with relevant authority.
2. Everyone wrestles with the names of cases.
   a. If you cannot remember the name of a particular case, *briefly outline* enough facts to enable the examiner to know which case you are referring to.
3. The best way to conquer cases for many students is to test yourself with case flash cards.
   a. Put the name of the case on the front of an index card.
   b. On the back put a brief summary of the facts, holding and the importance of the case.
   c. Look at the name and try to recite the information on the back. If you are correct put the card in a different stack. Keep going through the cards until you have them correct. Now turn the cards over and try reciting the name from the facts.
   d. Case cards are easier to carry and use than a full set of notes or books.

C. Answering the Exam Questions

1. **Problem questions** – test your ability to apply the law to the facts given.
   a. Many students find this type of question the most difficult.
   b. The best way of tackling this type of question is to treat it like a maths problem, i.e. **work** your way through it.
      (1) However, unlike a maths problem there is usually no single precise correct answer in most law questions.
2. **Planning your answer (problem questions).**
   a. *Read* the question.
   b. *Read* the question again.
   c. **Identify the potential criminal offences.**
      (1) Sometimes this is easy. If you find a question difficult, ask yourself the following questions.
         (a) What act or conduct has any person in the fact scenario performed?
         (b) What act or conduct has any person in the fact scenario failed to perform?
         (c) Has any harm been suffered?
         (d) Have any protected interests been impacted upon?

     (2) Remember – if you are asked to discuss Tom's potential liability you will earn few marks if you write a brilliant discussion of John's potential liability.

  d. **From the facts, what conduct may be a possible basis of criminal liability?**

     (1) Remember – the same facts may give rise to more than one criminal offence.

     (2) Unless you are instructed otherwise, it is probably best to begin with the most serious of the criminal offences.

     (3) **What interest of the victim has been injured?**

       (a) His person?

       (b) His property?

     (4) **How has the defendant conducted himself or herself?**

       (a) Performed an intentional act?

       (b) Performed a negligent act?

       (c) Performed no act? (Failed to act?)

       (d) Does the defendant have the required *mens rea*?

  e. **Identify the issues.**

     (1) Sometimes this too is easy. If not, try asking yourself the following questions.

       (a) What are the essential elements that the prosecutor must establish as a basis of liability for the offence?

       (b) Is each and every essential element present in the facts given?

       (c) Consider defences.

  f. After identifying the issue(s), select **one** issue.

     (1) It is better to take the issues one at a time than to skip back and forth in your answer.

  g. **Briefly outline your answer for each issue.**

     (1) Again, check to make certain that you are answering the question asked.

       (a) **Beware** – in exams it is easy to go off on a tangent.

     (2) All you want are a few basic *phrases*, *words* and *cases* to jog your memory to keep you from going off track or forgetting something.

       (a) Do not spend more than a few minutes outlining your answers.

     (3) If you do not like the flow of your proposed answer, just renumber the points quickly.

3. **Working out your problem question answer.**

  a. For a perpetrator.

     (1) Did his or her acts constitute the required *actus reus*?

(2) At the time of his or her acts did the defendant have the required *mens rea*?

(3) Was there a concurrence of the *actus reus* and *mens rea*?

(4) If the offence requires a specific result, make certain the required result is achieved.

b. For others.

(1) Can the defendant be held criminally liable because of his or her participation?

(a) As a co-conspirator?

(b) As an accessory by aiding and abetting?

(2) Can the defendant be held criminally liable because of vicarious liability?

(3) Can the defendant be held criminally liable for helping a perpetrator avoid arrest or detection?

c. Defences –

(1) Do the facts support a defence of:

(a) Intoxication

(b) Infancy

(c) Mistake of fact

(d) Insanity

(e) Necessity

(f) Duress and/or

(g) Defence of self or others?

d. Are there any legal limits on convicting the defendant?

(1) Constitutionally imposed limitations.

(a) Principle of legality – see [27] and [33].

(b) Principle of proportionality – see [32]–[34].

(2) European Conventions – see [37].

4. **Essay questions.**

a. Most students have less difficulty answering essay questions, but they often make the same types of mistakes.

b. **Read the question.**

c. **Read the question again**.

d. **The issue is usually identified for you**.

(1) Make certain that you answer the question asked.

(2) If you have prepared essay answers in the hope that the question will come up on the exam, make certain that you *tailor* your prepared essay to answer the question asked.

e. **Take a side.**

(1) Because most essay questions ask you to analyse some legal dilemma or problem, at times you will be required

to determine which side you want to take, so quickly determine which side you think you can put forth best.

(a) In doubt? What did your lecturer say about it?

(b) What do the legal commentators write about it?

(c) Has the issue been addressed by the Law Reform Commission?

f. **Ask yourself questions.**

(1) Why is this true?

(2) Why is this important?

(3) How can this be improved?

(4) How is this issue handled in other jurisdictions?

g. **Outline your answer.**

(1) Again, if you don't think that it flows well just renumber the points until you have it the way you like it.

(a) Do *not* write out a new outline.

(2) Remember – an instruction in an exam to **discuss, criticise** or **evaluate** does not signify that you should spend three pages stating the posture of the law as it now stands and two paragraphs on analysis.

(3) State the law, but spend the majority of your time and effort on the critical analysis.

h. **Start writing your answer.**

(1) Check to make certain you are answering the question asked.

(2) Cite authorities to back up your points.

(3) Cite any relevant works, including your textbooks.

i. **Reach a conclusion.**

(1) The best conclusions tie up many of the points raised in the answer.

(2) Merely answering the question asked isn't the best approach, but it is probably better than just ending abruptly.

II. Avoiding Common Mistakes

A. Answer the Question Asked

1. Many students spend hours revising by writing out answers to what they hope are the exam questions.

   a. One of the problems with this approach is that students often end up writing out their practice answer on the exam and do not answer what has been asked.

b. If you find it helpful to write out practice answers make certain that you alter the practice answer to answer the question asked on the exam.

2. Avoid those heart-stopping moments.

a. Ever leave an exam hall and learn that you advised the wrong person? Make certain you answer the question asked.

3. **Avoid killing your answer (and grade).**

a. **Shotgun approach –**

(1) Very seldom will you be asked to write everything you know about a particular area of criminal law. Yet many students spend most of their effort and time on writing every single detail they know about the subject in hopes that one or more of the points will hit the target. Blasting away with memorised material and writing pages on the subject and two paragraphs on analysis is not going to earn you many marks if a question asks you to analyse or criticise, for example.

b. **Shooting yourself in the foot.**

(1) Very few examiners will ask you to write an analysis on or critique something in law that is perfectly satisfactory as it stands. *Do not* merely write everything you know about the current status of that area of law and summarise that it does not need to be changed.

(2) Write a relevant summary of the status of the law, then:

(a) Discuss what is right with it.

(b) Discuss what is wrong with it.

(c) What has been proposed to make it better?

(d) Will the proposed changes make it better?

(e) What would you propose?

4. **Don't jump the gun.**

a. Many students lead themselves down the primrose path away from higher marks by jumping to a conclusion under the stress of the exam.

(1) This often happens when students only revise limited subjects or areas of the law, if they try to pigeonhole the criminal offences or rely on buzz or key words.

5. **Time is marks – do not waste it.**

a. Common time wasters include:

(1) Copying most of the facts given in the exam into the answer.

(a) The examiner knows the facts, so just briefly discuss the important or relevant facts in your exam answer.

   b. The use of two or three different colours of ink.
     (1) The examiner is looking for your knowledge of law, not your knowledge or use of colours. Stick with blue or black ink and save the time you would waste switching pens.
   c. Overuse of correction fluid.
     (1) There is nothing worse than picking up an exam script and finding the pages stuck together with correction fluid.
     (2) Instead of relying on correction fluid, quickly outline your answer before you begin to write your answer.
     (3) If you do make a minor mistake, simply and *neatly* cross through the mistake and continue.
     (4) And for those one-page big mistakes, do not waste time trying to paint over it. Cross through the offending page and continue.
   d. Underlining or highlighting words or phrases.
     (1) Unless you have been instructed otherwise it is a great waste of time to underline or highlight words or phrases.
     (2) Believe it or not, examiners read the answers and do not skim the papers looking for key or buzz words, cases or phrases upon which to award marks. Generally, underlining or highlighting words or phrases is simply a waste of time.

B. Do Not Make Reading Your Exam Answers a Trial

  1. Get the basics right.
   a. **Spelling** – every year students make fundamental mistakes with spelling legal and sometimes non-legal words.
     (1) If the examiner has any doubts about your ability it will be removed if you cannot spell automatism, insanity, *actus reus, mens rea,* etc. correctly.
     (2) It is always shocking to find third-level students who confuse weather for whether or use the numeral 2 for to or too.
   b. **Sentence structure** – write in complete sentences, but apply the kiss principle – **keep it short and simple.**
     (1) Many students try to emulate the styles of some of the great legal writers of the ages. This is quite understandable after spending a year reading their great works. However, the exam answers are your work and you must impress the examiner with your knowledge of the law. To do so you must be able to get your points across.

    (2) Long, difficult or contorted sentences are not the best way to get your knowledge across to the examiner. If an examiner has to reread a sentence several times to get your meaning, you are not helping your marks.

        (a) **Warning** – this study aid is in an outline form and many sentences are not complete. Make certain the sentences in your exam answers *are* complete.

c. **Paragraphs.**

    (1) Don't make your exam a chore to read! A paragraph gives the examiner a mental pause before continuing the ascent of your exam answers. Unfortunately, many students fail to see the importance of paragraphs and often write in bullet form or sometimes in a solid block.

    (2) Writing in paragraph form helps you to organise your answer and allows you to quickly glance over your answer to assess coverage of a topic.

d. **Punctuation.**

    (1) Is not optional – **use it**.

    (2) Your exam answer is not the time to experiment with new methods of punctuation. Stick to the conventional methods.

2. **Writing in the third person.**

a. Generally, legal writers write in the third person.

    (1) Yes, judges do often write in the first person, but as one of my law professors told our class, when you become a judge you too can write in the first person.

b. Some lecturers are fanatical about this, others are not.

ANSWERS TO REVIEW QUESTIONS

Chapter 1

1. The criminalisation decision concerns a discussion of the policy considerations of making certain conduct criminal. See [25]. There is no single correct answer to whether cheating on the leaving cert or university exams should be criminalised. You should discuss the liberal view (that criminal law is to prevent and deter harm to others) and the moral view (that criminal law should reflect and enforce the core moral values in society) in relation to:
   (1) What social interest might be furthered by criminalising the conduct of cheating on exams.
   (2) How the social interest might be furthered if the conduct of cheating on exams is criminalised.
   (3) What the costs of criminalising the conduct of cheating on exams are.
   (4) What the probable result of balancing the costs and benefits of criminalising the conduct of cheating on exams is.

2. Again, the criminalisation decision concerns a discussion of the policy considerations of making certain conduct criminal. See [25]. There is no single correct answer to whether dwarf tossing should be a criminal offence. You should discuss the liberal and moral views of the function of law in relation to:
   (1) What social interest might be furthered by criminalising dwarf tossing.
   (2) How the social interest might be furthered if dwarf tossing is criminalised.
   (3) What the costs of criminalising dwarf tossing are.
   (4) What the probable result of balancing the costs and benefits of criminalising dwarf tossing is. Since dwarf tossing is committed by willing participants, it is unlikely that criminalisation would be justified under the liberal approach, but under the moral approach it seems likely that criminalisation is likely to reflect the value society places on human dignity.

3. Again, there is no single correct answer to whether the conduct in the problem question should be criminal conduct. Here are some points that you might want to consider.

(a) Two consenting adults engaging in sexual activities in a public place; see [26].

(b) Vomiting in a shop. The biggest issue here would be the cost of criminalising the conduct. Potentially, ill persons would fall foul of the law and might refrain from going into a shop for essentials such as food or medicine when ill, etc. if vomiting in a shop is a criminal offence. Thus, to make it an offence to vomit in a shop is quite far reaching and could result in vulnerable persons doing without essentials or risking criminal prosecution for performing an action that is not always voluntary.

(c) Urinating in a shop or public place. Unlike vomiting, urinating in a shop or public place is generally a voluntary act and does not appear to be as far reaching. If a person has a medical problem and is prone to lose control, there are sanitary products available to alleviate the problem, therefore vulnerable individuals would not refrain from entering shops for essentials, etc.

(d) Kicking and damaging a door while intoxicated. Under both the liberal and moral theory it is likely that both theories would conclude that the conduct should be criminalised.

Chapter 2

1. (a) Yes, at the time Bart sold the sax he believed that Lisa owned it.

   (b) Yes, Bart sold the sax.

   (c) No. He did not perform the required *actus reus*. See [435]. A person is guilty of theft if he or she dishonestly appropriates property without the consent of the owner. Bart was given the saxophone by Lisa before he sold it. Therefore, Bart was the owner and although he did not know that he was the owner, as the owner he could not perform the *actus reus* of the offence of theft. Bart certainly had the *mens rea*, but he could not perform the *actus reus* because as the owner he consented to the sale when he sold it.

2. (a) No, the supposed corpse rule is used to deal with situations where the defendant commits two or more acts and there is no coincidence of the *actus reus* and *mens rea*. See [107]. The only acts that James committed were acts to defend himself from Les's attack. Perhaps James used excessive or disproportionate force in defending himself, but he did not cause Les's death. Even if you determine that James used excessive force in

defending himself, the actions of Tony were a *novus actus inter-veniens*. See [114]. While it might be foreseeable that a driver might not see Les and hit and kill him with a car, it is doubtful that it would be found to be foreseeable that Tony would come along and kill Les by throwing him into the river.

(b) No, although Tony believed that he hit Les and killed him with the taxi, Tony did not. He killed Les when he threw him into the river. At no time did Tony have the required *mens rea* to kill or cause serious injury to Les, therefore the supposed corpse rule will not apply. See [107].

3. Yes, Richard can still be convicted of raping Madge. This scenario is different than the case of *DPP* v. *Morgan*. In this scenario Richard's mistake was not centered on consent, but rather on the identity of his victim. In other words, Richard's mistake of fact was not in relation to an element of the offence. Richard had the required *mens rea* for rape and did in fact commit a rape. His mistake was that he raped the wrong victim. In *DPP* v. *Morgan*, the defendants were told by the victim's husband that she wanted to have sex with them, etc. Their mistake centered on the issue of consent, which is an element of the offence. See also [160] regarding transferred intent.

4. Probably. A victim's response to the defendant's unlawful conduct will not excuse a defendant's liability if the response could be reasonably foreseen by a reasonable person. *R.* v. *Williams & Davis* [117]. It is likely that it would be found to be reasonably foreseen by a reasonable person that Gráinne would attempt to escape after Joe pushed his way into her apartment, pointed a gun at her and put her in her bedroom where her only means of escape was across a roof.

5. Yes. Carmel had voluntarily assumed a duty of care toward her aunt. See [72] *et seq*. Criminal liability is not always premised on violence. Where a person is under a positive duty to act and he or she fails to do so, if another dies as a result of that failure to act, a manslaughter charge may be brought. See [350].

6. No. there is no concurrence of the *actus reus* and the *mens rea*. See [104].

7. No. Under the eggshell skull rule (see [120]), the defendant must accept the victim as she is. In the similar case of *R.* v. *Blaue*, the victim refused to undergo medical treatment involving a blood transfusion because of her religious beliefs and her refusal was held not to be a *novus actus interveniens*. The Court of Appeal noted

that the policy of the law has always been that those who inflict violence upon others must take their victims as they find them. This includes religious and spiritual values held by those victims.

8. *Ignorantia facti escusat; ignoranti juris non escusat.*
9. No. The *actus reus* requires a voluntary act that causes social harm. Mere thoughts cannot be criminally punished. See [53] and [54].
10. No. The *actus reus* requires a voluntary act that causes social harm. See [53]. While Rhonda certainly acted and caused harm, she did not act voluntarily, therefore she may rely upon automatism. See [58]. In particular, Rhonda may reply upon automatism induced by internal factors to escape criminal liability for injuring Ralph.

Chapter 3

1. (a) Yes. The Criminal Law Act 1997, section 7(1) provides that any person who aids, abets, counsels or procures the commission of an indictable offence is liable to be indicted, tried and punished in the same way as the principal offender. See [125] and [128]. Just because Richard raped the wrong woman is of no legal consequence to Ken's criminal liability, just as it was no defence to Richard's criminal liability.
   (b) Yes. See [160] *et seq.* Richard intended to rape Barbie, but instead raped Madge.
2. (a) Yes. See [126] *et seq.* Larry, Moe and Curly were present at the scene of the suicide, encouraging the young woman to jump to her death.
   (b) Perhaps. Counselling requires help or advice. The statement 'close your eyes and jump' appears to be advice, whereas the other statements appear to be more in the nature of encouragement. Therefore, Larry might be convicted of counselling the young woman to commit the crime.
   (c) Generally not. See [131]. Generally a failure to act, such as merely being at the scene of a crime, or failure to prevent a crime does not constitute secondary liability. However, be aware of the exception to this general rule. See [133].
3. (a) No. See [138]. If one person goes beyond what is tacitly agreed as part of the common design, the other person is not liable for the consequences of the unauthorised act. *R. v. Anderson & Morris.* There is no doubt that Bonnie exceeded the common design. The plan or agreement was to use fake guns and Bonnie produced a real machine gun. There is also the issue of withdrawal. When Clyde ran away from the scene and failed

to follow the planned escape, it could be argued that he withdrew and communicated his withdrawal by leaving abruptly. See *R.* v. *Mitchell* [140].

(b) No. Clyde was still part of the robbery, which was the basis of the common design. To avoid liability for the robbery itself Clyde would have had to withdraw prior to entering the bank and have communicated his withdrawal to Bonnie. See [140].

(c) Perhaps. Under the doctrine of common design [138], he probably escapes criminal liability for the robbery and murder. However, if he aided, abetted, counselled or procured the commission of the robbery ([125] *et seq*) he may be liable for the robbery, but not the murder.

4. (a) No. See [65]. This statute has an express requirement of conduct.
   (b) No. See [149].
   (c) Yes. See [141].

Chapter 4

1. Tyron might be able to avail of irresistible impulse, which is where the defendant is fully aware of his or her conduct and fully understands that his or her conduct is wrong, but due to some mental impairment he or she is not able to prevent himself or herself from committing the criminal offence. See [196].

2. It seems likely that intoxication will be a valid defence for John. One issue is whether the intoxication was voluntary or involuntary. It might be argued that because John voluntarily submitted to the surgery his intoxication was voluntary, but because he could not control any aspect of the anaesthetic administered to him for the surgery, the better argument would probably be that his intoxication was involuntary. Where involuntary intoxication results in an inability to form *mens rea*, it is a complete defence to any criminal charge. *R.* v. *Kingston*. See [200]. The *mens rea* for sexual assault is the intention to commit an assault that is indecent. See [423]. An assault under the NFOAPA 1997 is where a person without lawful excuse and without the consent of the other person directly or indirectly applies force to or causes an impact on the body of the other, etc. See [360]. Given the fact that John thought that Karen was his wife indicates that John did not intend to assault Karen, therefore he did not have the required *mens rea* when he sexually assaulted Karen.

3. No. Brian cannot avail of the defence of duress because it does not apply to murder. See [217].

4. Yes. Noel can avail of the defence of infancy. Due to the fact that he is less than twelve years old, Noel is *doli incapax*. See [175].

5. No. There is nothing to indicate that the driver was acting under threats. See [215].

6. (a) In order to avail of insanity there is a threefold test. See [186]. First, the defendant must be suffering from a disease of the mind. The disease must cause the defendant's defect of reason and lastly, because of the disease of the mind and the defect of reason, the defendant did not know the nature and quality of his or her acts or did not know the acts were wrong. It does not appear that Colin suffered a defect of reason from a disease of the mind. Colin did not lose his power to reason. He first planned to kill his mother, but determined that he could not do it without drawing attention to himself. It also appears that Colin understood the nature and quality of his conduct, and because he was worried about being caught by killing his mother he must have known that his plan to kill was wrong. Irresistible impulse does not appear to apply either. Colin was well able to stop himself from killing his mother because he feared being caught and selected a victim who would not draw attention to himself. Lastly, Colin might have a partial insane delusion that he is a vampire. The delusion must be treated as if it is real and then a determination must be made as to whether the law recognises the delusional situation as a defence to the offence. Assume that Colin is a vampire. The fact that Morticia allows Colin to draw blood from her arm shows that it is not necessary to kill to obtain blood.

   (b) Although consent is not really a defence, the fact that Morticia consented to the contact or impact to her body means that Colin cannot be convicted of assault, as lack of consent is part of the required *actus reus* of the offence of assault. See [360].

   (c) Merely planning a crime is not an offence. Colin clearly had the *mens rea* to murder his mother, but he did not perform an *actus reus*. If there is no *actus reus*, there is no crime. See [52].

7. Simon might be able to avail of the defence of intoxication if he was sufficiently intoxicated such that he could not form the required *mens rea*. See [210] regarding the Irish approach to intoxication. It is doubtful under the English approach that Simon would be able to avail of the defence of intoxication because assault is an offence of basic intent. See [208].

8. Under the Children Act 2001, section 52(1), the age of criminal responsibility was raised to age twelve. See [176].

 (a) Michael, fourteen – children aged fourteen or over are still conclusively presumed to be able to distinguish between right and wrong. The child may be prosecuted in the same way as an adult.

 (b) Larry, twelve – a child who is twelve but not yet fourteen is considered incapable of committing any offence, but this presumption may be rebutted by showing that the child knew the difference between right and wrong.

 (c) Joe, ten – a child under twelve is *doli incapax*, i.e. legally incapable of committing a crime.

Chapter 5

1. Under section 18 of the NFOAPA 1997, Natalie is allowed to use reasonable force to protect herself. See [237]. The issue is whether spraying hairspray in her attacker's face is unreasonable. This is a matter for the jury to decide [244] using an objective standard [256] based upon what a reasonable person would think or believe is reasonable under the circumstances. It is doubtful that a reasonable person would conclude that Natalie used excessive or unreasonable force in defending herself. Be careful that you do not fall into the trap of blaming the victim for being unreasonable for being a woman walking alone on the street with a large amount of money. Your answer should focus on whether it was unreasonable for her to spray hairspray into the face of her attacker in an effort to escape.

2. It is doubtful that James will be convicted of murder. James was attacked by Les and defended himself. Unfortunately, James used more force than was reasonable or necessary when he repeatedly hit Les in the head. See [256]. At some point after the first blow Les was no longer a threat to James, and James should have stopped. However, if James used no more force than he honestly thought was necessary, he should be convicted of manslaughter [344], not murder. If James knowingly used more force than necessary, he could be convicted of murder. Note that James must rely upon the common law of self-defence and not the NFOAPA 1997.

3. No. Necessity does not apply to murder. *R. v. Dudley & Stevens*. See [231].

4. Under the common law an individual is allowed to use reasonable force to defend another or prevent the commission of a crime. See

[257]. Lethal force is allowed so long as it was objectively reasonable, and where there is a mistaken but genuine belief that a threat to oneself or another exists, the defendant is entitled to be judged according to his or her mistaken view of the circumstances. *R. v. Williams (Gladstone)*. See [240]. If Wenceslas genuinely believed that his mother was being attacked by an intruder, the only issue is whether stabbing the intruder with a pointy star was objectively reasonable.

5. (a) Under the NFOAPA, section 18(1)(c), Rose is allowed to use reasonable force to protect her property from appropriation, destruction or damage. The issue is whether throwing stones at the twins is objectively reasonable force.

   (b) The problem does not indicate the age of the twins. If the twins are under the age of twelve, they may be able to avail of the defence of infancy. See [177].

6. The defence of necessity arises where the defendant intentionally commits a crime to prevent some greater evil where there is no reasonable alternative. See [228]. The issue is whether there was some other reasonable alternative to Joan stealing the food. The facts indicate that Joan made several attempts to obtain help, but she did not ask the manager of the supermarket for food, for example. It seems likely that Joan had a reasonable alternative and probably will not be able to avail of necessity.

7. No. At the time Alan hit the ringleader he was not acting out of self-defence, but rather out of revenge for the earlier threats made by the ringleader and his friends. Force used out of revenge is never justified. *People v. Coffey*. See [245].

8. Yes. Even though Richard indicated that he did not want Pearl's help, so long as Pearl used reasonable force in defending Richard, Pearl can still avail of the defence of another under section 18(1)(b) of the NFOAPA 1997. See [258] and [261].

Chapter 6

1. (a) No, Bonnie and Clyde cannot be convicted of conspiring to rob a bank. Conspiracy requires an agreement to pursue a common illegal goal. See [290]. Bonnie and Clyde have agreed to enter a creative writing contest, which is not an illegal act. The plans they make in order to provide authenticity to their writing are not illegal acts as they do not have the *mens rea* to commit the robbery.

(b) No. Bonnie does not have, for example, the required *mens rea*. In other words, Bonnie must have intended the person incited to commit the substantive offence. See [301].

(c) No. Bonnie and Clyde have not committed any acts other than purely preparatory acts. See [272].

2. (a) To commit an incitement Sean must have intentionally committed the *actus reus* by inviting, requesting, commanding, hiring or encouraging Moe and Larry to kill his wife. See [301]. The *mens rea* of incitement requires that Sean must have intended that the defendants commit the substantive offence. It is doubtful that Sean would be convicted of incitement. It is obvious that Sean is complaining as many spouses do in the pub, but it is only after he is drunk that he states that his life would be better if a lad took her off of his hands. Even if a reasonable person could conclude that this is an invitation or request for someone to kill his wife, a reasonable person hearing such a request from a drunk, upset spouse would realise that Sean is not serious.

(b) No. Larry and Moe cannot be convicted of attempted murder. See [271]. There has been no act in furtherance of the substantive offence, i.e. the murder.

(c) Yes. Larry and Moe have entered into an agreement to commit a crime. See [291].

3. Ken asked Richard to rape Barbie – this is incitement. See [301]. Richard agreed to rape Barbie – this is a conspiracy. See [291]. Note that there was no attempted rape of Barbie. It is true that the agreement was that Barbie was to be raped, but Richard raped the wrong woman. However, he did not act in furtherance of the substantive offence of raping Barbie, therefore there was no attempted rape of Barbie.

4. (a) No. Starskey and Hutch cannot be convicted of an attempted robbery because it was physically impossible for them to rob the ABC Bank. See [287].

(b) Yes, Starskey and Hutch have entered into a conspiracy to rob the ABC Bank. See [292]. The defence of impossibility will *not* apply because it arose after the conspiracy was complete. See [298].

5. Only if they entered into an agreement. Obviously they share a common illegal goal, but if they are acting independently there is no conspiracy. See [297].

6. No. Spouses cannot enter into a criminal conspiracy. See [294].

Chapter 7

1. (a) Yes. Provocation is the sudden and temporary loss of self-control, making the defendant incapable of refraining from acting. See [336]. In this case the victim (the husband) was performing an illegal act of bestiality (buggery). See [421]. This initial illegal act was not directed toward the defendant, but when she discovered his illegal act he attempted to kill her. Where the victim performs some unlawful act causing the defendant to suffer a sudden and temporary loss of self-control, this is sufficient provocation. See [338]. Either illegal act would probably be sufficient for a wife to suffer a sudden and temporary loss of self-control, therefore the wife should be able to avail of provocation.

   (b) Probably not. Ireland uses a subjective test, but under *MacEoin* there is still a requirement that there must be some acts done by the deceased to the defendant which causes the defendant a sudden and temporary loss of self-control. Where the victim performs some lawful act that causes the defendant to suffer a sudden and temporary loss of self-control, this was held to be sufficient provocation in *People (DPP)* v. *Kehoe*. See [339]. However, in this scenario the wife has done nothing more than enter her own home. In *Kehoe* the victim was the defendant's best friend and was found at the defendant's former partner's home. Additionally, a defendant cannot rely on the defence of provocation where he or she has deliberately brought about the acts of provocation. See [343]. The husband was deliberately making noise with the chicken, and this brought his wife into the house. If it was her presence that is the provoking act, he brought it about.

2. (a) Probably murder. See [325]. Section 4 of the CJA 1964 requires that the defendant must have intended to kill or to cause serious injury to some person for a murder conviction. Section 4(2) provides that a defendant is presumed to have intended the natural and probable consequences of his or her conduct. See [330]. It is up to the jury to determine whether death or serious injury is the probable consequence of throwing someone off of a bridge into a river, notwithstanding Tony's statement that he did not intend to kill his girlfriend. The *Nedrick Rules*, see [85]. However, if Tony cannot be con-

victed of murder because he acted recklessly rather than intentionally, he could certainly be convicted of involuntary manslaughter. See [348].

(b) Yes. There is no requirement that there must be a corpse to prove the victim's death. See [316].

3. (a) No, Rose cannot be convicted of murder. Murder requires that Rose caused the death of her mother. Rose did not. See [317].

(b) No, Rose cannot be convicted of either type of manslaughter. Manslaughter requires that Rose caused the death of her mother. Rose did not. See [346].

(c) No, Rose cannot be convicted of attempted murder. When Rose acted and attempted to smother her mother she was already dead, therefore it was physically impossible to kill her mother. See [287].

4. (a) No. Provocation is the sudden and temporary loss of self-control, making the defendant incapable of refraining from acting. See [336]. In this scenario there was a cooling off period between Elizabeth's act and Frank's reaction. Frank had a few pints then followed Elizabeth into the ladies' room, where he strangled her. Frank did not have a sudden loss of self-control. The longer the period of time between the victim's act and Frank's reaction, the less likely Frank will be found to have acted in provocation.

(b) Probably not. See [200] *et seq.* Intoxication only applies if Frank was so intoxicated that he could not form the required *mens rea*. He had a couple of pints and followed the victim into the ladies room. Frank may have been drunk, but it is not likely he was 'intoxicated' to the point where he could not form the *mens rea* to kill Elizabeth or cause her serious injury. Also, if Frank drank the pints in an effort to get the courage to kill Elizabeth, he cannot avail of the defence. See [211].

5. (a) Probably not. Attempted murder requires the intention to kill. Leopold shot over the heads of the workers, thus he did not intend to kill as required.

(b) Leopold should be charged and convicted of capital or aggravated murder under section 3 of the CJA 1990 for killing the detective. Under section 3 it is an offence to kill a police officer acting in the course of duty. See [335]. The prosecution must prove that Leopold knew that he was killing a police officer acting in the course of duty or that Leopold was reckless. Under the circumstances it seems clear that the workers left the area and the police arrived with thirty-five members of the force in uniform and five others not in uniform. In shooting the detective, Leopold was at the least reckless as to whether the detective was a police officer acting in the course of duty. If Leopold cannot be convicted under section 3, he could always be convicted of murder. See [325].

6. Infanticide probably will not apply. See [356]. There is nothing in the scenario to indicate that Sally's mind was disturbed as a result of the effect of childbirth or lactation. Rather, her mind may have been disturbed by her husband leaving her for a younger woman.

7. No. Attempted murder requires an intention to kill. When Spencer hit Louis in the knees, his intention was to cripple Louis, not kill him. Spencer cannot be convicted of attempted murder. However, had Louis died, Spencer could be convicted of murder because the *mens rea* for murder is the intention to kill or cause serious injury. See [325].

8. Yes. The doctrine of transferred intent will apply. See [159].

Chapter 8

1. (a) Yes. Section 2(1) of the NFOAPA 1997 provides that an assault occurs where the defendant, without lawful excuse, intentionally or recklessly, and without the consent of the victim directly or indirectly applies force to or causes impact on the body of the victim. See [360]. If Cousin Lenny attempts to argue implied consent, it does not apply (see [368]) because Lenny knew of Howard's phobias.

   (b) Possibly. The issue is whether Lenny's intentional and non-consensual contact caused harm to Howard. Under section 3 of the NFOAPA 1997, aggravated assault occurs where the defendant assaults the victim and the victim suffers harm. Section 1 defines harm as being harm to the body or mind.

2. (a) No, Shane cannot be convicted of assaulting Walter. See [360]. Leaving aside the issue of whether mere words can amount to an assault, Shane was speaking to Mags, not Walter, and made a future threat. Therefore, Walter was not placed in a reasonable apprehension of an *immediate* battery by Shane's words.

   (b) Probably not. Section 5 of the NFOAPA 1997 provides that it is an offence to make a threat to kill or to cause serious harm to any person and to communicate the threat by any means to any person, providing that the defendant intended that the recipient believed the threat. See [385]. Serious harm is defined in section 1 as an injury that causes a substantial risk of death, serious disfigurement or the substantial loss or impairment of the function of any organ or body member. A fat lip would not fit within the definition of serious harm. See [372].

3.	(a)	No, Shane cannot be convicted of coercion. See [388]. Section 9 of the NFOAPA 1997 defines coercion as compelling, without legal authority, the victim to refrain from doing something that he or she is legally entitled to do, or alternatively, to do something that he or she is legally entitled not to do by using violence or intimidation to the victim or the victim's family, injuring or damaging the victim's property, persistently following the victim, watching or besetting the victim's home, business or any other place where the victim happens to be, or following the victim with others in a disorderly fashion. Shane has not used violence or intimidation to Walter or to Walter's family, nor has Shane injured or damaged Walter's property, etc.

	(b)	No, in blocking the right of way Shane has not committed a false imprisonment. See [393]. Under section 15 of the NFOAPA 1997 it is an offence for a person to intentionally or recklessly take, detain, cause another to be taken or detained or otherwise restrict the personal liberty of the victim without the victim's consent. While it is true that Walter may not be able to access the right of way where he normally walks his dog, this is not an example of restricting Walter's personal liberty. For example, locking a person out of a room is not the same thing as locking a person in a room.

4.	(a)	Probably not. An assault is defined under section 2(1) of the NFOAPA 1997 (see [360]) as occurring where the defendant, without lawful excuse, intentionally or recklessly and without the consent of the victim directly or indirectly applies force to or causes an impact to the victim's body, or causes the victim to believe on reasonable grounds that he or she is likely to be subjected to an immediate force or impact. Leaving aside the issue of mere words, Peter's conduct, i.e. ordering Rodney to leave, would not generally cause a reasonable person to believe that an impact is imminent.

	(b)	There are two potential assaults.

		(1)	Rodney may be convicted of assault for threatening to spit on Paula and Peter under section 2(1) of the NFOAPA 1997. See [360]. However, these are mere words and it is not clear whether mere words can amount to a criminal assault under the NFOAPA 1997. See [362]. However, mere words in certain circumstances have been held in tort law to amount to an assault. In this scenario, given the fact that Rodney's bloody spit already hit Paula and Rodney observed her reaction, it could be argued that he knew how Peter and Paula would react to his words.

(2) With regard to the spit landing on Paula, it is unlikely that Rodney could be convicted of assault, for when his spit landed on Paula he was spitting into the gutter and the wind carried the spit. The wind would probably be viewed as a *novus actus interveniens* (unless the wind was already blowing strongly and Rodney should have realised that it was foreseeable that his spit would hit Paula or another person). See [114].

5. The gunman could not be convicted of assaulting Brenda unless Brenda has reasonable grounds for believing that she was likely to be subject to an immediate force or impact from the gunman. See [360]. Because Brenda is blind, she is probably not aware of the gun, and unless she is aware of it there can be no assault.

Chapter 9

1. (a) George might be convicted, but there are two issues that need to be resolved. First, whether a breast exam is indecent, and secondly, whether Nancy's consent to the contact is a valid defence. Under section 2 of the CLRAA 1990 (see [423]) George must have intentionally assaulted the victim and the surrounding circumstances are capable of being considered by right-minded persons as indecent. Some conduct is inherently indecent and some conduct is inherently not indecent. A real breast exam is inherently not indecent. A man pretending to be a doctor and performing a fake breast exam is indecent conduct to a right-thinking member of society. On the issue of consent, consent to the acts by a person over the minimum age that causes no harm or minor harm is a defence to a sexual assault. However, fraud as to the nature of an act may invalidate consent (*R. v. Flattery, R. v. Williams*). See [406], but in this case George told Nancy he was going to perform a breast exam and he did. His fraud went to his lack of credentials rather than the nature of the act. *R. v. Linekar*. It could be

argued that impersonating a doctor should be treated the same as impersonating a husband in rape. See [406]. However, even where consent is given, there are public policy considerations that may override the victim's consent. For example, in *R.* v. *Brown* the House of Lords held that while consent is a defence to violent sports like boxing, it should not be expanded to include sadomasochistic behaviour leading to grievous bodily harm. See [368] and [425]. On public policy grounds Nancy's consent should not be a defence to a person practising medicine without a license or any medical training.

(b) George might be convicted of rape under section 4 of the CLRAA 1990 for penetrating Nancy's vagina with the hand-held medical instruments. See [412]. The Act is silent on the issue of consent, but because rape under section 4 is a sexual assault it would appear that consent to the acts by a person over the minimum age that causes no harm or minor harm is a defence. See [360] and [423]. See answer above. On public policy grounds and in view of the fact that George performed internal exams using medical instruments where the risk to Nancy was much greater than the risk associated with the breast exams he performed, there are compelling public policy grounds for the position that Nancy's consent should not be a defence to a person practising medicine without a license or any medical training.

2. No. Billy will not be convicted of raping Marge, as he did not have the required *mens rea* for rape. See [404]. A man commits rape where he has sexual intercourse with a woman who he knows is not consenting or he is reckless as to whether she is consenting. In this case Billy did not rely merely upon Homer's statements (*DPP* v. *Morgan*). See [410]. Billy verified with Marge that she wanted him to donate sperm. If Billy honestly believed that sexual intercourse was the only way to donate sperm and Marge said she wanted his sperm, then Billy thought that he had Marge's consent for intercourse. Therefore, Billy did not have the required *mens rea* for rape, as Ireland probably uses a subjective test. See [409]. In other words, it does not matter what a reasonable person would conclude, it is the defendant's state of mind that is important, and in Billy's mind he had Marge's (and Homer's) consent.

3. (a) It is doubtful that right-minded persons would believe that removing a person's soiled clothes (and leaving that person in their undergarmets) would be indecent. See [423]. It is unlike-

ly that Adam would be convicted of any sexual offence for removing Susan's soiled clothing.

(b) If Adam has sexual intercourse with Susan he will commit the offence of rape. See [404]. A man commits rape if he has sexual intercourse with a woman who at the time of the intercourse does not consent to it and he knows that she does not consent or he is reckless as to whether she consents. If a woman is asleep or unconscious she cannot give consent. *R. v. Mayers.* See [407]. Note that had Susan given consent, Adam could still be convicted of statutory rape (see [413]), but where there is no consent the proper charge would be rape.

(c) Yes and no. If Neil became ill, passed out and Adam removed his outer clothing because Neil had soiled the clothing with vomit, it would be unlikely that Adam would be convicted of a sexual offence. However, if Adam had intercourse with Neil, Adam could not be convicted of rape. Instead he would be convicted of rape under section 4 of the CLRAA 1990. If Adam had Neil's consent for intercourse, then because of Neil's age Adam would be convicted of buggery under section 3 of the CLSOA 1993. See [421].

4. Outraging public decency. See [431].

5. Tina cannot be charged with incest due to her age. Tim can be charged with incest. See [416].

6. Sexual assault. See [423].

7. Probably not. Knowledge of the relationship is required. Recklessness is not sufficient. This is very similar to the case of *R. v. Carmichael.* See [417].

8. (a) None. A sexual relationship between a consenting adult male and his consenting maternal aunt is not contrary to the Punishment of Incest Act 1908.

(b) None. Same as above.

9. (a) Probably indecent exposure (see [430]), which requires that it occurs when a man exposes his penis to a female in a public place. So long as Fred was in a public place where it was possible that he could be seen by more than one person, it would be considered a public place. *R. v. Farrell.*

(b) Incitement to commit indecent exposure. See [302].

10. Common law buggery. See [420] and [421].

Chapter 10

1. (a) The flowers of the wild digitalis plant. Section 5(4) of the CJTFOA 2001 provides that wild flowers are not stolen unless the picker picks the flowers for sale or other commercial value. See [438]. If Samantha is using the wild flowers for her commercial potions, she will be deemed to have stolen the flowers from Farmer Finbar.

   (b) Three fallen apples in the orchard. There is nothing to suggest in the problem that the apples are wild. In fact, the apples are from an apple orchard. Therefore, section 5(4) of the CJT-FOA 2001 does not apply, because the apples are not wild fruit. Therefore, Samantha would be deemed to have stolen the apples from Farmer Finbar regardless if she uses the apples in her commercial potions or not.

   (c) The crow that Farmer Finbar shot. Under section 5(5) of the CJTFOA 2001, wild creatures cannot be stolen unless the wild creature has been reduced to possession and the possession has not been abandoned. The crow was reduced to possession when Farmer Finbar shot it. The crow has not been abandoned. Farmer Finbar is using it to scare away other crows, therefore the crow was stolen from Farmer Finbar.

   (d) Cow dung. There is no requirement that an item taken must have value. Even cow dung has some value as a natural fertiliser, but until it dissipates into the land it does not form part of the land and is therefore capable of being stolen. Under section 5(4) of the CJTFOA 2001, a person who picks wild mushrooms, flowers, fruits or foliage does not steal what is picked unless the picker does it for sale or other commercial purposes. While the Act does not address the issue of animal dung, particularly dung from domesticated animals, it seems likely that unless the dung is being used for a commercial purpose it would not be considered stolen. In this case, if Samantha uses the cow dung to make some of her potions that she sells, she might be deemed to have stolen the dung from Farmer Finbar. See [438].

2. (a) Yes. See [456]. The required *mens rea* for handling stolen property is receiving stolen property knowing it is stolen or being reckless as to whether it is stolen. Section 16(2) CJTFOA 2001 defines reckless as occurring where a person disregards a substantial risk that the property was stolen. Given George's

unusual conduct and the fact that Ted put the briefcase in his freezer, it would appear that he realised that the property was stolen. He may not have known exactly what property was in the briefcase, but he nevertheless appeared to realise that it was stolen and needed to be hidden.

(b) Yes. See [462]. Section 18 provides that possession occurs where a person without lawful authority or excuse possesses but does not steal the stolen property.

(c) Yes. See [456].

(d) Yes. See [462].

(e) Probably not. See [460–461]. At the time they asked the question the property had not been found in his possession. Further, he did not open the briefcase, therefore he did not know that it was filled with diamonds and emeralds.

3. (a) No. Section 12 of the CJTFOA 2001 provides that a person commits burglary if he or she enters a building as a trespasser intending to commit an arrestable offence, or being present as a trespasser, commits or attempts to commit such an offence. Tony certainly entered as a trespasser, but he did not have the required *mens rea* to commit an arrestable offence. He was only retrieving his own property and he was not damaging the land, etc. Therefore, Tony cannot be convicted of burglary.

(b) No. Section 13 of the CJTFOA 2001 provides that aggravated burglary is where a burglary is committed in circumstances where the defendant has with him or her a firearm, imitation firearm, weapon of offence or explosive at the time. See [451]. At no time did Tony have possession of the firearm. While he might be convicted of burglary (for attempting to possess the illegal handgun), he cannot be convicted of aggravated burglary.

4. (a) Yes. Under section 4 of the CJTFOA 2001 (see [435]), theft occurs where a person appropriates property without the consent of the owner and with the intention of depriving the owner of the property. Note that there is no longer a requirement that property must be taken and carried away. Once Noreen took possession of the property she usurped or adversely interfered with the owner's proprietary rights (see [436]), and when she attempted to leave the shop and threatened the manager she clearly showed that she intended to deprive the owner of his property.

(b) No. Under section 14 of the CJTFOA 2001, robbery occurs when a person steals and at the time or immediately before the theft, and in order to do so, he or she uses force or puts or seeks to put any person in fear of being then and there subjected to force. See [443]. Noreen committed the theft when she took possession of the clothes with the intention to deprive the owner of his property. She only threatened the use of force, i.e. threatened to bite the manager, in order to make her escape. She did not use force or threaten to use force before she committed the theft. Therefore, Noreen did not commit a robbery.

5. (a) No. Under section 12 of the CJTFOA 2001 (see [446]), a person is guilty of burglary if he or she enters a building as a trespasser intending to commit an arrestable offence, or being present as a trespasser, commits or attempts to commit an arrestable offence. Whether Patrick entered as a trespasser or not, he did not intend to commit an arrestable offence when he entered, nor did he commit or attempt to commit an arrestable offence after his entry. Patrick did not become a trespasser until he realised his mistake that his entry was a trespass. This is because he innocently entered the wrong flat. See [448]. The facts do not indicate when Patrick became aware that he had entered the wrong flat.

   (b) No. Under section 13 of the CJTFOA 2001 (see [451]), an aggravated burglary is where a burglary is committed in circumstances where the defendant has with him or her a firearm, imitation firearm, weapon of offence or explosive at the time. If Patrick has not committed a burglary (because he did not have the *mens rea* to commit an arrestable offence, nor is it apparent from the facts that he became aware until after the police arrived that he entered the wrong flat), he cannot be convicted of aggravated burglary.

6. Yes, in taking Archie's dog David has committed a theft under section 4 of the CJTFOA 2001. See [435]. The offence of theft no longer requires that it be proven that the defendant intended to permanently deprive the owner of his or her property. See [442].

7. No. It is not possible to rob a car. Robbery is where a person steals and at the time or immediately before the stealing and in order to do so he or she uses force or puts or seeks to put any person in fear of being subjected to force. Section 14 CJTFOA 2001. See [443]. Therefore, it is not possible to rob an inanimate object like a car or a house. For robbery, force or a threat of force must be made to a person. However, it is possible to rob a bank, because force is used or threatened against the tellers to hand over the money.

Chapter 11

1. Under section 17 of the Misuse of Drugs Acts, it is an offence to cultivate a cannabis plant. See [488]. The Act does not define cultivate. One ordinary meaning of cultivate is that it means to grow or raise. Technically, since Tony did not grow or raise anything from the seed, it could be argued that he has not cultivated a cannabis plant.

2. Under section 17 of the Misuse of Drugs Acts, Blanche has cultivated a cannabis plant. However, section 29(5) provides a defence if she can prove that she did not know, suspect nor had reasonable grounds for suspecting the existence of any element of the offence. Clearly, Blanche did not have the intent to cultivate a cannabis plant. She was told that it was an exotic Australian palm and the fact that she took it to a plant show tends to indicate that she was totally unaware of the nature of the plant.

3. While it might be suspected that the judge could be convicted of possession under section 3 (see [480]), it appears that possession of a drug in its natural state is not an offence. *R. v. Stevens.* Also, under section 29(2)(c) it is a defence to take possession of a controlled substance in order to hand it over to the police or to destroy the drug. See [484].

4. (a) Fred and Ginger will be convicted of disorderly conduct. See [467]. Section 5(1)of the CJPOA 1994 provides that it is an offence for any person in a public place to engage in offensive conduct between midnight and seven a.m. or at any other time after having been requested by the police to stop. Section 5(3) describes offensive conduct as unreasonable behaviour which, having regard to all the circumstances, is likely to cause serious offence or serious annoyance to any person who is or might reasonably be aware of the behaviour. It is likely that dancing and singing in the middle of the busy intersection is unreasonable behaviour that did cause serious annoyance to nearby residents and drivers.

   (b) There is nothing in the facts that indicate that Fred and Ginger are intoxicated to the point that they are a risk to themselves or to others. See [465].

   (c) No. Section 16(1) of the CJPOA 1994 provides that an affray is where a person in the company of at least one other person uses or threatens to use, by more than words, violence towards each other. See [473]. Fred and Ginger are dancing and singing, they are not arguing, fighting or threatening each other or another.

5. (a) No. Since Jackie was taking her young son to school it is doubtful that the conduct took place between midnight and seven a.m. See [467]. Therefore, for the offence of disorderly conduct to apply the police had to request the protestors to stop and the protestors must carry on after being requested to stop.

   (b) Probably not. Under section 6(10) of the CJPOA 1994, it is an offence for any person in a public place to use or engage in any threatening, abusive or insulting words or behaviour with intent to provoke a breach of the peace or being reckless as to whether a breach of the peace may occur. See [468]. While two of the protestors have engaged in abusive or insulting behaviour, the other eighteen did not join in the verbal abuse. It is doubtful that a one-off protest would be characterised as threatening unless it continued for a long period of time. In any event, eighteen of the protestors do not appear to have the intention to provoke a breach of the peace, nor seem indifferent to whether a breach of the peace occurs. Therefore, it is unlikely that all of the protestors would be convicted of engaging in threatening, abusive or insulting behaviour in a public place.

   (c) No. An affray under section 16(1) of the CJPOA 1994 is where a person in the company of at least one other person uses or threatens to use, by more than words, violence towards each other. There is nothing to suggest that the two protestors making the racial comments were threatening to use violence towards each other or indeed towards anyone else.

6. (a) No. The conduct took place on the footpath in front of the pub, therefore they were not on the licensed premises. See [476].

   (b) Not unless the activities took place between midnight and seven a.m. See [467].

   (c) No. See [469]. Under section 14(1) of the CJPOA 1994, it is an offence for any person to use unlawful violence in the presence of at least twelve people in any place, where unlawful violence to effect a common purpose is used or threatened, etc. Nothing in the facts indicates that at least twelve people were present and the unlawful violence was not to effect a common purpose.

7. (a) Sleeping in the intersection is not an offence under the Intoxicating Liquor Act 2003. It is, however, an offence under section 4(1) of the CJPOA 1994. See [465].

(b) Returning to the pub within one hour is an offence under section 8(1) as being disorderly conduct on licensed premises. See [476].

(c) Entering a pub while intoxicated is an offence under sections 6(1) and 6(2) of the Act. See [475].

(d) Returning to the pub within twenty-four hours after being told to leave the premises is an offence under section 8(1) as being disorderly conduct on licensed premises. See [476].

FREQUENTLY CITED SOURCES

Ashworth, *Principles of Criminal Law*, Oxford: Clarendon Press 1999.

Baker, 'Criminal Courts and Procedure at Common Law 1500–1800', in Cockburn (ed.), *Crime in England 1500–1800*, London: Methun 1977.

Charleton, *Criminal Law: Cases and Materials*, Dublin: Butterworths 1992.

Clarkson, *Understanding Criminal Law*, 3rd ed., London: Sweet & Maxwell 2001.

Dressler, *Understanding Criminal Law*, 2nd ed., New York: Matthew Bender 1999.

Hall, *General Principles of Criminal Law*, Indianapolis, IN: Bobbs-Merrill 1960.

Hanly, *An Introduction to Irish Criminal Law*, Dublin: Gill & Macmillan 1999.

Hart, *Punishment and Responsibility: Essays in the Philosophy of Law*, Oxford: Clarendon Press 1968.

McAuley, *Insanity, Psychiatry and Criminal Responsibility*, Dublin: Round Hall 1993.

McAuley and McCutcheon, *Criminal Liability*, Dublin: Round Hall 2000.

O'Malley, *Sexual Offences: Law, Policy and Punishment*, Dublin: Round Hall 1996.

Pollock and Maitland, *The History of English Law*, 2nd ed., Cambridge: Cambridge University Press 1968.

Smith and Hogan, *Criminal Law*, 8th ed., London: Butterworths 1996.

Wilson, *Criminal Law: Doctrine and Theory*, 2nd ed., Harlow: Pearson 1998.

Williams, Glanville, *Textbook of Criminal Law*, London: Stevens 1983.